VOICES from
The New York School for Psychoanalytic Psychotherapy and Psychoanalysis

Edited by Edwin Fancher
and Miriam Pierce

IPBOOKS.net
International Psychoanalytic Books

International Psychoanalytic Books (IPBooks),
New York • http://www.IPBooks.net

Copyright © 2015 New York School for Psychoanalytic Psychotherapy and
Psychoanalysis; edited by Edwin Fancher and Miriam Pierce.

Publisher:
International Psychoanalytic Books (IPBooks)
25–79 31st Street Astoria, NY 11102
Online at: http://www.IPBooks.net

ISBN: 978-0-9965481-7-5

VOICES from The New York School for Psychoanalytic Psychotherapy and Psychoanalysis

Contents

INTRODUCTION

The history of the New York School for Psychoanalytic Psychotherapy and Psychoanalysis (NYSPP) goes back to 1964 when Edwin Fancher, a Certified Psychologist in New York State, became a candidate for psychoanalytic training at the American Institute for Psychoanalytic Psychotherapy and Psychoanalysis. He was assigned Dr. Gertrude Blanck as his supervisor. Fancher was also a founder and director of the Washington Square Institute for Psychotherapy and Mental Health (WSI), which provided low fee treatment to the public. He was so impressed with Dr. Blanck that he arranged for her to become Director of Training at WSI. She and her husband Rubin Blanck, also a psychoanalyst, developed a two year program in psychoanalytic psychotherapy which she called the Core Program, designed for training the staff of WSI.

In early 1970 the Blancks left WSI to found The Institute for the Study of Psychotherapy (ISP) based on their Core Program and they also provided advanced courses for their graduates. In 1978 the Blancks decided to terminate ISP so they could devote more time to writing and lecturing. At that time, Edwin Fancher, MA, Jane Hall, CSW, Rosilie Korte, CSW, Miriam Pierce, CSW and Marjorie Tagart White, PhD, all students in their advanced seminars indicated to the Blancks a desire to establish a training program based on continuing their point of view of psychoanalysis. The Blancks agreed to support this project if it was independent of ISP. The Blancks spent a weekend at Mohonk Mountain House meeting with this committee to help them to formulate a new curriculum and a revised three year program of training in psychoanalytic psychotherapy.

The New York School for Psychoanalytic Psychotherapy (NYSPP) was chartered by the State Department of Education in early 1978 and classes started in September 1978. The new three year program featured an in-depth study of Freud, Malher, Winnicott, Kris, Hartmann, Spitz, Jacobson and the major object relations psychologists. The founders of NYSPP were social workers or psychologists who had studied with the Blancks for many years. They generally had years of courses, supervision, and all had had an analysis.

They shared the Blanck's dedication to providing the best training in psychoanalytic treatment available. They became the founding supervisors and faculty of the new school.

In 1984 the school changed its name to New York School for Psychoanalytic Psychotherapy and Psychoanalysis when we added psychoanalytic training for those of our graduates who were qualified for that training.

It seemed most appropriate to introduce this book with a speech made by Gertrude Blanck to the graduating class of 1996 of the New York School for Psychotherapy and Psychoanalysis (NYSPP). Dr. Blanck demonstrates her characteristic directness by posing the question "Why are we here?" She proposed that the thorny issue of the technique of treating the borderline patient was one of the central issues of psychoanalysis at that time. She is aggressive in demanding respect for psychoanalysis as a scientific discipline and as a valid therapeutic procedure.

Chapter two: It may seem strange to follow Gertrude Blanck's speech with another NYSPP graduation speech, one made by Jacob Arlow, MD in 1997. Dr. Arlow was one of the most respected members of the psychoanalytic establishment, Past President of the American Psychoanalytic Association and Past President of the New York Psychoanalytic Institute. as well as many other honors. But, Arlow, was independent minded and by the 1990's realized that psychoanalysis was lost to the psychiatric establishment which had dominated it for decades, and that the future of psychoanalysis was with non-medical analysts. Arlow then struck out boldly to teach seminars in psychoanalytic technique to non-medical therapists. Numerous faculty members and graduates of NYSPP joined Arlow's seminars. It seemed appropriate to ask Arlow to give a graduation speech the year after Gertrude Blanck had given one. Arlow critically reviewed the traditional curriculum for psychoanalytic training, but ended with an admonition "As analysts our courage is constantly being tested. Unless we have that courage, we begin to share our patient's fears; then we can not help them. To be an analyst requires courage that has to be renewed each day and each session."

The rest of the chapters of this book are papers our faculty or graduates have published over the years as contributions to psychoanalytic theory or to the techniques of psychotherapy or psychoanalysis .

Our next chapter is a sensitive treatment of the inevitable dilemmas of sibling conflicts. Joyce Edward points out the relative neglect of sibling problems in the psychoanalytic literature. She describes therapeutic techniques to reduce frozen sibling relationships and open up warmer family ties in our patients.

Fancher's contribution review the development of Freud's theory of the Superego and Arlow's revision of his theory. He proposes a technique where the therapist addresses the superego and the ego directly, as a way to challenging the patient's defenses directly.

Sheila Felberbaum's Memory, Mourning and Meaning in a Psychotherapist's Life recounts her personal experiences of loss and the way in which they intersect and influence her professional life. Ms. Felberbaum shows enormous courage in facing the death of her loved ones, and fear of her own death.

Jane Hall's contribution is a cry of rebellion: Relinquishing Orthodoxy: One Freudian Analyst's Personal Journey. Jane Hall described her orthodox training in traditional Freudian theory and ridged principles of technique, which dictated four times a week on the couch. She was taught that therapy with the borderline patients was hopeless, but learned from Gertrude and Ruben Blanck, how to modify analytic techniques with borderline patients. She also expanded her psychoanalytic understanding by reading widely in the relational literature and opened herself to a diversity of psychoanalytic approaches.

Our next chapter presents a case study of the treatment of a young woman identical twin with an eating disorder. The therapist, Lynn S. Lawrence, manages this extremely complex patient by resorting to the important psychoanalytic research on early infant behavior pioneered by Bowlby, Spitz, Stern and Winnicott. She shows how their insights led the therapist to help her patient to achieve a form of self differentiation that was essential to her successful treatment.

Miriam Pierce presents a very different kind of psychoanalytic case; a contemporary dyadic treatment informed by psychoanalytic developmental research. She tells us history. She tells us of a pregnant woman traumatized by the attack of the twin towers on September 11th. The mother gave birth shortly after the attack and went into a severe postpartum depression. Miriam Pierce followed the model of the psychoanalytic treatment approach, including home visits, originally proposed by Selma Fraiberg and other psychoanalytic "baby watchers" such as Spitz, Mahler, Winnicott, Emde, Stern, and Anna Freud. This psychoanalytic model of mother infant treatment proved invaluable for promoting growth and security in both mother and infant.

Maryam Razavi-Newman shares her profound emotional response to returning to her native country and family after 40 years of self exile. She uses her psychoanalytic understanding to master some of her painful feelings.

Naomi Schlesinger's case presentation focuses on the work of mourning with adult patients who have lost a parent at a very young age and treatment problems with such patients.

In a book review, Lucille Spira analyses the pain and depression suffered by many lonely widows. She discusses the role of relationship in promoting growth and security in these patients.

Iris Sugarman explores the psychopathology of the inability to mourn. She recognizes the defensive role of fantasies that the dead loved one is not really dead and discusses how to deal with them.

Toni Thompson presents an analytic case of working through the pathology of a woman who suffered trauma from the childhood seduction by a woman. Her patient experienced both strain trauma and shock trauma and treatment focused on the transference.

Our last chapter is by Patsy Turinni, faculty member and supervisor at NYSPP since 1978, and Diana Siskind, former faculty member and supervisor at NYSPP. They review the importance of the Blancks in applying Mahler's separation -individuation theory to clinical practice. Mahler's observational studies have been the inspiration for current study and research in development. Those findings have been integrated into psychoanalytic theory and have influenced practice. NYSPP includes this research in its curriculum and stresses its relevance for clinical practice.

This book is dedicated to the hope that the reader will come away with an increased appreciation of the enterprise of psychoanalysis and of the contributions of the New York School for Psychoanalytic Psychotherapy and Psychoanalysis over the past decades.

—Edwin Fancher and Miriam Pierce

WHY ARE WE HERE?

[Commencement Speech, New York School of Psychoanalytic
Psychotherapy and Psychoanalysis & The Society
of NYSPP November 15, 1996.]

If you ask the woman or man on the street, psychoanalysis is some pecu-
liar, old-fashioned, outdated, defunct aberration from the 19th century.
So why are we here?

Daniel Goleman and Jane Brody don't even mention psychoanalysis
anymore. They have long ago indoctrinated their readers to believe that
it is worthless. Except for us, readers of the NY Times believe they are
getting the scientific lowdown. They assume that a Times writer is objective and knows the scientific facts.

It is rumored, although I cannot confirm it, that very long ago a
member of the Sulzberger family had a failed analysis, so the policy of
the Times has been anti-analytic ever since. This is possible because, in
the days when analysts only knew how to analyze, they took on borderline cases but had no technique for diagnosing and treating them. Many
a disappointed patient was dismissed as unanalyzable in those days. I
knew some who suffered not only from their pathology but from the narcissistic blow of being declared unanalyzable. You have to understand
that in professional and intellectual circles in those days, it was essential
to one's social standing to be in to have been in analysis.

The history of psychoanalytically informed psychotherapy goes
back to the 1950's. Robert Knight was one of the first to try to tackle
it. Before that, if the analyst was not foolish enough to take a borderline
patient into analysis, but recognized that there was patient who had been
with a good analyst who did not know what to do with a man too disturbed for analysis. What he did was schedule the patient for the end of
the day so that they could have some scotch together. Don't laugh. It
wasn't bad. At least the analyst knew better than to try to analyze. I met
that analyst later on. He was a nice and knowledgeable person. At least
he did little harm, as compared with those who dismissed patients as
unanalyzable, who were banned for life. I said he did little harm, I did

not say no harm. I think that poor treatment is harmful. You will hear about that later on.

After Robert Knight, the American Psychoanalytic held an all-day panel on the as-if personality. They could not quite say borderline yet, so they used the concept of as-if to describe their unanalyzable patients. Helene Deutsch, who had written the paper on as-if, was invited to make comments at the end of the day. She said that the only as-if personality she had ever seen was an applicant for candidacy at the Boston Psychoanalytic Institute. She saw no reason not to accept him for training. Whatever that says about training in Boston I don't know, but was it an admission that she wrote her paper without having seen a single patient of that sort? We have a right to be unkind to her because of the damage she did in her work on female psychology. But that is another topic.

Then came a series of papers by Otto Kemberg given at several meetings of the American Psychoanalytic. It opened a door to this heretofore neglected pathology. That it was neglected is a historical oddity that came about because Freud analyzed himself. He discovered in himself the core conflict of neurosis—the Oedipus Complex. We do not know what would have become of psychoanalytic theory had he been borderline. Maybe we would not have any.

It was not my own quirks that led me to study borderline pathology. I had a borderline case in supervision. The supervisor was, as they say, supportive. He said that's right, go on supporting the ego. In effect, he said I was speaking prose and didn't know it. I went away pondering how to support the ego. I am, of course, indebted to Margaret Mahler who defined borderline as failure to have completed the separation- individuation process. She opened up a new world of the preoedipal determinants of pathology. As some of you know, I expanded this to take into account that preoedipal experience colors the Oedipus Complex.

Leaning upon the works of Hartmann, Jacobson, Spitz and Mahler, we (RB and I) worked out our theory and technique for the treatment of borderlines. It became the basis for our series of ego psychology books.

A word about ego psychology. No one knows what it means today. It used to refer to the work of Hartmann, his collaborators Kris and Lowenstein, and his successors. It still does in a way. But the designation ego psychology no longer does it justice. It is so much more than that. And the lay public thinks the ego is something else. To them the ego is usually too big. No theorist said it comes in sizes. "To the layperson too big is better than too small. Is it something else they are measuring?

I have tried, without much success, to alter the term ego psychology. We tried psychoanalytic developmental psychology. While accurate, it is not grabby enough to have caught on. My latest brainstorm is Structural Theory. That is also accurate. Modern psychoanalytic theory derives from the structural theory. But that may be the least of it. The most is that no one ever heard of it.

Back to the New York Times. In a recent article, Goleman wrote about a new discovery by psychoneurologists. They discovered critical periods, the developmental moment when it is essential that a number of developmental experiences must coincide if optimal development is to proceed smoothly. By avoiding any knowledge about that arcane pseudo-science that was called psychoanalysis, Goleman had no clue that Spitz had described critical periods in 1959. I follow the latest developments in the neurosciences and it is amazing to me how the ideas of the early ego psychologists are borne out. Too bad hardly anyone knows that. Goleman and others have convinced their readers that psychoanalysis was a mistake. So why are we here?

Philosophers of science condemn psychoanalytic theory on the ground that it is unscientific. There can be no greater pejorative in the scientific community. When I was a doctoral candidate they hammered at me that psychoanalysis cannot be replicated. Replication is the god of the physical sciences. Of course you cannot repeat an analysis, but their argument is spurious. Instead of having the method fit the data, they want the data to fit the method. But if psychoanalytic theory is unscientific, why are we here? Deconstructionist professors of English literature contend that Freud was not only mistaken, but dishonest. Those of you who know the rantings of Paul Rozan and Frederick Crews know that Freud abandoned the seduction theory because he lacked the courage to confront turn-of-the century Vienna with the prevalence of child abuse.

I took a course in T. S. Eliot at Duke University not long ago. Totally out of context, the professor managed to insert that Freud was a crackpot. It had nothing to do with Eliot, but a lot to do with professors of English having to establish their political correctness if they hope to get tenure.

If you read the NY Review of Books you know Frederick Crews who is on a mission to prove that Freud was a fraud and an adulterer. If you tell people you are Freudian they look at you with pity. You're not with it. How come you don't know better?

I have experienced that pity. Maybe you have too. I go to a dinner party and someone asks me what I do. I say I am a psychologist. Some pushy guest continues to try to make conversation. "What kind?" In an unguarded moment I acknowledge being a psychoanalytic psychologist. "Oh, isn't that old-fashioned?" He means you are too ignorant and have not kept up with things. Or she shakes her head. "I didn't think anyone believed in that anymore." They feel so superior and so sorry for me for being so stupid.

Psychoanalysis and psychoanalytically informed psychotherapy keep patients coming forever. Look at Woody Allen. A lot of good it did him. Any problem can be cured with medication or a few once-a-week sessions. So why are we here?

Psychiatrists, unless analytically trained, use DSM IV, which is atheoretical. They don't need theory; they have prescription pads. We wasted our time and money lying on the couch for years while pills can do the trick faster, better, cheaper.

Schools of social work have abandoned their base in psychoanalytic theory. Even Smith, the last holdout, where I taught ego psychology for many years, has caved in. The agencies no longer accept their students for placement if they come full of psychoanalytic nonsense.

We also have to contend with the fads, both semi-respectable and outright quacky. I remember dianetics, primal scream, EST, behavior mod and junk like that. Some fads came and went so that some of you have probably not even heard of them. But in their heyday they were so popular that I worried that they would get all the patients. I needn't have. They failed, and the patients came to us for repair. Matters are worse now because so many of the fads *du jour* are somewhat more respectable—self psychology, cognitive-behavioral, relational, intersubjective, British object relations, Winnicottian. You may be surprised that I include British object relations and Winnicottian my list of fads. Some of my best friends are Winnicottian. They take a piece of psychoanalytic theory and present it as a whole, stand-alone theory. Object relations was always a part of mainstream psychoanalytic theory. We don't need a separate theory.

Why do we persist in pursuing psychoanalytic developmental theory? Why will some of you, after graduation, continue in analysis, in supervision, in seminars that adhere to psychoanalytic principles when you cannot even say the P word at a dinner party if you want to be invited again?

And if you need to earn a living by affiliation with a managed care setup, do not even think the P word. So why did you undertake all this training? Why are we here?

We are here because ego psychology, or psychoanalytic developmental theory, or my latest designation—Structural Theory—works. It helps the patient. It helps the therapist. I can remember my own beginnings as a therapist—how hard it was at first, and the relief I felt when I could sit back and realize that I knew what I was doing, when every patient session was no longer a grope in the dark I did not have to function by the seat of my skirt. Knowing what I was doing gave me a better work day and helped the patient more. I went home relaxed. The patients got better.

The graduates of the original Institute for the Study of Psychotherapy, who are your teachers and my friends, can tell you that the theory they learned improved their practices. Some· of them tell me it has improved them personally. It gets into one's bones.

"Easy enough for her to talk about ego psychology," you may be thinking. "Doesn't she know that we have to work with the limitations of the fads that compete, with a public ignorant and disparaging of psychoanalytically informed treatment, with the horror of managed care? They don't want ego psychology. They want quick and dirty. She was in practice in the glory days when it was fashionable to be in analysis, when patients paid out of pocket, when a third party was something you went to on New Year's Eve."

To prove that I am not that much out of it, I want to deal with several current matters that vex us.

The first is violation of the patient's trust by telling managers more than they have a right to know. I do not believe that insurance carriers and employers need to know so much in order to pay for treatment. They practice a large slice of voyeurism. I had a patient who had some oddball sexual perversions. Blue Cross wanted to know all about it. Do you tell this to a clerk on the phone? Do you put it on a form? Do you refuse? Do you lie? Is there a point at which a white lie begins to look a little gray? I needed an X-ray for a minor thing. When it was over, I went to the reception desk where the clerk who was filling out the form asked me the diagnosis. I said I was there in order that the doctor be able to make a diagnosis. She said she would put down cancer, they always pay for that. Should we tell such outright lies? Does it matter? Do we have to be not only liars but snitchers in order to have the case approved for payment? What becomes of professional integrity if we let it be eroded?

The nonanalytic therapists have not heard of Edith Jacobson, but you have. Yet you may not know that she went to prison for refusing to reveal

9

a patient's confidences. She was treating a government official in prewar Germany whose state secrets the Nazis wanted to know. Imagine the courage it took to defy them? She was sent to a prison for noncriminal, political prisoners. She made the most of her incarceration by gathering data for her paper on Depersonalization, thus attaining mastery over an unbearable situation.

Before I am through, I hope to show you how to attain mastery. No, I am not proposing that you go to prison. This country is still a democracy, so there are other ways.

Squealing on your patient is only one way you are asked to compromise your professional integrity. And it is not only insurance companies that are the culprits. What about the law that you must report child abuse? Have any of you experienced the conflict of protecting your patient's privacy versus obeying that law?

Abuse is a global term. When I hear a case presentation referring to abuse, I want to know a lot more. I want to know what it means to the child. At what developmental level did this occur? How did it impair development? What became of the object relations pattern? What transpired between the self representations and the object representations?

Two therapists got into a tangle over so-called child abuse. One was treating a child, the other was treating the mother. In a. fit of anger, the mother slapped the child. The child's therapist phoned the mother's therapist to ask whether this had been reported. How ridiculous can we get?

Very. Take sexual harassment. How shall we define that? A six-year old boy has reached a major developmental milestone when he wants to kiss a girl. How many people know that it is a development triumph? What has been done to his developmental thrust to be punished for such phase-appropriate behavior? Would we rather he had not survived his oedipal crisis and moved on to a contemporary heterosexual object?

Those are not the only professional conflicts that the current scene gets us into. The insurers rob us of professional autonomy. Physicians have given in to that to a degree that shocks me. That most independent of professions bows to the decisions of the health uncaring managers. Why do doctors stand for drive through deliveries? I hope they are protesting more than we hear about.

How far should you bend and where should you stand pat? I neither want you to go to jail nor to be dismissed from the HMO roster if you need to be there to survive.

But here is your dilemma. Most, if not all, patients suffer in some way from having had parents who were not trustworthy enough. The *sine qua non* of therapy, no matter what kind, is that the therapist have absolute integrity. It cannot be taught or bought. If you do not have it, you cannot be a therapist.

This is not a new dilemma, only more so. You work in a setting where the administration dictates policy that goes against your professional judgment. Your supervisor tells you to do something that you believe is bad practice. What you do about it depends upon your independence. You can fight it. You can refuse to comply. You can resign your job. If you have to put up with it in the same way that some physicians do to earn a living, you are in a bad spot. I know that you would try to get out of it at the first opportunity.

It is not well known that the Institute for the Study of Psychotherapy was at first an in-service training program in a clinic. It became an independent institute because the administration of the clinic demanded some unethical practices. Ed Fancher and I are the only survivors of that. We had the freedom to leave an untenable situation. I am aware that that is not always possible.

I am going to conclude by describing a case. How to deal with it under optimal conditions, which means without interference by managers. How to deal with under limitations of other kinds. How deal with it under managed care. I shall not discuss the political aspect. You have able people doing that and I hope that you will join them. They need all the help they can get. I am going to discuss the technique of treating the same case under a variety of conditions.

Let me say at the outset that we have always had limitations. The patient lives too far away to be able to come as frequently as is indicated. The job does not allow sufficient time off. There is not enough money for optimal treatment. If we were in training, we had the supervisor and the institute sometimes not agreeing with us. These dilemmas are not new, only made more so now by third party interference.

I am going to play around with a case now to show how to handle limitations in treatment A 35-year-old man is still living with his mother. He was the youngest of three boys. The brothers were ten and seven when he was born. His mother was 38. The parents did not need a third boy, but would have welcomed a girl. As the baby in the home he got what lay people call lots of attention. That means that he was sort of a plaything. Mother welcomed his company because the older kids were in school. This impaired his separation thrusts because or her need. Brothers played with him as a toy. Father was too tired to do much with him. In all it was not a bad situation, just not good enough. He had a hard time going off to school at age five, and this was repeated when he went off to college in another city. In high school he had tried some dating. Didn't like it much. Was able to stay in college only because he found a young woman with similar problems and they stuck it out together. Sex was not their main preoccupation. Togetherness was. They did not marry because, she did not want to live in his home town after college, so he returned home alone and has been there ever since.

Without taking the time here to walk you through all of the diagnostic criteria, let me just say that he tilted on the neurotic side of the fulcrum, with many preoedipal hangups. He had an uncertain gender identity because unconscious compliance with the mother's wish for a girl enabled him to feel closer to her. He also had masculine identifications with father and brothers. He was structured, had intact defenses, and his preoedipal problems were more regression than fixation.

He came for treatment because he was having trouble on the job. His coworkers would taunt him about still living at home, being single, not dating much. They called him Sissy, Mama's boy. Maybe he was gay. Maybe he was impotent.

Our diagnosis tells us that job performance is only the tip of the iceberg, not the real problem at all. What was? You have just spent three years learning how to recognize a separation problem and what to do about it.

The ideal thing to do is analyze him. I am not going to detail how to do that, only to point up that this would be optimal treatment.

Let's suppose that time and money do not allow for analysis. Then I would recommend two or three times a week and use what Kernberg calls expressive therapy—that is, exploration of unconscious fantasies short of analysis.

What if he could only come once a week? Then I would try to help him see that the job problem is a deflection from the real problem, which is separation. I would hope that he would find a way to increase the time so that we could deal with it.

Since the presenting problem is job performance, one that insurance would surely find acceptable, the manager did accept it and decreed six sessions.

What can you do in six sessions? It may be shocking to hear that I would still take the time to diagnose. What, waste one or two of those precious sessions to formulate a developmental diagnosis! You still have to know what you are dealing with.

The nonanalytic therapists that abound these days would accept the presenting problem at face value and go on to help him find devices for dealing more assertively with his colleagues. The employer, manager, and everyone else would think it a great success—a model of how you don't have to spend a lot of time in therapy. I think it would do harm. It would be a deflection akin to Edward Glover's concept of inexact interpretation. The patient is happy to have the therapist fall for something that gets him away from the source of his anxiety. It does harm because life is not forever. He will handle his coworkers better but continue to live with his parents until they die. A wasted life. Maybe a breakdown when his parents are gone.

I want to wind up with the simple thought that brief therapy, although a drop in the bucket, has to be the right drop. You have to know what the contents of the entire bucket would consist of so that you can insert the drop that will fit in with the total problem. The drop, in six sessions, is to seize on whatever manifestations of reluctance to separate you can find. Maybe he finds it hard to leave when the session is over, maybe he is reluctant even to get started because he is afraid of getting involved. Very likely he will want to stay with the job problem. Then he needs to know that it bothers him so much because some of the things they say hit home.

If you are granted ten sessions, you may be able to provide two drops. Then you can deal with his passivity as a defense against the anger at his colleagues for touching his sore spots. You are not telling him what to do, but helping him know where it hurts. I have not gone into the political aspects of our current health care problems.

I have shown how to do what is right within the system while working politically to change it. It is said that happiness is when the superego smiles at the ego. Taking this approach should make you happy all the time.

COMMENCEMENT ADDRESS
by Jacob A. Arlow, MD

[New York School of Psychoanalytic Psychotherapy
and Psychoanalysis, September 12, 1997.]

Ordinarily a commencement address becomes an exercise in platitudes and, coming to think of it, perhaps that is just how it should be. After all, the occasion is a happy one. A course of study has been mastered, hurdles have been overcome, one has been tested and one has prevailed. It is indeed an achievement and congratulations are in order. To all of you graduating, my congratulations! You deserve it, perhaps more than you realize. I say that because these are not ordinary circumstances. These are not ordinary times.

Over the past several years, you have acquired special training as mental health professionals with a psychoanalytic orientation at a time when future rewards for your skills, both in terms of finance and prestige, may not be commensurate with the dedication and effort you have put into your training. But today we are witnessing a fundamental revolution in the healthcare system in our country. Both financial remuneration and professional independence are being progressively and inexorably curtailed, and this is especially true in the field of mental health therapy. Even the idea of therapy is being subverted by a concept of counseling.

As troubling as these developments in the field of mental health delivery may be, the situation is even worse in your case, because the specific orientation and the skills that you have acquired, that is, psychoanalysis, is under continual attack. The dangers are real and present, and for you to have undertaken this special form of training speaks of your conviction and dedication. You chose this course of study because you felt it was the best medium for apprehending the depths of the human soul, so, above all, I consider it a sign of courage, of mental fortitude. Therefore, in addition to my message of congratulations, let me now add a message of admiration, not only for your dedication but, above all, for your courage.

I like words and I hate to see them abused. The word "courage" has a very precise meaning. Webster's *Dictionary* says it consists of "facing and dealing with anything recognized as dangerous, difficult or painful, instead of withdrawing from it." All too frequently people disregard that last phrase of the dictionary definition, emphasizing "facing" instead of "withdrawing." Having known many times what it meant to be facing danger, General William Tecumseh Sherman wrote: "I would define true courage to be a perfect sensibility of the measure of danger and a mental willingness to endure it." The dangers are real and present and you have chosen to confront them.

In preparing these remarks, I was struck by the fact that, in the psychoanalytic literature, there is a vast number of contributions on the subject of fear but very little on the subject of courage. Perhaps this is to be expected because fear is ubiquitous, while courage is rare indeed. The pursuit of psychoanalysis is, in itself, an exercise in courage. We have before us the courage that Freud exemplified, particularly, as he said, in maintaining a state of independence from the compact majority. He had the courage of his convictions. But I am thinking of courage in terms of a broader and a perhaps more basic sense, the kind of courage that is a fundamental part of the psychoanalytic enterprise. Ask the average preschool child "what is courage?" and, surprisingly, he will give you a definition very close to that contained in the dictionary. "Courage," he or she might say, "is when you are afraid but you keep on going." "Going?" The answer you would most likely get would be "going into the dark." "And what are you afraid of in the dark?" "You know," will come the answer, "all kinds of terrible things can happen to you."

This is really what psychoanalysis is all about. With our patients we enter into the dark recesses of the mind, not knowing for sure what kind of dangerous monsters lurk within. Someone might object, "The demons that lurk in the mind are not real. The dangers are imaginary." Not real? They are real indeed. The dark, unconscious forces of the mind can wreak havoc and destruction on the patient himself, on those in the circle of his existence and, at times, even on society at large, as we have learned only too well in this century. As a young candidate in training, gaining access to the hidden recesses of the human soul, I once said to my wife "Considering what goes on in people's minds, it's a wonder that the fabric of our society holds together." If we have learned anything in the 20th Century, we have come to know how the most unimaginable, uncivilized, savage tendencies may be carried into action, even on a massive scale, as the Holocaust has demonstrated.

It takes courage to be a psychoanalyst and to practice psychoanalytic psychotherapy. If we give in to our fear of the unknown, if we withdraw in the face of unimaginable danger, we will lack the courage to be true analysts. It is this fear that all too often lurks behind the attacks on psychoanalysis. For example, in his debate with Heinz Hartmann on the validity of analytic findings, Sidney Hook did not raise questions directly about the methodology of analysis. What he wanted Dr. Hartmann to do is the following, namely, show me a case that doesn't have an Oedipus complex. An analyst has to learn to navigate in the dark, even as he comes upon the demons concealed in the recesses of the mind. Some are old evils, already identified and made commonplace in the textbooks of psychopathology. But there are always new demons, unsuspected, perhaps even more dangerous and unfathomable. As analysts our courage is constantly being tested. Unless we have the courage, we begin to share our patient's fears and withdraw; then we cannot help them. To be an analyst requires courage that has to be renewed each day and each session. Often, when our courage fails, we call it countertransference, a response to fears that arise within ourselves. It takes courage even as we peer into the darkness, on one hand, and face up to hostile critics, on the other. When facing powerful adversaries, flight is easy. Moral courage is hard. Moral courage is at least the equivalent of physical courage. True courage comes hard. In parting, I want to leave you with a message from *The Ethics of the Fathers.* Rabbi Tarfon said, "The day is short, the work is long, the laborers are sluggish, the reward is great and the master is urgent. It is not your duty to complete the work but neither are you free to withdraw from it." I congratulate you on your success, I admire you for your courage, I wish you well.

Comments on the Psychoanalytic Curriculum

From my experience as a teacher, a supervisor, an editor and a participant in various psychoanalytic panels, both as a discussant and as a presenter, I have reached certain impressions and conclusions about how psychoanalysis is taught.

One of the reasons for the shortcomings in psychoanalytic education relates to historical developments. Psychoanalysis began as a movement clustered around an heroic figure and consolidated around a myth of struggling against hostile enemies. I have discussed some of the issues in several previous publications, notably, "Myth and Ritual in Psychoanalytic Education" (unpublished) and "Some Dilemmas of Psychoanalytic Education" (1972). Other factors, the specific nature of the psychoanalytic experience, the master-apprentice relationship, serve to influence the philosophy behind the psychoanalytic curriculum.

Psychoanalysis should be taught as a natural science and not as a received tradition. The major portion of many psychoanalytic curricula consists of an historical reading and review of Freud's writings, sometimes beginning with preanalytic contributions, contributions that Freud often repudiated (e.g., "The Project"). In many places, it is possible for a beginning candidate to go through the entire first year having read no author other than Freud. We are, in fact, the only science that uses textbooks that are almost 100 years old. As a result, our candidates are indoctrinated with what psychoanalysis was and not what psychoanalysis is.

With these considerations in mind, I would propose the following approaches so that psychoanalysis can be taught as a natural science, divorced from the trappings of faith. It might be useful to use the analogy of medical school education. As the beginning medical student is introduced to the basic fundamentals of anatomy and physiology, so the beginning analytic candidate should be introduced to our current understanding of the nature, development and functioning of the human psyche. This means that, in the first year, emphasis should fall on the development of the mind. The concepts of determinism, dynamics, topography and the genetic principle and the pleasure principle serve as a conceptual background against which current knowledge of the development of the mind is explored. This would include fundamentals of child development, the evolution of the self and the object concept, the theory of drives, psychosexual development, the development of psychic structure in the course of the individual's life.

Parallel to this approach, which roughly corresponds to the "anatomy" aspect of the educational experience, should be a course in psychoanalytic theory and methodology. While the theory of drives has to be touched on in discussion of development, in this aspect of the experience the physiology of mental functioning should be explored. This should concentrate on the structure of the psychoanalytic situation and the nature of the psychoanalytic process. This course should be based primarily on demonstrations from actual sessions, with detailed process notes. Conflict and compromise formation and the nature of mental mechanisms, whether used for defense or other purposes, should be illustrated from real experience. The methodology of psychoanalysis would belong in this track. How does one reach conclusions? What is the nature of psychoanalytic evidence, the difference between an anamnesis and the conclusions one can draw from it and process material and the conclusions one can draw from that. This would be combined with the principles of psychoanalytic technique. Clinical presentations from process material should be used to illustrate the evidence for and the usefulness of the basic concepts of psychoanalysis, e.g., determinism, dynamics, drive, comfort, compromise formation, etc.

For the purpose of orienting the student to the analytic concepts and to enable him to appreciate Freud's writings in particular and the literature in general, there should be a third track for the first year—the history of psychoanalytic concepts—a *rapid overall* survey of development of Freud's concepts and later elaboration by other contributors up until the present time. In this track, emphasis should be placed on the observational considerations that led to changes in psychoanalytic theory and practice. The student should come away with an idea that certain things have indeed been discarded while other things remain valid up until the present time. He should also have some appreciation of why certain proposals for change, even though not yet accepted, are offered by what is called "deviant" approaches.

The important overall principle guiding this first introduction to analysis and to the way analysis in general should be taught is to get away from the need for each individual in training to recapitulate the entire history of psychoanalysis, and also to have an objective understanding of the relationship between observational data (information derived within the psychoanalytic situation which is our laboratory instrument) and theoretical constructs. A specific objective would be to offset the tendency now widely used to impose comfortable and familiar I paradigms on certain configurations of the clinical material, without regard for their dynamic setting. This approach would suggest the omitting from the syllabus of many of the sacred cows of the psychoanalytic literature. Much of early Freud could be covered in summary fashion. I see no reason to include "The Project" in any syllabus. The "Studies in Hysteria" are interesting historical remnants. That work should not represent an introduction to psychoanalytic theory or practice, but that is how it is being used. The fact that there are germs in

"The Project" and in Chapter 7 of "The Interpretation of Dreams" of ideas that Freud developed later does not justify spending a student's time by going into detailed analysis of them. All the papers about the actual neuroses and the contributions concerning pent-up libido being transformed into anxiety could be covered in summary fashion. "The Moses of Michelangelo" has no place in the syllabus. It is a bit of applied analysis which might be used in an elective dealing with that subject. The Schreber case is not a case; it is an exercise in analysis applied to an autobiographical book. Freud wrote that book before he had the dual instinct theory. Would anybody today try to explicate the phenomenology of schizophrenia or psychosis in general using only libido theory? These are the kinds of questions that we have to face up to. When we do so, we realize how much we are prisoners of tradition. What is required is a bold fresh look at what we make our candidates read, especially in the first year.

REFERENCES

Arlow, J.A. (1972). Some dilemmas in psychoanalytic education. *Journal of the Ameriacan Psychoanalytic Association* 20:556–566.

THE LOVING SIDE OF THE SIBLING BOND: A FORCE FOR GROWTH OR CONFLICT

[Edward, J. (2009). *Issues in Psychoanalytic Psychology* 25:27–43.]

At the time I began preparing today's remarks, by a strange coincidence, I found in my files a note from a patient I had seen many years ago. Ms. Waters, as I shall refer to her, then a 20-year-old college student, was referred to me after she had made a serious suicidal attempt. Several years after she concluded her five year, twice-a-week treatment she married and moved to another state. I heard from her at the birth of each of her two little daughters, and for some years received holiday cards. Several times she phoned me when she was in the area visiting her family. In her note, Ms. Waters expressed her regrets that she had been unable to reach me during a recent visit to Long Island. She wrote: "When I called you, we were out on the Island at my brother's house, whom I have not seen in years. My children were beyond the point of exhaustion and I was beginning to feel badly that I had brought them out to Nassau County. Our stay was brief. Somehow for some reason, I have the need to see brothers and sisters whom I have not seen in so long a time, regardless of what the past may have been. Something about just being a unity for so long that I will probably always feel some strong attachment to them."

As I read, my thoughts went to Ms. Waters' family. She was the youngest of five children. Her father was an alcoholic who mistreated his children and both physically and emotionally abused his chronically depressed wife. *As* the sisters grew older they had banded together, supporting each other and their mother as best they could. Her two brothers, the eldest children in the family, however, mistreated their younger siblings and sexually abused her two sisters. Yet, despite the pain of the past, and her ambivalent feelings towards her brothers, Ms. Waters, as she indicated, had maintained a bond with them as members of her family and wanted to preserve some connection.

While Freud (1916–1917) recognized siblings as constituting a child's first love object, he was not speaking of the kind of bond, Ms. Waters was referring to. Rather he meant that like parents they were the objects of each other's early erotic, incestuous wishes, as well as serving as displacement or substitute objects for their Oedipal parents. For Freud, non-erotic feelings between brothers and sisters either represented aim inhibited manifestations of old sexual longings (1905), or served as defenses against what he regarded as the earliest attitudes between siblings—namely envy, hostility, and murderous wishes. "Even when siblings feel love for one another, and are bereaved at each other's death," Freud (1900 p. 251) maintained, that they "harbor evil wishes against them in their unconscious, dating from earlier times". It was this negative, hostile side of sibling relationships to which Freud gave most of his attention, though in fact his writings on our topic were limited.

Following Freud, sibling rivalry and discord tended to dominate psychoanalytic thinking on the subject (Neubauer, 1983). It was left to biographers as well as novelists to consider the positive feelings between siblings and the constructive roles they frequently play in each other's lives. Think of the novels of Louisa May Alcott, Caron McCullers or Jane Austin. Positive sibling relationships are often central in their writings (Hudson, 1992). In *Mansfield Park* (1995), for example, Austin wrote "Children of the same family, the same blood, with the same first associations and habits, have some means of enjoyment in their power, which no subsequent connections can supply;" She doubted, as she expressed it that "the precious remains of *this* (italics mine) earliest attachment are ever outlived."

Siblings have, as we know, played critical roles in the lives of many well known persons. One is reminded of the relationship between Vincent Van Gogh and his brother Thea. In his book, *Blood Brothers, Siblings as Writers,* Norman Kiell (1988) has shown how important their siblings were to the creativity and success of such writers as James Joyce, Aldous Huxley and Henry James. Those of you who have read Leonard Shengold's (1989) book *Soul Murder* may recall his moving account of the relationship between Rudyard Kipling and his sister, Trix. After what appears to have been a happy early childhood, Kipling at the age of six and Trix, who was three, were sent to England, and placed for the next six years in the care of extremely sadistic guardians. Kipling was the primary target of his foster mother's sadism. While, as Shengold points out, such children often deflect their rage away from the tormenting caretakers and displace it on a sibling, this was not so with the Kipling children. Instead, Kipling treated Trix as if he were the protective parent that they both so much needed. She, in turn, responded to his care with love, gratitude, and deep loyalty. Shengold regards this relationship as having been crucial for both children's development.

In the last twenty years or so psychoanalysts have, as this conference attests to, begun to appreciate that the bonds between siblings are far richer and more complex than previously thought. While continuing to recognize that envy, jealousy, rivalry and hatred, as well as incestuous, erotic longings between siblings may lead to pathology, they are beginning to identify ways in which siblings can make valuable contributions to each other's development, and how in many families they serve important supportive and restitutive functions (Agger, 1988).

In what follows, I shall briefly review some of what is still a limited body of literature on our topic. I will then share a case vignette of a young woman patient, focusing on how her love as well as her hatred for her older brother affected her development, her character, her pathology and her life. I will try to show how important siblings can be in dleir own right, even as they may also serve as displacement or substitute objects for their parents, how envy and rivalry between them may at times serve to defend against conflictual loving feelings, and how the vicissitudes of their relationship may lead to pathology, even as the relationship may at the same time favor growth. Finally, I hope to demonstrate how our attendance to sibling issues in the treatment of our patients may enrich our clinical efforts and enhance our therapeutic outcomes.

THE ROLE OF CULTURE

One caveat before I proceed. While the nature of any particular sibling relationship is determined by a multiplicity of unique personal and familial factors, it is important to bear in mind that the culture in which siblings develop also can play a role in shaping their relationship. While American families hope that their children will relate harmoniously to each odler, it is not an essential goal in our country. As a nation that places a high value on autonomy and competitiveness, sibling rivalry, up to a point, may even be considered a valuable training ground for success. This is not so in some parts of the world (Nuckols, 1993) where individuation from the family is seen as an aberration and competition is not regarded as a positive attribute. There are some countries in which siblings are expected to be lifelong participants in each other's lives. The obligations they share are not fleeting or optional but are expected role attributes that last a lifetime.

LITERATURE REVIEW

One of the most prolific contributors to our understanding of sibling relationships is Judy Dunn, an English psychiatrist, who along with various collaborators has studied siblings for many years. Though not an analyst as far as I can tell, her work has been drawn upon by many psychoanalysts. In the 80's in collaboration with her colleague, Carol Kendrick, (1982) she studied siblings from forty working class, intact, middle class English families who were between the ages of one and half to two years, when their baby siblings were born. All of the older children showed signs of unhappiness and responded to the new infant with envy and hatred. At the same time, though, they exhibited considerable interest in and affection for them. Regardless of their initial discomfort by the age of three these older brothers and sisters frequently acted as teachers and comforters as well as sensitive companions to them, and became highly skillful at reading, anticipating and responding to them. Unlike Margaret Mahler (1975), who when observing similar positive behaviors among the siblings she studied, regarded them as defensive, Dunn and Kendrick saw these affectionate expressions as indicative of a budding sense of empathy. In turn the young siblings often looked to their older brothers or sisters as a source of comfort and security, and when they were absent frequently showed signs of missing them, which these researchers interpreted as a sign of attachment.

Attachment between siblings was considered by Bowlby (1973) more than forty years ago, when he studied a group of children, ranging in age from thirteen to thirty months, who had been place temporarily in a residential nursery. The children who entered the nursery whether accompanied by an older or a younger sibling fared better and remained calmer than the other children. They cried less and showed fewer outbursts of marked hostility. During the early days of the placement especially, brothers and sisters sought each other's company, talked and played together. To outsiders they presented a united front, insisting to others that "She's not your sister, she's my sister."

In our earlier preoccupation with issues of rivalry, we have tended to pay less attention to attachment between siblings and its implications. In the case of children who have lost a brother or sister, for example, we have I think sometime focused overly on the impact of the surviving sibling's hostility and guilt, without sufficient attention to their loss of an also much valued object. Erna Furman reported on a case (1974) of a one-year-old child whose several-years-older brother had recently died. She was impressed by the fact that such a young child could be so acutely upset and inconsolable at the loss of a sibling.

Henry Parens (1988) has been among a number of psychoanalysts in our own country who has considered the role that siblings play in each other's development. He observes that siblings begin to be valued during the middle of the first year of life, and proposes that they engage in a kind of symbiosis with one another as well as participating in a form of separation individuation from each other. Leichman (1985), has detailed the steps that he believes siblings traverse in this process, likening them to the stages Mahler (1975) has outlined, albeit different. Siblings also aid, Parens proposes, in the child's separation from parents. As members of the extra-familial as well as the familial world and as peers as well as family members, they can serve as bridging or connecting objects to the other-than-mother world. According to Parens erotic activities and incestuous fantasies between siblings, which he regards as commonplace, can also be developmentally useful. Viewing erotic exchanges between siblings and the fantasies about them as primarily displacements of Oedipal longings for the parent, he regards them as helping to facilitate the necessary transformation of parental incestuous fantasies into age-appropriate peer sexual fantasies.

Contrary to Parens, Sharpe and Rosenblatt, (1995) have concluded that siblings also experience an erotic attraction to each other as persons in their own right. They have gone on to suggest that siblings experience an "Oedipal like" configuration in relation to each other similar to the parent child-constellation but different, thus the term "Oedipal-like." Given that there are greater opportunities for erotic and sexual activities among siblings, as well as the fact that taboos about such play are less severe than in the case of the parents, they believe that such strivings are less likely to be fully repressed and may not be relinquished as easily nor as soon as in the case of the parents. They have concluded that more individuals' romantic lives may be dominated by a continuing quest for an idealized, loved sibling who has been won or lost in an earlier oedipal struggle, than has been taken into account. Sander Abend (1984) has also proposed that while sibling love, may be used defensively, in some cases it may leave an "ineradicable stamp on the pattern of object choice in later life" (p. 426).

SIBLING INCEST

Consideration of the erotic ties between siblings raises the issue of sibling incest, about which relatively little has been written in the psychoanalytic literature, since Annie Reich's 1932 paper on her analysis of a young woman who from her sixteenth to her twentieth year had had an incestuous relationship with her one year older brother. Reich regarded this as evidence of severe pathology, which she related to her patient's early deprivation, abuse, and constant exposure to sexuality, as well as to the poor socio-economic conditions facing her family.

It has been estimated that if one defines incest as vaginal intercourse and/or oral-genital contact between brother and sister (Banks, 1982) sexual relations between siblings occur far more frequently than parent child incest (Gebhard et al. 1965, Wiehe, 1990). In many cases, sibling incest, as we know, has nothing to do with attraction or love but rather is motivated by the wish to achieve power (Bank and Kahn, 1997). When such is the case sexual relations are usually exploitative and coercive and frequently involves deliberate mental or physical cruelty. On the other hand incest that is prompted by more affectionate ties frequently occurs by mutual consent and contains elements of erotic pleasure, loyalty, compassion and love. In both cases incest is most likely to occur when relationships with parents are deeply troubled (Bank and Kahn 1997).

CASE STUDY

Let me now move on to my work with Ms. Fine, the name I shall give the patient. In presenting the following material, you will appreciate that I am narrowing my focus to highlight the contributions that her relationship with her brother made to Ms. Fine's development and her life. In doing so I am omitting the role of her own endowment, the contributions of each parent and their relationship with each other and with her brother, as well as other crucial factors, which affected and were affected by her sibling relationship.

Presenting Problems

Ms. Fine began her twice-a-week treatment after medication by her internist failed to relieve her severe depression. Her dysphoria had followed a promotion she had received at work some five months previously. An attractive, intelligent, sophisticated 36 year old, articulate businesswoman, she was married and without children. She had been in once-a-week psychotherapy for several years, some five years earlier, and felt she had derived much from that treatment. With that therapist's support and encouragement, she had gained greater self-confidence and had been able to complete her MBA. She would have preferred returning to her former therapist but he had retired. She was surprised that she once again could feel so badly, for she had thought she had gained more strength than it seems she had. Those difficulties that had not been relieved by her former treatment, she felt she had learned to live with. These included her anxiety around sex and her inability to achieve orgasm on the rare occasions when she and her husband did have intercourse. This felt to her like a flaw and she seemed to feel more ashamed than deprived. Though she wanted a child she had not yet been able to bring herself to seek medical help for her infertility. While her efforts at work had been rewarded by increases in salary and more recently by her promotion, she always felt on the brink of failure. She had acquaintances but no close friends, which she attributed to her inability to attract people. On those rare occasions when she began to get close to someone, and incident inevitably occurred which made her feel slighted, rejected or excluded, and which then led her to break off contact.

History

Ms. Fine came from a middle class family composed of her parents and an 8 year older brother, Peter. When treatment began her father was elderly and infirm and was being cared for by a homemaker. He lived across the country, so that she rarely saw him but spoke with him weekly. Ms. Fine described him as brilliant, distant, self-preoccupied, and critical. A man who was devoted to his work and to her brother and too little involved with herself or her mother, in the past and now with herself in the present.

Her mother, according to Ms. Fine, had been a weak, chronically depressed chronically ill woman, who lived an isolated life, limited to caring for her children and her home. Ms. Fine saw her as intrusive and clinging. She slept witll Ms. Fine during her adolescence. Ms. Fine grew up wanting to be as different from her mother as possible. With considerable guilt, she acknowledged that she experienced her mother's death, some five years prior to her treatment, as a relief, for she was convinced she would have had to become her mother's caretaker for life, had her mother lived.

Ms. Fine described her brother Peter, as successful, highly intelligent, and adventurous. As an adult he was quite renowned in his field.

He was the pride of her parents' when growing up and always remained, she believed, their favorite. In her weekly phone calls to her fatller, he continued to regale her with her brother's most recent accomplishments. Never an inquiry into what she was doing or feeling! As adults, brother and sister had for many years been geographically and emotionally distanced. She was both enraged and saddened by what she regarded as her brother's lack of any interest in her.

Ms. Fine's husband was a successful attorney, who appeared to be devoted to her, sometimes seeming to assume a parental role. To him she took all of her hurts and disappointments. He would spend hours listening to her and sympathizing. Husband and wife shared equally in the running of their household, enjoying a variety of interests together, and were as she said each other's "best friends." Mr. Fine did not seem concerned about their very limited sexual life, and she recognized that while he seemed to be trying to be sensitive to her difficulties, the arrangement somehow suited him as well.

Treatment

During the first months of Ms. Fine's treatment, she spent most of her sessions detailing incidents with her father, brother and colleagues past and present, in which she felt slighted or aggrieved in some way, often weeping as she recounted her experiences. It seemed to me that she herself frequently had unwittingly provoked the situations she complained of. She responded to any effort I made to engage her in looking at what had happened in one situation or another, as if I were criticizing her and implying that she had some responsibility for what had transpired. What she needed from me, she said was support, encouragement, and empathy, not analysis. When I did offer such, she often found my interventions insufficient or condescending. There was little I could do right during the first six months of her twice-a-week treatment.

However, after about seven months or so, a session occurred which was followed by some shift in her participation in the treatment. In the session I am referring to she had complained of a number of things. After about twenty minutes she paused, and I inquired about the first thing she had said in the session. She became enraged, noting that she had shared a number of thoughts, but I was only interested in what interested me. I was like her family. She began to weep and refused to say another word during the rest of the hours. When I inquired as to what she might have found more helpful for me to have responded to, she cried more loudly.

A little later I went on to say that while I regretted I had so upset her, I was not clear as to what was so offensive in what I had done. After sitting in silence for a while, I said I sometimes wondered at such times, when she was so profoundly hurt by me, whether without knowing it, she somehow wanted or needed to experience me as a hurtful person. She made no response.

Much to my surprise Ms. Fine returned for the next session, saying that she had thought about the session later and wondered if her tears had not been false. She could see that I had not really done anything that warranted such an extreme response. She had wasted the whole hour. I was right, when I once said that no matter what I did it was wrong. She was aware that she could experience the simplest question as hurtful. Sometimes when she left the session she herself wondered what could have been so upsetting in what I had done. Why was this happening? I encouraged her to think further about her question, particularly since what was occurring between us was what she often experienced with other people. Perhaps if we could get a better idea of why this was occurring in our work together, it might shed light on the difficulties she had with others outside the office.

It was shortly after these exchanges that the following hours pertaining to Ms. Fine's brother occurred. Brother and sister were at that time in greater contact over the phone around needed health care planning for their father. Though Ms. Fine acknowledged her brother was trying to be helpful, she was nonetheless disappointed, hurt and angry after each call, at what she experienced as his lack of concern for her.

Session I

This session followed an hour during which I had informed Ms. Fine of my upcoming vacation. She began the hour by telling me how unhappy she had been since our last meeting. She had been thinking of the exciting things I would probably be doing on my vacation, while she would be home leading her usual dull life. She started to weep, expressing how uninteresting a person she is in comparison to me. Then she spoke of her brother and his taking off on his ski trips during school vacations, while she was stuck at home. Everyone was interested in him. He was exciting, attractive and successful. In comparison she is "boring," and she knows her brother sees her as such. On the rare occasions when they meet now that they are adults he "suffers" her company. I pointed out that it seemed as if she was experiencing me as her brother, and letting us know how envious she had been of him, how limited she seemed to feel in comparison to him, and how painful that was for her. Gradually her crying ceased and she somewhat disinterestedly went on to talk about a work assignment for the rest of the session. As she rose from her chair to leave, she informed me that her brother had sent her a birthday gift recently. She sounded delighted for a moment, but by the time she reached the door she added bitterly, that it had arrived late. I think it was at that point in our work that I began to wonder if her focus on her envy, central as it was for her, might at times be in the service of defense.

Session II

During the two weeks I was gone, Ms. Fine sustained a slight physical injury to her arm which somewhat limited her activities. She expressed some concern as to whether she might be exaggerating the extent of this injury. According to her doctor the damage was sufficient to account for her discomfort. Yet she could not rid herself of the idea that she was making more of the condition than was warranted. She never quite knew how to assess the severity of a physical problem. She attributed this to her parents having minimized her physical ailments, which, as we discovered later, was actually not the case. While she was thinking about this she began to recall an afternoon when she was recovering from a stomach upset, and her mother had left her at home to purchase some groceries in a nearby store. Her brother came home from school and found her in intense pain. He put her on his bicycle and rushed her to the doctor whose office was nearby. She recalled with obvious pleasure that her brother had been very kind and attentive. He had remained wither until her mother arrived to take over. Suddenly her mood in the session changed and she resentfully added that then he went off to join his friends. I appreciated how disappointing it must have been to have so enjoyed his attention and then to have him leave her. However, wasn't it surprising, given all she had said about her brother's complete indifference to her to discover that there was at least one time when he had been attentive to her? Well she said it hadn't lasted. "Yes," I said and that seems the part that has remained with you. I wondered if there was something troubling about this obviously pleasant encounter with him that made her, in the end, want to view it as another unhappy event. I reminded her then of the time she had told me about his gift to her, but then immediately complained of its late arrival. It seemed to me that there was something about positive feelings between her and her brother that was troubling. She didn't know.

Session III

In the next session Ms. Fine began with her recollections of her brother visiting her in an apartment she had rented after her graduation from college. One night he went off to a club dinner to which only men were invited. When he returned they spent most of the night speaking of politics, philosophy, literature and she said with some obvious embarrassment "of all things, premarital sexuality." She was so pleased that he treated her as an equal and recalled how much it meant to feel herself on a par with him intellectually. She had found it strange though to be talking about sex with him, and here she made a slip, using her husband's name instead of her brother's She gave an indication that she noted the slip, but then quickly launched into a long tirade against male organizations that excluded women. I noted that once again after recalling an intimate experience with her brother, she had shifted to her feelings of resentment and envy. I thought that our last sessions, including today's, suggested that despite all of her resentment and criticism, she had also loved her brother dearly and that he had not been as indifferent to her as she had suggested he was. I thought that in using her husband's name instead of her brother's, she was expressing, without being aware of it that she wished her brother could be her husband and that they could make love. Her picture of her brother as an arrogant male with special privileges and of herself as an angry, envious, woman seemed to me, to some extent to guard against such uncomfortable wishes. After some moments of silence, Ms. Fine began to speak with feeling of her deep admiration for her brother. When he was home during their childhood, he brought light to an otherwise drab household. While she envied his ability to liven up the family, she was happier when he was home. I thought that she often did envy her brother and felt very angry with him. These were strong feelings in themselves, but from what she was saying today I thought she sometimes focused on her envy and hatred to avoid the loving feelings that seemed more difficult for her to deal with. After a rather long silence Ms. Fine said she had been thinking about whether or not her brother might not have similar feelings towards her. Perhaps his distancing from her was also protective? She now remembered his hugging her sometimes when she was a little girl. Once when she was around six years old, he took her on his lap and she could recall feeling very good but also as if they were doing something wrong. This memory was followed by her commenting that she suddenly felt happy. The idea of his wanting to be close to her made her feel attractive. As soon as she said this, she began to criticize him for having been inappropriate with her. This was followed by a burst of anger against her mother, whom she had told about the incident, and who hadn't taken it seriously. I drew her attention then to her once again becoming angry with her brother immediately after she expressed good feelings about him and about herself, feelings that were both affectionate and sexual. Perhaps she needed to keep any thought of his longing for her as she longed for him out of her mind, since such feelings between them felt wrong. Unfortunately in protecting herself against these thoughts she had to perceive herself as unattractive and unlovable, thereby further diminishing her self-regard. We could see from what she said that to think of herself as attractive was to think of closeness with her brother. This meant something forbidden, something incestuous.

Session IV

In the following session Ms. Fine began by describing a phone call from her brother. Their father's health had worsened, and her brother had offered to visit him. While her brother lived somewhat closer to their father than she did, it still meant a long trip and taking time off from his professional responsibilities. He had often in the past made extra efforts on behalf of both their parents and she always had found herself resentful. She saw it as his way of ingratiating himself and making her look inattentive. She was surprised that she could look upon what he was doing now as an effort to spare her. She felt gratitude and warmth towards him and had expressed her appreciation for his help. This made her feel good about him and about herself.

Session V

In the next session Ms. Fine reported that her mood had been fluctuating. She was warmed by the exchange with her brother, but felt she was becoming increasingly inept at work. She referred to herself as "hopeless." She questioned whether her discomfort had anything to do with what we had been talking about with regards to her brother. After our previous session she had sent a holiday card to him. Last night she had been tormented with thoughts of her worthlessness. There is a battle taking place in her mind, she said, between a criticizing part of her and a part that feels criticized. She recognizes that she needs to beat up on herself. When she woke up this morning she felt no one liked her. She was beginning to wonder to what extent she created these bad feelings about herself. Now she can see that as soon as she feels good, she begins to think about how limited or inadequate she is. It is as if she needs to destroy the good feelings.

At this moment Ms. Fine became visibly troubled. After a few moments of silence, she explained that an old fantasy had crossed her mind. Beginning to cry, she explained that she suffers in the fantasy but she is also aroused and excited. She imagines herself being tied up and a man forcing a scarf into her mouth. If she spits it out she will be beaten.

Like all psychic phenomena this fantasy was multiply determined (Waelder, 1936). However, in this hour, we understood it as indicating how she could allow herself to enjoy the fantasy of sexual pleasure with her brother provided someone else was put in his place and she could imagine being forced to submit and tolerate pain. Suffering was the condition for enjoying sex. In our later work, we came to see how the thoughts of herself as a hurt, demeaned woman, as a victim of domineering, insensitive others, of being beaten if you will, represented derivatives of this fantasy as did her beating herself mentally and provoking ill treatment from others. Here we can observe a type of masochism, described by Freud (1919) in which pain serves as a form of sexual gratification and at the same time provides a means of punishment.

After we considered the fantasy together in that session, Ms. Fine was silent for several moments. Then she began to speak of a book she had read when she was a teenager. The story was about a girl who was deeply admired and loved by her older brother though he constantly castigated and hurt her. She stoically endured his ill treatment. When they grew up they became increasingly estranged. Ultimately her brother refused to see her at all for he erroneously believed she was involved in a scandalous love affair. At the end of the book there was a catastrophic flood. Ms. Fine was not clear whether the sister tried to rescue the brother or vice versa. However, they both drowned. She concluded her account of the book by saying that finally in death the sister and brother were joined.

Many of you will recognize that the book she was referring to was *Mill On The Floss* by George Elliott. Elliott says of her characters' last moments "brother and sister had gone down in an embrace never to be parted: living through again in one supreme moment the days when they had clasped their little hands in love and roamed the daisied fields together" (p. 557). The book ends with the inscription written on their tombstone "In their death they were not divided."

Let me remind you that *Mill On The Floss* deals with at least two of Ms. Fine's unconscious fantasies—one to die with her brother and one to be in a position to rescue him. The latent content of the first fantasy can be understood as a wish to have intercourse with him and the second to have a baby with him. You may recall that Ernest Jones (1911) regarded the wish to die with another as suggesting a wish to sleep and lie together. Where there is a belief in an afterlife such a wish, he proposed, suggests the hope that after death, what has been denied in life will finally be granted. The rescue fantasy according to Freud (1910) can possess the significance of giving a child to someone or bearing mother or father's child.

Progress in treatment

Unfortunately Ms. Fine was forced to conclude her treatment after the fourth year, which we both thought was premature. However, our work together around her relationship with her brother seemed to have proven beneficial, though it is of course difficult to ascertain with surety what particular strands of her multi-faceted treatment enabled her to move ahead. Yet our efforts together seemed to have enabled her to see how she sometimes had provoked his ill treatment in the past, and before the treatment ended she was able to change sufficiently so that they achieved a greater cordiality in their limited exchanges. Unfortunately, she nonetheless had to face the fact that her brother was not interested in a more intimate relationship with her. What helped to soften the impact of this realization was her recognition that he tended to isolate himself even from his wife and children. She no longer assumed the onus for their lack of closeness. She became much less preoccupied with him, and when she thought about him it was with less hurt and anger. He came to exert much less influence on her thinking and her life. Interestingly, though she did not gain a more meaningful relationship with her brother, she did become better able to make and maintain friendships. I attributed this in part to her greater awareness of the way in which she had often related to colleagues and friends as displacement objects for her brother, as well as to her need to provoke in others the hurt and disappointment that had become masochistically gratifying for her.

This work also had an impact on her sexual anxiety, and before the treatment ended she had begun to experience desire for her husband, and to seek intercourse. As one might expect what was a gain for her was a problem for him. He was unable to respond and with difficulty she finally persuaded him to seek treatment, but he ended after only a few sessions.

DISCUSSION

Why, one might wonder, did this sibling relationship become so influential? Largely, I think this was due to the failures of the parents to partner their daughter more adequately as a result of their own psychological problems. In such situations, siblings often overly turn to each other as parental substitutes seeking to have needs met that are beyond even a much older sibling's capacity to respond to adequately. Peter could not be the mother or the father that she developmentally needed and wanted. That he was significantly older than her, was a matter of developmental consequence itself. On one hand she could not successfully compete in many areas with a sibling eight years her senior ` which seemed to have increased her envy and resentment of him. On the other hand as an older brother he was a more attractive, romantic figure than a sibling closer to her age might have been. She was unable to win out over him nor to win him. At the same time, it is important to note that Ms. Fine also feared competing with Peter lest he retaliate, and she' feared winning him lest she be punished for an "oedipal-like" victory (Freud, 1916). Unfortunately, due to the vicissitudes of her early development, she lacked those narcissistic resources which ordinarily help cushion such childhood failures and disappointments.

Yet, despite these considerations, Ms. Fine's brother also served to aid in his sister's development. For example, in view of what appears to have been her father's minimal role in her upbringing, her love for her brother helped her, I believe, to separate from her mother to the degree that she did. If she had not been so drawn to him and if her mother had not had Peter to focus some of her maternal attention on, I believe Ms. Fine's development might have even been more compromised. Her brother also acted as a spur for her growth. There were many interests she adopted in order to please him, and he clearly served as an object for identification. Her love of sports, her interest in travel, her political activities all represented interests of his, which she had emulated, and which she was able to tap into, as the treatment progressed.

CONCLUSION

According to research (Gold, Woodbury and George, 1990), rivalry and discordant feelings between siblings ordinarily tend to lessen as they age. Those who feel they have been hurt by their brothers or sisters earlier in life, often see themselves as mellowing, forgetting or forgiving old hurts and conflicts. However, for many individuals, their sibling conflicts remain unresolved and powerful. Early unmodified representations of brothers and sisters continue to remain overly influential and demand the continual attention of their adult minds (Volkan and Ast, 1997). Unfortunately, in the past, when we paid less attention to sibling relationships in treatment, such individuals were apt to conclude their therapy, despite having made appreciable changes in their interpersonal relationships with their parents, with their siblings unchanged (Balsam, 1988). I am hopeful that our increased interest in the understanding of the potential roles that siblings may play in one another's development and lives, will lead us to accord sibling relationships to more central place in our clinical work. This means becoming more alert to sibling transferences (Schecter, 1999) as well as sibling countertransferences, something I have failed to consider in this presentation, largely because I was not as mindful as such in the years I treated Ms. Fine. I would hope that would not be the case today.

I should like now to conclude this presentation with a few words from Arthur Miller's play *The Price,* (1963), which I think conveys something of what it can be like when sibling relationships remain frozen in the childhood past, and brothers and sisters arc thus deprived of the friendship, as well as the comfort and support, they might offer to each other had their relationship had the opportunity to mature. *The Price* (1963) is a drama about two adult brothers, who have long been separated, and are brought together by their father's death to dispose of his estate. The two brothers are very different. One, the elder, Victor has been educated, and is rich, and self-indulgent; the other, Walter is undereducated, poor, self-sacrificing, and a policeman. Victor gave up college and the pursuit of his chosen career as a scientist in order to support their father. His hurt and resentment of his brother's failure to help out are with him always. When they meet in the play, Walter has had a breakdown, has been hospitalized and I assume has had some treatment. He is trying to refashion his life, and is seeking to form a closer relationship with his brother. Expressing his regret over what has transpired in the past, he reveals that he actually had made efforts to help his father out, which their father had refused and had not advised Victor. Victor remains unmoved as far as one can tell and despite Walter's efforts, continues to respond to him as the brother of the past. I quote from the play:

> *Walter:* . . . we're brothers. It was only two seemingly different roads out of the same trap. It's almost as though . . . we're like two halves of the same guy. As though we can't quite move ahead alone. You ever feel that way? . . . (Vic is silent) Vic?

Vic answers him:

> *Victor:* Walter, I'll tell you there are days when I can't remember what I've got against you. (He laughs emptily in suffering) It hangs in me like a rock . . . And you can go crazy trying to figure it out when all the reasons disappear—when you can't even hate any more (Miller, 1969, p. 91).

REFERENCES

ABEND, S.M. (1984). Sibling love and object choice. *Psychoanalytic Quarterly.* LIII:525–430.

AUSTIN, J. (1995) *Mansfield Park.* New York: Modern Library.

BALSMI, R.H. (1988). On being good: The Internalized sibling with examples from late adolescent analyses. *Psychoanalytic Inquire.* 3:66–87.

BANK, S.P. & KAHN, M.D. (1997). *The Sibling Bond.* New York: Basic Books.

BOWLBY, J. (1973). *Attachment and Loss* Vol II. New York: Basic Books.

DUNN, J. & KENDIRICK, C. (1982). *Siblings Love, Envy & Understanding.* Cambridge. Mass: Harvard University Press.

ELLIOT, G. (1994). *Mill on the Floss* New York: WW Norton.

FREUD, S. (1900). *The Interpretation of Dreams 4 & 5. Standard Edition.* London: The Hogarth Press.

(1905). Three Essays on Sexuality. 7:125–243.

(1908). On the sexual theories of children. 9:205–22.

(1910 a). Five Lectures on psycho-analysis. 11:3–59.

(1910 b). Contributions to the psychology of love. 11:164–175.

(1916). Some Character-Types met with in Psycho-Analytic Work. Those Who are Wrecked by Success. 14:316–331.

(1916–1917). Introductory lectures on psycho-analysis. 16:243–448.

(1919). 'A Child is being beaten': A contribution to the study of the origin of sexual perversions. 17:175–204.

FURMAN, E. (1974). *A Child's Parent Dies.* New Haven: Yale University Press.

GEBHARD, P.H., et al. (1965) *Sex offenders: An Analysis of Types.* New York: Harper & Row.

GOLD, D.T., WOODBURY, M.A. & GEORGE, L.K. (1990) Relationship classification using grade of membership analysis: A Typology of sibling relationships in later life. *Journal Gerontology.* 45:543–551.

HUDSON, G.A. (1992). *Sibling Love and incest in Jane Austen's Fictions.* New York: St. Martins Press.

JONES, E. (1911). On "dying together" *Essays on Applied Psychoanalysis.* 1:9–15 London: Hogarth Press. 1951.

KIELL, N. Editor (1983). *Blood Brothers. Siblings as Writers.* New York. International Universities Press.

Leichtman, M. (1985). Influence of .an older sibling on the separation-individuation process. *Psychoanalytic Study of the Child* 40:111–162.

MAHLER, M., PINE, F. & BERGMAN, A. (1975). *The Psychological Birth of the Human Infant.* New York: Basic Books, Inc.

MILLER, A. (1969) *The Price.* New York: Bantam.

NEUBAUER, P.B. (1983). The importance of the sibling experience. *Psychoanalytic Study of the Child* 38:325–336.

NUCKOLLS, C.W, Editor. (1993) *Siblings in South Asia.* New York. London. The Guilford Press.

PARENS, H. (1988). Siblings in early childhood: some direct observational findings. *Psychoanalytic Inquiry.* 8:31–50.

REICH, A. (1973). *Annie Reich: Psychoanalytic Contributions.* New York. International Universities Press.

SCHECTER, R.A. (1999). The meaning and interpretation of sibling-transference in the clinical situation. *Issues in Psychoanalytic Psychology.* 21:1–10.

SHARPE, S.A. & ALLAN D. ROSENBLATT. (1994). Oedipal siblings triangles. *Journal of the American Psychoanalytic Association.* 42:491–523.

SHENGOLD, L. (1989). *Soul Murder.* New York: Fawcett Columbine.

VOLKAN, V. & AST. G. (1999). *Siblings in the Unconscious.* New York. International Universities Press.

WAELDER, R. (1936). The Principle of multiple function. *The Psychoanalytic Quarterly.* 5:45–62.

WIEHE, V. (1990). *Sibling Abuse. Hidden Physical, Emotional and Sexual Trauma.* New York: Lexington Books.

MY CONVERSATIONS WITH THE SUPEREGO AND THE EGO: AN EXPERIMENTAL APPROACH TO PSYCHOTHERAPY TECHNIQUE

[Fancher, E. (2014). *Psychoanalytic Review* 101(1):81–94.]

The author traces the history of superego theories in Freud's work and shows how latter contributions to psychoanalytic theory by Gray, the Novicks, and Arlow have provided theoretical foundations for innovative treatments in psycho-analytic psychotherapy. Arlow's insight into the continuous debates and discussions within our patients provides us with an opportunity to join in these discussions. Vignettes from two mildly obsessional male patients seen twice and twice a week provide demonstrations of this approach in psycho-analytic psychotherapy.

The technical recommendations for psychoanalysis were developed for treatment for patients seen four to six times per week on the couch. The modifications of technique adopted for psychotherapy patients seen once or twice a week sitting up have always been unclear. Freud saw patients six times per week and complained of the "Monday crust" which inter-fered with the momentum of the treatment and made working through more difficult. Recently, Marion Oliner (2008) pointed out that therapists who see their patients once a week have to contend with a "six-day crust." As an analyst who also practices once- and twice-a-week psycho-analytic psychotherapy, I have been interested in exploring how such less-frequent treatment might be improved. I have found that a review and revision of superego theory has provided me with useful formula-tions for the treatment of some once- and twice-a-week patients.

The procedure of psychoanalytic psychotherapy is aimed at provid-ing the therapist with insight into how the patient's mind works, in such a way that he or she can share this insight with the patient through inter-pretations. The goal of treatment is to help patients understand how their mind works so as to increase their ability to take better control of their life and help them reduce their symptoms and inhibitions. To provide this help the therapist must have at least a rough model of how the mind works.

DEVELOPMENT OF THE STRUCTURAL MODEL

Freud experimented with several models of the mind before he developed the "structural theory" based on the systems of id, ego and the superego (Freud, 1923, 1933) and a revised concept of anxiety as an unconscious signal of psychic danger (Freud, 1926). In a recent history of psycho-analysis through the lifetime of Freud, *Revolution in Mind,* George Mahari (2008) asserts that the proper translation of Ego, Id, and Superego should be "I," "It," and "Over-I" He complains that "the use of Latinate terms stripped the words of any connection to ordinary internal experi-ence" (p. 464). More recently, Mark Solms (20 13), editor of the forth-coming *Revised Standard Edition of the Complete Psychological Works of Sigmund Freud,* reviewed this issue and decided to continue the use of Strachey's terms, ego, id, and superego.

Freud described the superego as that portion of the ego that repre-sents the voice of conscience, derived originally from conflict during the oedipal period. Although he regarded superego functioning as normal, most of his discussion was directed to the role of the superego in patholo-gies such as obsessive-compulsive neurosis, depression, masochism, and so on, but he also recognized that the superego provided the functions of self-observation and self-regard (Freud, 1933, p. 60). The superego was regarded by Freud as an independent agency at times, but at other times as merging with the ego itself. He posited that the superego is always expressed in words of admonition, either positive or negative, and con-scious or unconscious, and it originates in early childhood identifications with parents or other authorities.

I first became interested in the clinical use of superego concepts many years ago when one of my mentors, Gertrude Blank (personal communi-cation, 1965), mentioned that she believed that the greatest advancement in psychoanalysis in the coming decades would be in a greater under-standing of the superego. I was also influenced by another of my early teachers, Karen Horney (in her 1948 lectures at the New School for Social Research), who emphasized the role of "the tyranny of the should" in her lectures on the psychopathology of neurosis. A few years ago I became particularly interested in the problems of clinical interpretations of superego elements when I reviewed *A Primer of Clinical Interpretation,* by P. F. D. Rubovits-Seitz (2002), for the *Psychologist-Psychoanalyst* (Fancher, 2003). This book provides examples of how many analysts from various schools actually word their interpretations. I was struck by how few of the interpretations reported in the book dealt with superego issues.

One of the early theoreticians of the new "ego psychology" was Robert Waelder (1936), who presented a theory of psychological over-determination in which the ego was burdened by the simultaneous need to satisfy, in various degrees, the demands of the id, or drives, the superego, reality, the repetition compulsion, and the needs of the ego itself. Behavior and symptoms were understood in terms of compromises the ego made between these various pressures.

After World War II, ego psychologists led by Arlow and Brenner (1964) and Charles Brenner (1982) developed a refined version of the structural school of psychoanalysis, which emphasized that the three elements in the structure interacted with each other in terms of conflict and compromise formation. They also posited that each of the three agencies of the psyche, including the superego, were formed in terms of conflict and compromise formation, and that they interacted with each other on the basis of conflict and compromise between each of them. Later, Brenner (1994) again revised his assessment of the structural theory and of the role of the superego as a separate agency. He proposed that the superego concept be replaced with "one of the calamities of childhood, the calamity of parental disapproval"—a reflection of the verbal criticism by the parents which had been internalized (p.483).

In 1960, Joseph Sandler wrote a paper complaining about the vagueness of the superego concept and the difficulty his researchers at Anna Freud's Hampstead Clinic had in pinning down superego elements in their Index of psychoanalytic terms. He felt that "the concept itself . . . is one which is indistinct, and it has become increasingly so with the absorption into our day-to-day thinking of advance in ego psychology" (p. 145).

Roy Schafer (1960), in the same issue of that journal, made a very different contribution by describing the history of superegolike ideas such as guilt in Freud's work from the earliest days through the end of his life. In his paper "The Loving and Beloved Superego in Freud's Structural Theory," he also demonstrated the broad range of superego influence in Freud's work other than guilt and showed how the importance of positive superego love for the self contributed to self-esteem and to healthy psychic functioning. He saw that positive superego functioning plays an important role in psychic health and is an element in cognitive functioning, something Freud had noted in 1933 (p. 60).

Several years later, Jack and Kerry Kelly Novick (2004) followed up on Schafer's theme by developing a clinically interesting reformulation of the superego in the form of a "dual-track model of two modes of superego functioning: the 'closed' sadomasochistic, omnipotent superego and the 'open' competent, loving, reality-attuned superego." They demonstrate the value of their formulation of a dual-track model with several clinical examples.

The most important recent contribution to superego clinical theory is found in a series of papers by Paul Gray (1994). He was one of the few analysts who emphasized the clinical importance of superego analysis in the 1980s and 1990s in psychoanalytic treatment. His paper on '"Developmental Lag' in the Evolution of Technique" (1982) called attention to the neglect of the insights of ego psychology to our clinical work. In a series of closely reasoned papers, he describes in detail superego analysis in resolving defenses and the value of "close process observation" in the analytic situation. Gray emphasized the need for focused interpretation of the defensive role of superego elements in the treatment of neurotic patients (see Levenson, 2007, for a review of Gray's work).

The person who has most influenced my understanding of the clinical aspects of the superego is Jacob Arlow. In 1982 Arlow returned to the issues Sandler had discussed in 1960 and broadened our understanding of the range of superego functioning. In his paper "Problems of the Superego Concept," he explained,

> The superego is by no means a uniform, coherent, integrated harmonious structure. It is a mass of contradictions, fraught with internal inconsistencies, or as we say in our technical language, intrasystemic conflicts. Its functioning is neither uniform nor reliable . . . . The superego is a conglomeration of many identifications derived from experiences with objects, from fantasies and imagination and stemming from almost all levels of development, not necessarily exclusively those of the oedipal or postoedipal period (p. 234).

In one of his last papers Arlow (1995) followed up on the insights of his 1982 paper. He did not write about the superego directly, but pointed out the dialogue in the mind which I feel is between elements of the superego, or superegos, and the ego. He pointed out,

> When we intervene, it is not to enter a conversation with the patient. What we do is elucidate for the patient the nature of the conversation that has been taking place. But it is not a conversation between a patient and ourselves that we have been privy to. It is a conversation, or more appropriately a debate, that has been taking place within the patient We have been observing how different voices within the patient have been asserting themselves, demanding unbridled pursuit of wishes, condemning hostile erotic, or self-centered pursuits, cautioning against the realistic and unrealistic consequences of thought and action, and so on. (p. 231)

Arlow's descriptions of the internal dialogue between various internal voices can be best understood as a debate between ego and superego elements that occurs continuously in our patients.

Clinically, I try to listen for every evidence of the internalized voice(s) of the other(s) as reflections of the superego, both conscious and unconscious. I listen particularly to the voices of the "should" and of the contradictions from the variety of "voices" and how the ego responds to them.

A few years ago I began to experiment with ways to focus on superego issues in some psychotherapy patients and interpret these issues in a fairly direct way. I euphemistically called this approach "conversations with the superego and the ego," but it is really an attempt to intervene on the side of the ego in a conversation between the ego and the superego that has been frozen in compromises reflected in symptoms and inhibitions. I try to enter the conversation by calling attention to those superego "voices," conscious and unconscious, pressuring the patient, so that he or she can better understand them and so, hopefully, his or her ego can respond to them.

CLINICAL VIGNETTES

I will provide some clinical data demonstrating my use of focusing on superego dynamics in the treatment of two professional men, about twenty years apart in age, but with somewhat similar problems. Both have obsessive-compulsive tendencies, problems with time management, and complaints of "clenched jaw" syndrome when they started treatment. Both men have administrative positions at work and both have problems disciplining their subordinates. In presenting these few vignettes from ongoing treatments, it should be recognized that these interventions are small pieces of "working through," and that the dynamics exposed were focused on over and over again before the patients were able to modify some of the symptoms and inhibitions that brought them to treatment.

I will call the older man Mr. Olds. He is a bright professional man in his mid-fifties, and is in once-a-week therapy for self-defeating habits and for problems about time. He complained that he went to work each day with an agenda of work that he planned to accomplish, but that he always gets sidetracked when someone phones him or comes into his office, so he can play the "good guy" to everyone. The result is that he very often has to work late into the evening to finish his schedule and then feels that he has been a victim. He leaves at the end of the day frustrated and angry with himself. This symptom is one among many, but is typical of others. I said to him: "When your secretary told you there was a call, the 'voice' of your agenda told you to tell her to take a message and call back, but another 'voice' argued with the first and said, 'No, I don't want to hold to my original intent, I want to be interrupted so I can fail at my plan and feel sorry for myself, so I'll take the call.' The problem is that the second voice was unconscious, so you weren't fully aware of the argument going on in your head." This interpretation led him to associate to other examples of his masochistic behavior. He reported a new fantasy/metaphor for how he acted. He saw himself as Dr. Jekyll and Mr. Hyde. We analyzed how he played the role of the "good guy," Dr. Jekyll, especially with his employees and colleagues up to a point, then he would suddenly switch to Mr. Hyde and yell at the very people he had just indulged. I suggested that his role of Dr. Jekyll led to an anxiety attack because he felt out of control and felt he was being taken advantage of by others. I regard this approach as a way of dramatizing the role of the unconscious superego in conflict with the ego. It is a way of making the conflict underlying the symptom more real and accessible. It is also an opening for the ego to talk back to the superego(s) and thus to take a more active role in the treatment.

This same patient is also in a perpetual race against time. He evaluates exactly how much time it will take to get to his commuter train, both going to work and going home, and races every day to just make the train with no time to spare. He doesn't always win this race. He is often late to his sessions, for the same reason. I interpret to him that he has a narcissistic fantasy that he is a superman and can win any race (an omnipotent ego-ideal) but is constantly frustrated by the limitations of reality and ends up in a rage against his colleagues and employees. I interpret to him that he is driven by an internal "voice" that requires him to compete against everyone, and even against time. For the same reason he found it hard to determine what was important or unimportant in his work because his perfectionism required him to do every task perfectly, no matter how unimportant it might be in reality.

When we started treatment he was in a rage against his colleagues for not appreciating him enough, or paying him enough. He admitted that he frequently attacked them, and gave them plenty of reasons not to love him.

He had a dream: He was walking the plank, not ten feet or fifteen feet from the end, but a few inches. His association was that he is always worried about making a mistake at work, even a very minor one. I pointed out that he had a voice in his head that said he would be killed if he made even the smallest mistake. A few weeks after that dream he woke up thinking about his fear of "being found out," as in the Holocaust, because he might send out a letter with an error. I pointed out that there were two voices in his head about the letter. One voice said it would be a Holocaust if he sent it out with the wrong punctuation, so he had better hold on to it and stay late to review it. The other voice is the voice of reason which points out that the letter is really not very important anyway, and if there are any errors they will be minor, and ·hardly a Holocaust. These two voices are having a dispute, and I suggest to Mr. Olds that he will have to decide which side he will take.

Mr. Olds is concerned that he should be seen as virtuous and wants to be seen as a model for others to admire for his modesty and frugality. He drives a ten-year-old wreck to demonstrate to his neighbors that he doesn't put on airs. He competes with everyone at work. He assigns work to his assistants but then competes with them by doing the work himself and feels virtuous that he did the work, and is superior to them because he did it better than they could. He has a fantasy that his subordinates will see how hard he works and follow his example, but becomes frustrated and angry when they fail to imitate his model of intensive devotion to work.

When he achieved a very important goal in business, he realized that he could not enjoy his achievement. His harsh superego told him that it was not important, that he has no right to feel satisfaction with his successes, and that he should get on to the next task. He mentioned that he often feels like a private in the army who has to take orders from everyone. If someone asks him to do something he can't say "no." I interpret that there is a voice in his head that orders him to try to do everything for others, and that they will praise him as a hero, a super-man, for doing so much, but at the same time another voice tells him that he has been a victim and he is cheated. Then, there is a third voice that says, "Wait a minute, what is the most logical and realistic decision to make for this situation?"

Recently Mr. Olds reported that he was ten minutes late to therapy because he had misplaced his car keys. He said," Usually if that had happened I would have run around the house hysterically calling myself stupid and bad, but today, I was calm and looked until I found them." I said, "Today, you listened to the voice of reason, that your lost keys did not constitute a Holocaust." "Yes," he agreed.

To whom do we speak when we interpret? Traditionally we say we address the ego, of course, in its conflict with id and superego elements. In clinical work there are often several superego voices involved in conflict with the ego, and sometimes there are conflicts between superego voices themselves.

Let me give another example:

I will call the younger patient Mr. Young. He is a professional man in his mid-thirties with obsessional problems that make it hard for him to make decisions in his love life or finish a variety of tasks at work or home. He is seen twice a week sitting up. When I called the analyst who had referred Mr. Young to me, he said "What? I gave him your name two years ago. It has taken him this long to come for treatment." Mr. Young told me that he had come to see me only because his live-in girlfriend had threatened to leave him if he didn't come into therapy. They have lived together for several years and she wants to buy a home, marry, and have children, but he resists.

Mr. Young is head of an office of twelve to fourteen employees, for a firm headquartered elsewhere. In addition to his "clenched jaw" syndrome, he complains that when he is angry or anxious, he often can't return phone calls or e-mail at his job. He hadn't filed his taxes for the past few years, so he hadn't collected reimbursements he was entitled to. He arranged for his company to deposit his pay in a bank account, but since he often doesn't open his mail he never knows how much money he has. He knows that this behavior is crazy and wants to change it, but is very threatened by the idea of psychotherapy.

Unlike Mr. Olds, he is never late, and in fact, is always exactly on time, to the minute, but during the first few years he would usually be silent and often start the hour with "I have nothing to say today."

One day Mr. Young sat down, and as he retied his shoelaces he said, "I need new shoelaces, these are falling apart." *[Silence.]* "I have nothing to say today."

THERAPIST: You have already said something when you mentioned that you needed new shoelaces.

MR. YOUNG: Oh, yes, but I might not buy them for several weeks. I will forget that I need them when I leave here, and remember to buy them only when they are so frayed I can't use them any more at all.

THERAPIST: So you hear the voice of several "shoulds." One voice says you should buy new shoelaces because that is a sensible thing to do before they fray completely. But another voice says, "No, play the role of a victim who can't afford new shoelaces, or doesn't deserve them, and then you can feel sorry for yourself and present yourself to the world as virtuous and frugal." You tell yourself that you can buy the shoelaces only when you will be forced to do so by reality. This is like the voice that we have talked about that says you don't have to remember what we talk about here after you leave.

MR. YOUNG: That reminds me that I have postponed calling X back for weeks at work, and I should, and I don't know why I can't. I tell myself that it is so long now that I will look foolish if I call now, so put it off even more.

THERAPIST: So there are three, and maybe four "voices" operating in your mind at any one time, now. One voice says you should call X, it is the right thing to do. Another voice is your defense attorney, providing you with rationalizations for your defiance of that "should," a defense which you don't really believe yourself. And the third voice is unconscious and not too clear, but it is defiant, stubborn, and says you will not give in to that "should" to call X, although you don't know why. You are just so angry at X for making demands on you. So you are paralyzed by all these conflicting "voices." And I am part of the confusion, because I keep giving you another "should" that you should talk about whatever is on your mind here, which you rebel against also.

COMMENT: Similar superego conflicts are reflected in Mr. Young's relations with his live-in girlfriend, his friends, and his colleagues and other people connected with work, as well as his attitude toward money.

Let me give another example of superego elements in this same patient's therapy.

MR. YOUNG: *(Started the hour)* You know I am superstitious.

THERAPIST: How do you mean?

MR. YOUNG: I always walk exactly the same route from my job to your office. I know that if J deviated from this exact route, nothing bad would happen, but I think that somethi~g might go wrong. When I was a kid, if I was watching a sports game on TV and switched channels, and later switched back to my team, I had the thought that my team might loose because I was not loyal and had switched them off, and shouldn't have done that. [superego fantasy]

THERAPIST: So you have a fantasy that you have been unfaithful to your favorite team and that they will be hurt magically by that. This is a fantasy that you are guilty of not loving your team enough, and that they will read your mind and blame you for losing. You have said that you have a similar fantasy about me, that I can read your mind and do something to make your symptoms go away magically if I wished to.

MR. YOUNG: Well, you should know how to do that. You are the expert. At least you should know how long it would take. I know that I don't do everything at work that I am supposed to do, but I'm not too bad. I make up for it by not taking vacations, and I am always in to work on time.

THERAPIST: You have a raging debate going on in your head all the time between "You should do more work, and finish certain tasks," versus "No, I won't give in, but you can't punish me because I punish myself by not taking vacations and by coming in on time." You know that your bosses don't care about your vacations or coming on time, but you feel guilty about not doing your job more efficiently, as you are supposed to. There is another voice, a higher authority in your head, that evaluates your virtue or defiance and judges you all the time. And, if you take another route to come see me, something bad might happen to you or to me, especially since I make you come here and haven't cured you of your problems yet, as I am supposed to do.

Recently Mr. Young arrived at his 1:30 appointment and said he felt a little dizzy. He had arrived by plane at 4 a.m. and had gone into work without having anything to eat. Why not? It had something to do with feeling superior to other people-Look how much he can deprive himself. How virtuous this is. Would anyone else know about this virtue? No, but he would know. Also, he could have bought a sandwich for $3, but by not doing that he had saved that $3. Could he not afford $3 for a sandwich? Yes, of course, but it also has to do with a sense of virtue. This pattern is related to his masochistic failure to file his income tax for a refund, and to fail to file for reimbursement for therapy, and to fail to invest his money, or even look at his bank account, or open his mail, as if handling money is beneath him.

He is contemptuous of his friends who marry, and especially if they have children. He and his lady were "holdouts," morally above their friends.

However, recently, his partner accidentally became pregnant. To my amazement my patient suddenly became excited by the prospect of being a father, and even began to think of marriage.

COMMENT: As therapists, we believe that we should always analyze all three components of the neurotic conflicts, that is, the ego and the id in relation to the superego, as Anna Freud suggested. But, in once- and twice-a-week therapy, we sometimes must make choices of where to focus our interventions. I have found that special sensitivity to the "shoulds"—the myriad voices of the "others," both conscious and unconscious—often leads to important insights into symptoms. Addressing superego derivatives directly stimulates a more active engagement of the patient's ego in the task of breaking out of neurotic stalemate. It is an attempt to reduce the influence of the "six-day crust" on the momentum of the psychotherapy process. This experimental approach to technique seems to be effective with higher-level neurotic patients in psychotherapy once or twice per week.

In both of these cases there have been significant improvement in symptoms. Mr. Olds has become far less angry and depressed. His relations with his colleagues and his wife have improved a great deal He still has issues with time, but now leaves his office at 5:30, takes vacations, and is more focused on how to spend his time by having fun, something his wife encourages him to do. He expresses gratitude for the changes in his life that therapy has helped him make.

Mr. Young has filed one of his tax returns, and received a tax refund, and plans to file the other one soon. Now that he is a father, he feels that he will be able to deal with his denial of money issues because he will be forced to do so by reality. He seems happy that fatherhood is forcing him into an adult mode of life, and has married his partner He now questions his previous contempt for his friends who had gotten married and had children. His defensiveness of "I have nothing to say today" is completely gone, and he now talks freely in the therapy hour and continues to work on the intrapsychic conflicts that continue to inhibit him. He even talks now about how to invest his money for the future of the family.

REFERENCES

ARLOW, J. (1982). Problems of the superego concept, *Psychoanal. Study of the Child, 37*:229–244.

———— (1995). Stilted listening: Psychoanalysis as discourse. *Psychoanal. Quart., 64*:215–233.

———— & BRENNER, C. (1964). *Psychoanalytic concepts and the structural theory.* New York: International Universities Press.

BRENNER, C. (1982). The concept of the superego: A reformulation. *Psychoanal. Quart. 51*:501–525.

———— (1994). The mind as conflict and compromise formation. *J. Clin. Psychoanal., 3*:473–488.

FANCHER, E. (2003). *A primer of clinical interpretations: Classic and post-classical approaches* by P.F.D. Rubovits-Seitz (Book review]. *Psychologist-Psychoanalyst, 23*(3):71–72.

FREUD, S. (1923). The ego and the id, *The standard edition of the complete psychological works of Sigmund Freud,* 24 vols. London: Hogarth Press, 1953–1974. *20*:3–66.

———— (1926). Inhibitions, symptoms and anxiety, *Standard ed., 20*:77–174.

———— (1933). New introductory lectures, *Standard ed., 22*:57–80.

GRAY, P. (1982). "Developmental lag" in the evolution of technique for psychoanalysis of neurotic conflict. *J. Amer. Psychoanal. Assoc., 30*:621–655.

——— (1994). *The ego and analysis of defense.* Northvale, NJ: Aronson.

LEVENSON, L.N. (2007). Paul Gray's innovations in psychoanalytic technique. *Psychoanal. Quart., 75*:257–273.

MAKARI, G. (2008). *Revolution in mind.* New York: Harper.

NOVICK, J, & NOVICK, K.K. (2004). The superego and the two-system model. *Psychoanal. Inq., 24*:232–256.

OLINER, M. (2008, May). Graduation speech, New York Freudian Society.

RUBOVITS-SEITZ, P.F.D. (2002). *A primer of clinical interpretation.* Northvale, NJ: Aronson.

SANDLER, J (1960). On the concept of superego. *Psychoanal. Study of the Child, 15*:128–162.

SCHAFER, R. (1960). The loving and beloved superego in Freud's structural theory. *Psychoanal. Study of the Child, 15*:163–188.

Solms, M. (2013). Notes on the *Revised Standard Edition. Psychoanal. Rev., 100*:201–210.

WAELDER, R. (1 936). The principle of multiple function: Observations on overdetermination. *Psychoanal. Quart., 5*:45–62..

MEMORY, MOURNING AND MEANING IN A PSYCHOTHERAPIST'S LIFE

[Felberbaum, S. (2010). *Clinical Social Work* 38:269–274.]

In this paper the author, a psychotherapist specializing in bereavement, recounts her personal experiences of loss and the ways in which they intersect and inform her professional life. One clinical vignette explores how unresolved grief in a patient and anticipated grief in a therapist emerge in transference-counter-transference issues. Another vignette illustrates a way in which supportive therapy can open the door to intra-psychic work with the ill or dying patient and how psychoanalytically informed psychotherapy with the aged can help them to reimagine their lives and to form different relationships, in their minds, with significant others in their past.

> The last half of life can be lived with conscious knowledge of eventual death, and the acceptance of this knowledge, as an integral part of living. Mourning for the dead self can begin.
>
> —*E. Jaques* (1965, p. 11)

> Little by little, we are more and more peopled by the dead . . .
>
> —*May Sarton* (1997)

Tibetan monks spend days creating a brilliant mandala sand painting with colors so vivid that sun, ocean and earth appear to shimmer and vibrate throughout. The mandala, a "three dimensional visualization of an imaginary palace, represents a journey from the outside to the inside" (Ray 2008[2006]). Upon completion, all of the colored sand is blown away; an exquisite metaphor for non-attachment to the physical world, for the impermanence of life, for transience (Freud 1916[1915]; Von Unwerth 2005). My life-mandala spins like a pin wheel, outside-inside, attaching-detaching, constructing-deconstructing; connections lived in the moment and revived in memory, circles embracing circles. Here are some of the circles.

Lillian

Trees outside the upscale independent-living facility were just shedding summer's greenery for autumn's complex shading of red, burgundy, ocher and amber. I park my car and walk through automatically opening front doors. I am greeted by lush blue-green sculpted carpets and brocaded easy chairs. What distinguishes my patient's facility entrance from an ordinary hotel or apartment reception area is the end table supporting an ornate double frame. The face of a smiling woman is on one side, an announcement on the other:

> *Sophie Morseman, October 3, 1920–May 24, 2005*
> *Services to be Held at Shalom Jewish Center on May 27, 2005*
> *Memorial Service in the Community Room on June 1, 2005*

Here it is: the right-in-your-face acknowledgement of the perpetual presence of death. Welcome to tomorrow, I thought.

Lillian was waiting for me in her lovely two bedroom apartment with a full view of the newly constructed waterfall. For the past few months and in the years to come, that view, along with her books, opera CD's and television, all enjoyed from her black leather recliner, occupied a great deal of Lillian's time. Eighty-seven years old with brilliant, blue eyes, she looked me over from top to bottom, inside-out. As the months turned into years, and the transference-counter-transference tango danced on, I became her mother, father, siblings and children while she switched places with my mother and mother-in-law.

During that first session, rigidly perched at the edge of her chair, Lillian described an incident from the previous month that she would mention repeatedly over the next 4 years.

> I have a rare blood disorder. I began to bleed from my gums and was hospitalized. They found my platelets were almost gone, can you believe that? The worst thing was that I was given large doses of steroids and I went into a frozen state. I couldn't talk or move-it was if I were glued to the chair. I lost my mind. Finally after they treated me I regained myself. My internist came to visit me in the hospital. I asked him how Annie, the nurse, was.

> She is such a lovely, caring gal. Dr. M said to me: "imagine that, here you are, in the hospital, hardly a platelet left, dying, and you ask about my nurse?" So here I sit, waiting to die, it could have been then and it can be now, at any moment.

In a subsequent session Lillian quoted another statement that haunted her. When she asked her hematologist for a note for her dentist to work on her teeth; he said, "I can give it to you for this week because your blood counts are O.K.; I can't vouch for next week." "All of my stomach symptoms got worse," Lillian exclaimed. She then revealed another example in which her body reflected anxiety. and some of her death fears.

> There was a woman dying in the bed next to mine in the hospital. The priest came in the middle of the night and mumbled over her. I think I heard someone say, "the body is cold." I had a dream about a white shroud, white fabric wrapped around like a mummy. I think of cold related to death, when I had that psychotic time, I felt cold from my knees down and I was certain that I was dying. [She begins to cry.] I never got to say goodbye to my mother. She died alone, in the middle of the night in a hospital.

What had begun as crisis intervention related to steroid overdose (labeled as catatonia in her medical records) and an acute post-traumatic stress reaction, transitioned into weekly psychoanalytically oriented psychotherapy sessions. The crisis of acute illness offered her an opportunity for change, and a door was opened for intra-psychic work. Lillian was able and eager to shift her focus from the fear of imminent death to curiosity about early childhood deprivations as well as realistic concerns about dying. She was capable of attaining higher levels of functioning (Goldstein 1984).

Another significance of her panic reaction regarding her brush with death related to fear experienced when her father moved to a foreign country for 3 years returning for a few months after the first 2 years only to leave again for a year. "Mother said everyone cried except for me (indicating that she was a cold unfeeling child); I developed sties around my eyes that required eye drops." "Those sties were your tears," I replied. This was the first symptom of many illustrating what would become a life-long pattern of somatization. She was left with a mother ill-equipped to cope with three children under the age of six. As the oldest, Lillian coparented her siblings; she had to think of others and care for them when she herself needed so much. Inquiring of her physician, "How is your nurse?" was, at least partially, a re-enactment of this earlier experience.

Generally, the tone of a positive transference colored our sessions, as exemplified by her heartfelt statement, "You're my kind of person." I had reciprocal feelings towards her. Although I was in my sixties and she was in her late eighties when we began, we had a meeting of the minds and heart. Negative transference reactions also had an important place in our work (Casement 2006). When I would return from a long separation, Lillian imagined I'd joyously travelled to exotic locations: she experienced troubling feelings of disconnection and anger towards me. Memories of her refusal to kiss or talk to her beloved father when he returned from his trip resurfaced (Hall 1998). Sibling rivalry, longing for her mother's love and appreciation, desire to be her father's special one- many of the usual issues associated with psychoanalytic exploration at any age and stage flourished in our sessions reinforcing the notion that psychological change and emotional growth are possible from birth until the moment of death (Edward 1976; Mahler eta!. 1975; Neugarten 1979).

Images and thoughts of death often crept into our sessions.

> I don't believe in an after-life, Lillian stated. I want to be cremated. Each day in this place, I watch people deteriorate, changing from something to nothing. There's an assisted living and an Alzheimer's wing here. Knowing it's here, visiting folks who end up there, it's a constant reminder of death. You could be laughing at dinner one night and be in assisted living the next, just like that. Rationally I could say it would be good to die at eighty-eight but I don't want to.

Two years later Lillian stated that she hoped she could feel peaceful when she died, and that what she wished for the most was not to be alone. She wondered, "Would that be too hard a thing to ask of you and of my family?" Lillian continued to mull over thoughts of aging and the passage of time, she said that as a young woman she had a recurring dream of looking in a mirror and seeing herself grey-haired and old. She felt happy about this at the time. "I'm pleased to be turning 90, I want to be alive for my party next month, but always I think of myself as a year older than I am."

Lillian began to view her mother's harsh treatment of her as a child . . . being made responsible for heavy domestic and child rearing duties and constantly being referred to as less attractive than her siblings, from the vantage point of her mother's projection of her own poor self-image onto her, the eldest daughter. As she became able to verbally express the anger and resentment she experienced towards her father for leaving her when she was a child, she was able to feel compassion for her mothers' situation. This was illustrated in the following dream:

> I am with the kids, the telephone rings . . . someone says your mother is on the phone, will you talk to her? I'd be happy to talk to her I said. When I awake I think, I don't hate her anymore. She had a hard time.

Together, we could re-imagine her life. She was able, at the age of 90, to develop an "internal reconciliation" (Omin 1989, p. 330) a new relationship in her mind with her parents. This appeared to lessen her anxiety about death and enabled her to have more energy directed toward enjoying and appreciating the good life she had with her husband, children, grand and great grand children. She had what Therese Ragen (2009) describes as "a renewed sense of vitality" (p. 24).

The day before I was to leave for a month's vacation Lillian was admitted to the hospital. She was pale, had not been eating and had oxygen to help her to breathe.

> "I'm so glad you came" she said, "I have my best friend and my husband here. I am such a lucky person, but I'm so tired, of all this."
>
> *Are you talking about being tired of fighting? I asked.*
>
> "Yes, I'm worn out. I don't want to do it anymore"
>
> *Are you talking about dying?*
>
> "Yes", she responded, "I've had enough, after all I'm 92 years old."
>
> *You're only ninety-one,* I said. The three of us laughed.
>
> *Bill, do you hear what Lillian is saying? She's saying she is ready to die.*
>
> Bill shakes his head yes, but appears bewildered.
>
> *How are you feeling Lillian, are you in any pain?*
>
> "My belly problems are there and the medicine isn't working. If a doctor came and offered me two more years of life like this, I would refuse it."

We hugged and said a final good-bye, both of us knowing she was dying. Lillian was transferred to the skilled nursing facility on the grounds of her independent living home where she received compassionate palliative care. Her family visited her daily encircling her with their presence and their love as she died. Lillian got her wish, she was not alone.

Sylvia, My Mother

I often thought about my mother when exploring Lillian's abandonment issues. In my mid-forties my mother moved to Florida, not far from two of my three siblings. She gave me a box filled with all the cards and letters I had ever given her. This was a mixed blessing for me; happy as I was that she had saved them, especially since I did not have any toys or dolls from my childhood, in my heart I wanted her to keep those cards and letters forever. How could she part with them, how could she part with me?

My mother would stand on the balcony of her Florida condo in her washed-out cotton housecoat, waving goodbye to me, tears streaming down her cheeks, as I left to fly home to Long Island. I would look up from the parking lot wishing she would just enjoy the visit; why did I have to feel guilty for leaving? Years later, as my daughter stood in the hallway of our home, bags-packed, hand on the front door knob, ready to drive back to her college dorm she said to me "There's that look on your face, every time I go."

I have been surrounded by loss and death in my professional life since I entered nursing school at the age of seventeen. After I'd earned a masters degree in social work, completed psychoanalytic training and analysis, worked with bereaved and terminally ill patients, I imagined that I understood loss. Not so. It wasn't until my mother's death when I was 55-years-old, followed by the death of my mother-in-law 8 years later, that those external occurrences converted into an internally focused, visceral understanding of grief (Silverman 2004:11). I experienced a sense of frozen emptiness deep within my stomach and a crushing heaviness in my chest. Tears came unbidden, I sighed frequently, and the world appeared to be drained of color. A new marker of time had been created: before and after their deaths.

My mother was 81-years-old when she was diagnosed with lung cancer. From that moment on I reacted much more emotionally when listening to patients who were in deep mourning. I had to work hard at staying present in the session, at combating excessive tearfulness and feelings of fatigue. My thoughts would jump from my patient to my mother; I would either be hyper vigilant in terms of therapeutic outcomes, hospital and hospice scenarios or my mind would wander and ideas about shopping or vacation fantasies would drown out painful information. Because of these countertransference issues I temporarily stopped accepting new patients who were in active mourning or who had been newly diagnosed with end of life issues.

I struggled with treatment issues concerning my mother. Clinical training, analytic theories, rights to self-efficacy, all of these constructs faded as I considered my own mother undergoing painful and debilitating procedures. I wanted her to have the best quality of life possible. I had seen and heard too much as a nurse and therapist; too many days, weeks and months chasing promised cures, too many painful interventions with minimal results. Her options: surgery, radiation, or chemo? "Or do nothing," I suggested. My mother chose to fight for time, time to watch her great-grandchildren grow.

My Patient, My Mother, Myself

Marsha, a 40-year-old health care professional, transformed my statement of a family emergency into a daily, intrusive mantra, imagining that my mother had died even though I never mentioned who was ill. There were many similarities between us and our experiences with our mothers' illnesses and deaths. She shared the following memory of staying with her mother in the hospital just after she died:

> I stood over my mother, guarding her body like a soldier. I watched the staff nurse wrap her in a plastic shroud, it looked like a garbage bag. I wished it could -have been made of cloth instead. There was her little body, eaten up by cancer, her once big, strong self, gone. All the while my father hounded me to go home. He couldn't understand why I wanted to stay with her throughout her death, how much it meant for me to have her for myself, just this once, without my older and younger brothers and sisters all fighting for a piece of her.

Listening to this material was painful. I identified with her wish to be the special daughter, to use her professional skills as another link of connection, to want her mother to be treated with dignity, even in death. I visualized my mother taking her mother's place. It was easy to see myself behaving just as my patient had. Heeding Arlow's (1991) advice, I realized that an excessive lingering at identification with my patient "implies merging and can be detrimental to the therapeutic work" (p. 222). "While we need to feel *with* the patient temporarily, we must be able to appreciate that what we felt is *about* the patient and make use of that understanding" (Felberbaum 1996, p. 253). It was important for me to remind myself that although there were similarities between us, our individual differences still existed. If I disclosed aspects of my own life to my patient it would be important for me to be aware, as much as possible, of my motivations for doing so. Would it be in my patient's best interest, "to facilitate the therapeutic process" (Sherby 2005, p. 501) or because I needed to feel more connected to her because of my own feelings of vulnerability?

As my patient spoke of her mother's death she queried:

> I wonder if you are bored with me always talking about death. I feel that I should, at least sometimes, entertain you with happy things though I know that's not correct in terms of how therapy should work.

> "Perhaps you are worried about me because someone close to me is ill," I reply. Tearfully, she says:

> I never want to inflict that pain on anyone. I look into your eyes and I see you reflect back what I am feeling.

I suggest that she also accurately gauged my reactions and was trying to protect me. I encourage her not to censor herself so that we might both understand what her needs are. I reassure her that if talking about death becomes too difficult for me or if family needs are too pressing, I will take time off or use other supportive measures to take care of myself outside of our sessions.

News from the oncologist informing me that my mother's cancer had metastasized forced me to do just that. My mother entered an inpatient hospice in Florida for 3 weeks; I spent the last days of her life with her there. I covered her room with pictures of her four children and their spouses, her eight grandchildren and six great grandchildren. My mother was happiest when with her family or when she was traveling to exotic places. In a place of honor was a picture of her in Paris looking glamorous and mysterious. I wanted the hospice staff to know what a special woman she was, that she once was beautiful and vibrant.

The nurses and social workers supported me as well as my mother. I was able to choose the staff members who would bathe and .reposition her. I could be my mother's daughter instead of her nurse. This was a transformative time for me. For as long as I could remember I had hidden behind the pseudo-safety of helpful care-giving, concentrating on the skills I had learned to keep my mind and body active. I'd worked hard to ward off the psychic and emotional pain of loss. Now, it was freeing for me to be with those feelings with my mother. I could pay attention to the sensory environment we were in, swabbing my mother's gums with the taste of coffee, her favorite beverage, and talking to my sister Maralyn about. our lives as we watched and heard my mother take her final breath. There was no other place I needed or wanted to be. I felt great sadness but also peace.

Florence, My Mother-in-Law

At the same time that I was visiting Lillian in her independent living facility, my mother-in-law, Florence, was similarly ensconced in a residence in Florida. She had begun to have hospice visits due to a diagnosis of "failure to thrive".

The hospice nurse stoops down and speaks at wheelchair level: "Tell me about how you hate the food. I want to hear you in there." Turning towards the commanding, lilting voice, my mother-in-law Florence struggles to open heavily weighted eye-lids, takes a deep-throated breath and responds, "The food is tasteless, I don't care about it, what's the point? The problem is . . . was . . . I found myself outside in the dark, I don't know why." Florence had begun to mix her days and nights: her time sense was no longer sharp. Her last 2 years had been spent in a residence called "Sunny Gardens". She described it as more closely resembling "Grey Gardens," feeling that rather than assisted living it felt more like witnessed dying. An increase of medication to control pain threw her into a semi-comatose state; the nurse felt she was on the verge of death. My husband and I spoke to Florence as she drifted in and out, urging her to fight to live for the ninety-fifth birthday party we had planned, just a few weeks away. I was torn; on the one hand I didn't want her to suffer, yet I knew how she loved parties and how much it would mean for her grandchildren and great grandchildren to see her one more time. The medications were reduced, she rallied and she was alert enough to recognize and interact with them all.

Seven months later, just 1 month before she died, Florence refused the Methadone prescribed for her bone and belly pain. "I want to save it for when I need it," she says. "You mean you want to stock pile it," I reply and I am rewarded with a glint of a smile, a flash of who she had been to me, the all-knowing, powerful, physician-mother-in-law, Loretta Young and Dr. Welby all rolled into one whom I had known for 45 years, was revived. This was a woman who, when she was in her late 80s, just moments before being wheeled in for a hospital procedure instructed me to apply hair dye mousse to her roots ."No one respects you if you look too old" she said. Florence had become superfluous in this world she now inhabited, severely vision-impaired, locked in a skeleton that moved slowly, each movement needed to be carefully plotted, one step at a time. The stroke 15 years previously, macular degeneration, a torn rotator cuff and 95 years of wear and tear conspired to rob us of who she had once been. And yet there were moments in which Florence would, once again, leap out. In the Town Center Shopping Center, propelled in her stream-lined cherry-red walker complete with chair seat, she eyeballs a huge sign—"Spend $150.00 Get a Free Tote Bag"—and asks "what do I have to do to get the bag?" The sale-bargain lingo etched so deeply in her brain, as it is in mine, allowed for a giant synaptic leap. She's back, and for a nano-second the world is once again spinning correctly on its axis. The phone rings at 5:00 a.m. "This is Sunny Gardens calling, Florence died at 4:30 this morning, they found her in her bed during rounds, it must have happened in her sleep." I awaken my husband. "She waited until the New Year," I sobbed. "Mom died alone, without us. She didn't want to live this way another year." Twice during the past 10 days we had received calls alerting us: "She is unhurt, it is our policy to call and let you know, your mother did not know how she ended up on the floor." I think she was trying to go home, to the big house on Bennet Place in Amityville filled with closets and sub-closets, where her children's toys were stored. My children loved going inside that hidden closet, emerging triumphantly with treasures; an old doll wearing a nurse's uniform, a picture dictionary book, a miniature Singer sewing machine and Lionel trains. I would marvel at one of the closets in her bedroom, the one I named the goody closet, filled with foreign travel trophies, French perfumes and silk scarves and parasols, fine English bone china, Waterford crystal, leather wallets, pocketbooks and gold embossed serving trays from Italy. That closet of abundance will always represent Florence to me.

Epilogue

What stands out most clearly for me as I reflect back both on my patients and my own experiences of end of life issues is the importance and mul-tiplicity of meaning imbedded in the concept of connection. Psychoanalytic exploration and a strong relational tie with me enabled my patient Lillian to form a more positive connection .in her mind, with her parents, long after they had died and I was able to more clearly process and rework simultaneous interactions with my mother-in-law before her death . I was also in a better position to understand Marsha's grief over the loss of her mother as I struggled with similar issues with my mother; I connected with Marsha just as she connected with me. Mary Sue Moore's statement that "Pieces of my own experience has woven its way into the work I do." (2009) resonates strongly with me as does the following quote from "Learning from Experience: A Guidebook for Clinicians" (2004), written by Marilyn Charles.

> I sat in my therapists' chair through those long months of not peak form, knowing there is a benefit to being thrust head long into the harsh realities in life, in that it enables us to sit with our patients' pain so much more profoundly without running and hiding from that particular peril (p. 66).

Donnel B. Stern, in his foreword to Therese Ragens' book *The Consulting Room and Beyond* (2009) correspondingly expresses this idea: "In clinical practice, the patient's experience is contextualized by the analyst's, and the analyst's by the patient's" (p. xi). Working with patients and their families as they deal with end of life issues engenders a variety of affects to all who are involved; sadness, wonderment, laughter and tears to name a few. Practitioners are not exempt or uninvolved in this life long process. Confronting our mortality allows us to be more fully present with our patients, our friends and family members during what can be an incredibly rich period (Felberbaum 2003, p. 10–11). After my last visit to Sunny Gardens I felt that I too had grown older; if I lived to be my mother-in-law's age then two-thirds of my life was already gone. Gratefully escaping back home, I hug my husband, children and grand-children, go to lectures, see my patients, visit with friends, write poetry and rush off to some wonderful trip, cramming in as much living as possible while I can still see and walk without noticing every step. Although my defensive parent-as-buffer-against-death is gone, and some of my counter- phobic activity, a way of "outrunning death" (Von Unwerth, p. 194) remains; remembering and writing the following poem about experiences at my mother's death bed has helped to lessen my fears about dying, especially the fear that most of us have, the fear of dying alone.

Close as a Breath

> *There was a beauty to your dying as we stayed together*
> > *close as a breath.*
> *Five days of night and day blended seamlessly.*
> > *Time flowed boundary free.*
> *I slept with you as if you were an infant,*
> > *in need of holding.*
> *I heard you call out Ma-Ma, Ma- Ma,*
> > *your arms out stretched*
> > *into your mother's embrace*
> > *reaching from the grave.*
> *Someday, when it is my time,*
> > *if I am blessed,*
> > *my daughter will be holding me,*
> > *and my mama will be waiting.*

REFERENCES

ARLOW, J.A. (1991). *Psychoanalysis: Clinical Theory and Practice.* Madison, CT: International Universities Press.

CASEMENT, P. (2006). *Learning from life: Becoming a Psychoanalyst.* New York: Routeledge.

CHARLES, M. (2004). *Learning from Experience: A Guidebook for Clinicians.* New Jersey: The Analytic Press.

EDWARD, J. (1976). The therapist as a catalyst in promoting separation and individuation. *Clinical Social Work Journal* 4(3):172–186.

FELBERBAUM, S. (1996). Psychoanalytically oriented psychotherapy with the HIV-infected person. In J. Edward & J. Sanville (Eds.), *Fostering Healing and Growth: A Psychoanalytic Social Work Approach* (pp. 244–260). New Jersey: Jason Aronson.

——— (2003). Fantasy death exercise: Life and death, a labor of love. *The Clinician: Newletter of the NY State Society for Clinical Social Work* Spring:10–11.

FREUD, S. (1916 [1915]). On Transience. *Standard Edition* 14:305–307.

GOLDSTEIN, E. (1984). *Ego psychology and Social Work Practice.* New York: The Free Press.

HALL, J. (1998). *Deepening the Treatment.* New Jersey: Jacob Aronson.

JAQUES, E. (1965). Death and the midlife crisis. *PEP Web. International Journal of Psycho-Analysis* 46:502–514.

MAHLER, M.S., PINE, F., & BERGMAN, A. (1975). *The psychological birth of the human infant.* New York: Basic Books.

MOORE, M.S. (2009, February). Developmental aspects of trauma, Washington Center for Psychoanalysis. Paper Presentation, New Directions Weekend Conference on Trauma, Washington, DC.

NEUGARTEN, B. (1979). Time, age and the life cycle. *The American Journal of Psychiatry,* 136(7):887–893.

OMIN, R.F. (1989). To die in treatment: An opportunity for growth, consolidation and healing. *Clinical Social Work Journal* 17(4):325–336.

RAGEN, T. (2009). *The Consulting Room and Beyond: Psychoanalytic Work and its Reverberations in the Analyst's Life.* New York: Routledge.

RAY, R. (2008 [2006]). *10 Questions for the Dalai Lama* (Documentary) WNET, PBS Channel 13.

SARTON, M. (1997 [1978]). *A Reckoning.* New York: W.W. Norton & Company.

SHERBY, L.B. (2005). Self-disclosure: Seeking connection and protection. *Contemporary Psyclwanalysis* 41(3):499–517.

SILVERMAN, P.R. (2004). Introduction. In J. Bezoff & P.R. Silvennan (Eds.), *Living with Dying: a Handbook for End of Life Healthcare Practitioners* (pp. 1–17). New York: Columbia University Press.

VON UNWERTH, M. (2005). *Freud's Requiem: Mourning, Memory, and the Invisible History of a Summer Walk.* New York: Riverhead Books a Member of Penguin Group.

RELINQUISHING ORTHODOXY: ONE FREUDIAN ANALYST'S PERSONAL JOURNEY

[Hall, J. (2008). *Psychoanalytic Review* 95:845–871.]

The word orthodox, from the Greek *ortho* ("right," "correct") and *doxa* ("thought," "teaching," "glorification"), is typically used to refer to the correct worship or the correct theological and doctrinal observance of religion, or other forms of intellectual activity shared by organizations or movements, as determined by some overseeing body. In Judiasm, and for the purposes of this paper, *reform* stresses ethical teachings and frequently simplifies or even rejects traditional beliefs and practices to meet the conditions of contemporary life.

Some of my ideas about technique have changed from an orthodox Freudian psychoanalytic approach to what I call *patient centered psychoanalytic work*. With the many new theories and the reviewing of older theories of technique today's analyst can tailor (without being called eclectic) the treatment to fit the patient. For instance, much of Kohut's work can apply to the narcissistic individual. Contemporary life demands that we reevaluate the issue of frequency of sessions and telephone sessions. I am sure that this is not a new idea but much of the literature, particularly the conservative literature, appears to support a strict attitude.

During my years as a candidate there were many taboos and expectations that seemed not to be in the patient's best interest. Along the road, which I continue to walk, I have learned to be flexible, to use my common sense, and to speak in my own voice more and more. I appreciate the classical training that has been my foundation, but have learned to question what I refer to as "received wisdom". I find myself impressed by both the classicists like Waelder, Fenichel, et al as well as by many of the relationalists of my generation like Mitchell and Greenberg. More than anyone, Loewald (1960) gave my generation the idea of analyst as new object, through the new discovery of objects. My idealization of these dedicated and erudite theoreticians and clinicians, however, is tempered by my own experience and by my most important teachers: my patients.

A BRIEF HISTORY OF MY EDUCATION

My private practice, begun in the early 1970s while still in classes and supervision, was predominantly psychoanalytic. I would shift practically all my patients from the chair to the couch, from twice a week to five times a week over the course of a year or sometimes more (Hall, 1998). Being a candidate and immersed in classical psychoanalytic theory of technique, it seemed that deepening the treatment was not only in the patient's best interest, it was also necessary to complete my education. The clinic patients who came with me to my new office were curious about the couch and before long, after an explanation of deeper psychoanalytic work, four out of five of them began three, then four, then five times a week work.

Before beginning my analytic training, I attended Gertrude and Reuben Blank's Institute for the Study of Psychotherapy and for several years, both programs over-lapped. I learned both classical analysis and how to work with the "so called" borderline in psychotherapy. This double exposure provided me with a unique experience. Most, if not all of my teachers believed and practiced in a strictly orthodox manner, not using the couch until a patient was deemed "analyzable" and willing to be in 4- or 5-times-a-week treatment on the couch. (If for any reason the analysand stopped using the couch for a period of time, those hours were not counted towards graduation by the training committee.)

Gertrude and Ruben Blank had definite ideas about the "so called" borderline and narcissistic patients whose object constancy they saw as compromised and whose egos they felt needed strengthening before beginning psychoanalysis proper. The Institute for the Study of Psychotherapy focused on the works of Hartmann, Kris, Lowenstein, Spitz, Jacobson, and Mahler. Some of us were privileged to have seminars with Margaret Mahler herself. Those were the days when infant research and child development became a major focus.

Five plus years of postgraduate seminars with Martin Bergmann, William Grossman and others, reading the contemporary literature, and listening to my patients broadened my mind. Three recent books stand out as especially transformative: *Hate and Love in Psychoanalytic Institutes: The Dilemma of the Profession* by Jurgen Reeder (2003), *The Brain That Changes Itself by* Norman Doidge (2007), *The Dream Interpreters* by Howard Shevrin (2003). Reeder gives a scholarly history of the Eitington model of education and shows clearly how institutes infantilize the candidates. He discusses the issue of training analysis versus personal analysis, favoring the later. Doidge shows in detail how the brain, once thought of as permanently wired, is now seen as plastic. The chapters illustrate how the brain finds new pathways and there is a moving chapter on psychoanalysis. Shevrin's book is a beautiful presentation, in prose form, of seven analyses conducted at a mythical institute. It is a page turner mystery that should be read by all those interested in analysis. The prose form lends itself beautifully in showing the process of analytic sessions along with the political climate in the institute.

ATTITUDE AND TECHNIQUE

In my mind the analytic attitude had changed over the years from a strictly scientific endeavor to a humanistic one, even though there are many who persist in trying to measure its success statistically. Freud, in the position of having to prove the scientific aspect of his creation, and his early (and present) followers believed in certain core concept's as the bedrock of psychoanalysis: libido and aggression, the Oedipus complex {negative and positive), and psychosexual phases (oral, anal, phallic, genital), with diagnostic categories such as hysteria, obsessive compulsive neurosis, and certain character disorders treatable by resolving a transference neurosis. Simplistically speaking, the return of repressed memories were originally thought to be curative; resistances were to be analyzed away; signal anxiety and both the topographic and structural models, were used to understand the patient in psychoanalysis. The analyst was trained to interpret the complexes by making the unconscious conscious so as to alleviate the symptoms or improve compromise formations as they appeared in the transference neurosis. The analytic treatment practiced by the classicists was based on the patient's free associations which gave the analyst material to interpret. This method is now referred to as a one-person model of analytic treatment as opposed to a two-person model that took its place when object relations came into the forefront. Loewald (1960) opened the door to thinking about the analyst as new object. In his paper *The Therapeutic Action of Psychoanalysis* he carefully explained the need for the analyst's objectivity. *"This objectivity cannot mean the avoidance of being available to the patient as an object . . ..through the objective analysis of [the patient's distortions] the analyst becomes not only potentially but actually available as a new object."* For me, Loewald stood at the crossroads between orthodoxy and reform. True to Freud's efforts, he expanded and deepened concepts of how and why to work with transference. But he also spoke of the analyst as potential new object—and this mention of a new object heralded the blossoming focus on object relations for me.

The analytic process had been authority laden, with the patient literally at the feet of the wise and all-knowing analyst. Both abstinence and neutrality were practiced strictly so that the transference neurosis could form. It was thought that any information about the analyst would contaminate the formation of a true transference neurosis. Using the couch and attending 4 to 5 sessions per week remain part of the analyst's understanding of practicing psychoanalysis. Some analysts still practice the orthodox form of treatment. In fact, this is the public perception of the classical analyst, frequently displayed in the *The New Yorker* magazine cartoons.

But, over the years, patients have not fit the original Freudian model and have been unable or unwilling to undertake a classical analysis. In America, analysts, starting with Kohut and Kernberg, have expanded their vision to include treatment of the narcissistic and so called borderline patients (my qualification of borderline with "so called" is because I do not think the concept of borderline is useful.) Since *The Widening Scope* paper (Stone, 1954), analysts, whether social workers, physicians, psychologists, and others, are treating all kinds of people, not just the normal neurotic. Many clinicians have thought that so called heroic work often requires modifications in the traditional models of psychoanalytic work. My experience has been that if the therapist can explain to the patient the reason for the frame and all that it includes, most patients can work with this model The frame is, in fact, reassuring and provides a sense of constancy and reliability to a person who has never experienced safety and consistency. Even those patients who begin by saying they do not want a silent analyst eventually understand that in order to get to know them I must listen and that a lot of talk from me will get in the way. I always promise that when I feel I can contribute, I will. Each patient is different in requiring active versus a more passive style and both patient and therapist work out an optimal manner of discourse.

The Relational School of thinking, led by Greenberg and Mitchell (1983), practices analysis by focusing on the here and now, stressing the relationship between patient and analyst as paramount, and doing away with Freudian drive theory. Coming t9 this way of thinking midway into my career gave me more food for thought and though at first I wanted to cling to what I thought I knew, I became intrigued by some of the relational reasoning. As long ago as Fairbairn (1958) the real wish of the patient was seen as connecting to the object and it does seem possible to me that old theory and new will find a more common ground. When treating patients, relational psychoanalysts stress a mixture of waiting, and authentic spontaneity. Some relationally oriented psychoanalysts eschew the traditional Freudian emphasis on interpretation and free association, instead emphasizing the importance of creating a lively, genuine relationship with the patient Winnicott's idea of the holding environment is embraced by some relationalists and I would imagine that Bionians' theory of containment fits in too. Relational analysts focus on what happens between patient and analyst with the goal of changing the patient's repetitive relationship patterns that they believe maintain psychopathology.

FREQUENCY AND COUCH

The debate about psychoanalytic psychotherapy and psychoanalysis proper still goes on, some seeing the two modes on a continuum (Gediman, 1991; Hall, 1998); others believing that these forms of treatment are different (Turo, 2007). Rothstein (1990) sees most patients as candidates for analysis and blames the analyst's countertransference on not recommending analysis. My experience has shown me that each dyad determines what is best, possible, and appropriate and that psychoanalytic work goes on whenever a psychoanalyst is part of the treatment. I continue to strive for optimal frequency and using the couch when appropriate, explaining my reasoning to the patient. There is a freedom that comes with not having to look at each other and there is also a need to see the other. My patient and I explore which mode is preferable. In general, more time together assists the dyad in their exploration but this is based on experience, not on rules.

THE ABUSED PATIENT

Some patients have had chaotic childhoods with severely diminished capacity for trust. These patients have helped me understand that being attuned to their needs and abilities along with providing constancy within a safe therapeutic environment is the main challenge. In such instances, the therapist's talent in making and maintaining a connection is paramount and cannot be dictated by theories and rules. There are however important references to working with the more challenging patients and I have been most helped by Shengold's work (1989). He discusses patience:

> One must never assume that the analyst will be felt by the patient as working for the patient's welfare; even with the "average expectable" patient, these anticipations of benevolence are at best intermittent. The analyst and the patient must be able to last it out. Given enough time, the near delusion that only the worst is to be expected, sometimes initially unconscious, can be modified by *the reliability of the analytic situation: a time and place that can be counted on, the dependable, continuing presence o(a generally accepting, nonpunitive parental figure, the persistent attempt to empathize and understand.* . . . Interpreting aggression toward the analyst in such a way that the patient can make use of it requires great skill, perseverance, and (again) patience" (pp. 331–316, my emphasis).

Many patients have come to my office over the years, some functioning on a high level, but unable to form meaningful relationships. Time and again I have learned about these patients' childhoods of abuse and neglect, not enough and too muchness, under-stimulation and overstimulation, both psychical and emotional, and I have learned from such patients that psychoanalytic treatment must be based on attunement and patience. None of the techniques learned in orthodox schooling prepared me for this *patient-centered* work. The techniques of tact, timing, and the knowledge that the abused patient is attached to the abusing parent both as tormentor and victim, and will engage the analyst in a sadomasochistic struggle is necessary to doing analytic work. With a good enough therapist some of the damage may be softened. But it is important for therapists to have the humility and the ability to tame their own grandiose fantasies of cure (Hall, 1998).

CHANGES

Since Freud's Dora case, technique was centered on the transference, free associations, dreams, and actions of the patient, with the analyst making interpretation when he/she felt it appropriate. According to Strachey (1934) mutative interpretations occurred only in the transference with the analyst as transference figure. Improvement was expected when repressed memories were brought to consciousness using the patient's free associations interpreted according to Freud's theories. Countertransference was for many years considered problematic and more analysis was recommended if the analyst could not overcome these *distractions.*

I like what a colleague said in a recent discussion regarding technique, *"Freud was a brilliant thinker in his time but that was not our time."* He suggested:

> We might take our eyes off the rear view mirror and try to look ahead using what has accrued in neighboring disciplines since Freud's era. The interaction in the analytic setting "gets curiouser and curiouser" as we learn about reciprocal social roles, "mirror neurons" and the "non-dynamic" unconscious and so on. Just what and how the analysand elicits a reaction in the analyst overt or covert seems more complex today than it seemed just yesterday My teachers here in Washington, DC taught and wrote about the analyst's counter-resistance which was for them a response to the analysand's resistance. They foreshadowed what we now can appreciate is a multi-dimensional com ing to grips with human dilemmas that seem to me to be poorly managed by 'conventional' analytic discourse. The real analytic situation has a more powerful and complex influence than we can fathom (Gross, 2008).

We have traveled far from these early days of classical analysis, although it is still taught and practiced in many schools. Today, thanks to M. Klein, Loewald, Mahler, Winnicott, Kemberg, Kohut, Mitchell and Greenberg, Fonagy, Schafer, Aron, Jacobs, the English Middle School, Fairbairn, Bion, Lacan, and many others too numerous to mention, the present day analyst lives in a pluralistic world. Ideas from all just mentioned and others, have given rise to a richer form of psychoanalytic work—a form that includes, in my way of thinking, the patient as co-worker.

MY CHANGING PERSPECTIVE OVER THE YEARS

My change in perspective seems not so much a matter of conversion, but rather one of evolution. I now see analytic work as a journey with the analyst as guide, experienced in traveling different terrains, with the patient as explorer. The goal is that the analysand takes over the guide's function as the trip progresses. Both partners row the boat. In fact, while in training, one of my supervisors stressed that if the patient did not begin interpreting the material after a certain period of time, something was going wrong (Nass, 1974). It seems only natural for a person to become interested in what lies beneath a symptom or inhibition, or anxiety once they have exhausted treating the surface problems with medication and behavioral techniques. It is the psychoanalytically educated psychotherapist who is equipped to travel beneath the surface where the unconscious influences our lives and it is her conviction that reaches the patient. Naturally, the travelers develop a unique relationship during the journey.

Although theory often lays the groundwork for technique, if it becomes too much of a guiding principle, the patient ends up being shaped by the theory. For instance, when studying the Oedipus complex the clinician tends to hear the patient's productions in those terms, often neglecting or not hearing the preoedipal issues. When studying the psychosexual phases of development, we tend to see patients fixated at one of these phases (the anal character, for example). When learning about the power of transference everything is heard as transference. But many theories of development and of technique, if and when internalized and metabolized, give the analyst her own unbiased ears and her own voice that resonates, and can sing many roles depending on the special needs of the analysand. (Learning to sing Aida does not keep the soprano from learning Carmen.) This approach has been called eclectic and it is not the right label. I prefer to see it as *patient centered work* as opposed to theory centered. Psychoanalytic technique is a subject of constant, worthy debate. Requirements such as using the couch and frequency of sessions must not be written in stone. The clinician must also realize that stages and phases of development, while convenient for theoreticians, are not clear cut and in fact overlap making the individual far more complex than once thought.

Although there have been many competing schools of theory and technique including Jungian, Kleinian, .lderian, and Bionian, Kohut was the first to influence the main stream Americans. At one point there was a possibility that Kohutians would break away from the American Psychoanalytic Association to form another Association. Due to the work of many, this did not happen and Kohut's theory of the narcissistic personality disorder and the technique he espoused, Self Psychology, has become part of what has been referred to as a paradigm shift. Kemberg's stress on analyzing the negative transference by confrontation has also influenced many and is part of most analysts' repertoire as was Reich's analysis of character armor before him.

Both Kohut and Kernberg opened my mind and allowed me to consider techniques I had not been taught in the institute—particularly Kohut with his explanations of how the narcissistic person related to the analyst by responding in either an idealizing, mirror, or twinship manner. Kohut felt that if one of these types of transference developed the patient had a narcissistic personality disorder. Mirroring and empathy were Kohut's major technical contribution and very useful ones with certain patients and at certain times in treatment. He proposed the idea that there was a narcissistic line of development and based his technique on that theory. Whether or not analysts use the narcissistic model of development Kohut's techniques which stress empathic listening are often helpful.

Relational psychoanalysis which was launched by Mitchell and Greenberg is anti- Freudian drive psychology. It is less monolithic and more diverse. Greenberg introduced his own drives—safety and effectance. Relational psychology has evolved to the point where many relational analysts keep the treatment in the here and now, without linking behavior to past development. The analyst's self-disclosure is a technique meant to enhance the here and now relationship.

As an analyst who continues to attempt integration of both classic and modern trends, I have still not learned what determines analyzability. Anna Freud (1965) has said that both diagnosis and analyzability are not known until the end of a treatment. I prefer to assess with each patient what will work best during the consultation period and as treatment progresses. If a person strongly wishes to begin once a week, I agree suggesting that we reevaluate the plan after a period of time. The continuity and consistency that comes with more frequency is valuable to most people and I say that in the beginning. Depending on the patient, I mention psychoanalysis and using the couch early on as a possibility. When there are deep character problems and a degree of motivation from the patient, I recommend analysis right away. I have found that character work requires the intensity of four to five times a week. The wish to decrease sessions is another problem. This wish has meanings that are worthy of exploration before taking action. In most cases I do think more is better. A patient's wish to increase sessions is usually found in his/her material. Things like leaving a dream to the end. of a session, references to never having enough time, and coming on the wrong day are clues.

During my institute years I was employed by a clinic that treated people from all socioeconomic classes and nationalities with drug related problems. Some patients were abusing heroin, barbiturates, amphetamines, and/or marijuana. I learned that each person had traveled a different road to drug abuse, and that the ones who were able to form a connection with me were amenable to psychoanalytically oriented psychotherapy. I also learned that psychotherapy could be deepened into more intensive work, and when I left the clinic, five patients came with me to private practice and four began analysis.

Since orthodox psychoanalysis was being taught I learned such things as the necessity of four or five times per week, on the couch work. I learned the value of silence and of not answering personal questions, instead deflecting them back to the patient. I explained to the patient that his/her fantasy would be more important than my answer. Today, I am more inclined to answer but ask the patient to work with my answer. I was not very successful in the diagnosis course as I always experienced patients as complex individuals who did not really fit the categories I was learning. Many so-called borderline people were quite well put together and took to analysis readily, and many so called neurotics were unable to take advantage of psychoanalysis.

Over the years my repertoire of technique has expanded and includes first and foremost listening with open ears, hearing the patient as an individual. I have seen that patients relive their pasts in some way or shape in the present and that the analyst becomes an amalgamation of earlier perceptions (transferential elements); a vehicle for projection; and a real person. By using explanation (not written about enough), questioning, sharing my own thoughts and associations, mirroring, confronting, and most importantly, by being genuine, I have found many troubled people who can take the analytic journey.

Being genuine is a necessity in analytic work. One patient recently reminded me of my initial reaction when she announced she was pregnant after a long period of trying to get pregnant by the IUV method which involved a long period of using hormones that affected her moods. My reaction to her good news was spontaneous, enthusiastic, excited, and genuine. That reaction, in some analyst's minds would not be kosher. It reminds me of the debate between Leo Stone and Charles Brenner described in Janet Malcolm's *The Impossible Profession* about how the analyst should react when a patient's loved one dies. Stone argued for expressing condolences, Brenner felt that silence would permit the patient leeway in expressing both negative and positive feelings. In this case my spontaneous reaction proved that I truly cared about her. I might not have reacted so openly with another patient with different needs, but this woman's evocation of my enthusiasm allowed her to deepen the treatment.

Each patient must have the freedom to create her own theory and it is the analyst's job to be attuned to what best elicits speaking spontaneously and freely. Listening with the patient in mind and focusing on the way the dyad interacts leads to what I call "open-minded understanding" as opposed to theory-based understanding. New information about child development and the plasticity of the brain (Doidge, 2007) contribute to the analyst's ability to hear more intricate and sophisticated themes. The Oedipus complex as central to neurosis has been challenged. The myth of Persephone (Kulish, 2008) has been applied to women. The work on mirror neurons challenges analysts to rethink the benefits of the couch with certain patients. And the real relationship between partners. in the dyad is ripe for discussion much of the time.

In sum, it was during the years after graduation and becoming a training analyst that my own learning curve deepened. My new teachers were my patients.

MY PERSONAL ANALYTIC ATTITUDE

I believe that everyone who crosses my threshold wants a second chance and that in-depth treatment, whether it is called psychoanalytic psychotherapy or psychoanalysis, is the treatment of choice. I have always disliked labels for I believe they lock us in, inhibiting our openness to new ways of listening and interacting. Instead, I see each patient as a unique human being with myriad ways to deal with conflict and to resume development. I actually see psychoanalytic work as a developmental phase.

Although I do not consider myself a "relationalist," I am convinced that the success of the psychoanalytic work depends on the relationship between patient and therapist. As with all relationships there are rough times and smooth times all to be explored.

Regarding psychoanalytic technique I think of a quote from Ella Sharpe (1950) that has shaped my clinical approach:

The fundamental interest of a would-be clinician must be in people's lives and thoughts. The dross of the infantile super-ego in that fundamental interest must by analysis be purged. The urgency to reform, to correct, to make different, motivates the task of a reformer or educator. The urgency to cure motivates the physician. *A deep-seated interest in people's lives and thoughts must in a psycho-analyst have been transformed into an insatiable curiosity which, while having its recognizable unconscious roots, is free in consciousness to range over every field of human experience and activity, free to recognize every unconscious impulse, with only one urgency, namely, a desire to know more and still more about the psychical mechanism involved. . . . When we come to a habit of thought. a type of experience, to which we reply: "I cannot understand how a person can think like that or behave like this," then we cease to be clinicians. Curiosity has ceased to be benevolent.* (my emphasis)

Benevolent curiosity when embraced by the patient eases the super-ego's burden and allows the ego to take over the work.

The wish on the analyst's part to understand people and what makes them tick is really a calling. A calling, in my mind, is a pull that tugs strongly at the heartstrings—and that keeps you going—no matter what.

Benevolent curiosity has shaped my work.

SHIFTS IN TECHNIQUE: YESTERDAY AND TODAY

- *Greetings:* Addressing the patient by his/her formal title and staying with that professional form versus using first names if preferred by the patient is a personal issue in my mind. I was trained to always use the formal title in greeting a patient with the rationale that this was professional and that first names colored the potential transference expectations. I was taught that if the patient did not follow suit, it was to be analyzed for the benefit of understanding the transference. My attitude has changed and I now take the patient's lead. If he/she prefers to call me Jane I see no reason to interfere. In fact, Mrs. Hall or Jane both have meaning but early in treatment does not seem the right time to challenge or analyze this issue. Whether my change of heart is a cultural one or an issue of taste and respect is not crystal clear to me—and of course there are exceptions. Sarcasm, condescending tones, and other hostile clues should be explored early on. Growing up in a time where the teacher was called Mrs. X, and adults were addressed formally, I was conditioned to this way of greeting others. Today, everyone seems to be on a first name basis and some people don't even have last names (Cher, Bono, etc.) A colleague spoke of a child patient who calls her Dr. Alicia.

- *Vacations:* Freud took vacation during the summer months and in America analysts became accustom to taking August off every year. This is still practiced by many analysts but it is not at all uncommon to take shorter and more frequent periods of relaxation. I continue to see that any separation in the dyad is meaningful and always address the break in sessions. (Hall, 1998)
- *The Couch:* Orthodox training meant using the couch with only four- to five-times-a-week patients based on the idea that the couch leads to regression and that if regression occurs, less than four sessions per week is dangerous. I have never seen evidence of this and have changed my policy. If a patient wants to use the couch, I see no reason to dissuade him/her. Just like anything else, the couch means different things to different people and can be assessed by the parties involved. Freud used the couch originally because he did not wish to be looked at all day and this is understandable. Each analyst has different experiences with using the couch just as each patient does. I think using it or not should be left up to them. Personally, I have never heard a patient complain about not being able to look at me once they decided to use the couch.
- *Histories:* Taking a history in the consultation phase makes sense to analysts who are trying to make a diagnosis before recommending a course of treatment. Phyllis Greenacre took many interviews getting a detailed history. Others believe in letting a person's past unfold as treatment progresses. Still other analysts are not interested in a patient's past and keep the interaction in the here and now. I have found some history useful in getting to know a patient and I let my intuition guide my approach. I usually start with "How can I help" or "What brings you?" "Tell me about yourself?" My tone is inviting and benevolently curious.
- *Working relationship:* My early education implied that the analyst was the interpreter and the patient provided the material. This has changed drastically and with the two-person model, both parties in the dyad make interpretations and use their reactions to each other to

understand and to grow. My patient's pictures of me include elements from past parental images to the real me and to everything and everyone in between.

- *Free association:* In the past, the patient was expected to free associate. In my practice both parties associate. A patient's productions often kick off an idea that comes to me and I share it often quite spontaneously. I consider everything a patient says, if not interrupted, free association.

- *Telephone sessions* are more and more accepted today. Again, this seems to be a personal decision. Originally, I could not imagine telephone therapy. I was quite set against it. But, once when a patient was away, we tried the telephone and its success has led me to use the phone when necessary. I prefer in person work but some people do quite well with the phone.

- *Termination:* This is not a comfortable word. Joseph Schachter has suggested replacing it with "graduation" (personal communication). I prefer Ending. Ending an analysis can be seen as a phase, just as beginning an analysis is often seen as a phase. Usually, the analytic dyad sense when the work is reaching a conclusion. The patient perceives the world differently and with certain weights lifted. The analyst is satisfied that growth and change have occurred. Both parties have learned from each other and so they discuss ending their external relationship. A date is agreed upon and the good byes are poignant. Each dyad experiences the end of sessions differently. After many years of weekly contact, saying good bye is an emotional moment filled with pride, sadness, and hope. Both parties go through a period of mourning. As for post-analytic contact, this happens when the analyst and analysand are part of the same institute and it is a normal part of life. With people not in the field, I leave the wish for another contact up to the patient. I do feel that a period of not seeing each other provides potential for growth and independence.

EDUCATION

Regarding the future of psychoanalytic education, I suggest teaching in a less militaristic, infantilizing manner. Terms like "training analysis" and "control case" make the education of adults sound both infantilizing and unfriendly. Reeder 2003) has a lot to say on this matter. The Future of Psychoanalytic Education Conference, held in New York each year is ecumenical and provides a platform for exchange of ideas. Working ecumenically is growth promoting and although there is debate involved, mutual respect is fostered. In 2007 the theme of who do we teach and what do we teach was discussed. In 2008 the theme will be innovation and preservation.

CLINICAL MATERIAL

The Shift to Psychoanalysis: from Support to Reflection

A, mid-twenties, came to her first interview in tears. Her sister, with whom she had been sharing an apartment for two years, was moving out of town. A was the middle sister and had recently had a self-described breakdown. She was diagnosed as having a mild bi-polar disorder and in her manic phase she let loose at her boss who fired her. She came to see me right before my August vacation and we had phone sessions twice a week during which she cried throughout the hour. (It is only since the late 1990s that phone therapy has been condoned by the establishment). I was supportive and when I returned she began medication. She settled in to twice weekly therapy and by the 3rd year finished a graduate program and got a job. Supportive work deepened into problem centered work and after a year of bemoaning her difficulties with friends, men, and work she took eagerly to my suggestion that she use the couch and let herself say whatever came to mind. The treatment has deepened and she has shifted her focus to her inner life. An analysis has begun.

Listening to the Patient's Requirements

B began once a week therapy with the strict instruction that I not ask her to come more often. She had left a twice-a-week therapy with a classical analyst a year before calling me. I agreed to her insistence on once a week therapy saying that as we proceeded we might revisit her adamant decision. After several months B saw the value of more sessions. She also saw that I was not authoritarian, intrusive, and open to moving at her pace. Rothstein (1990) states that if the recommendation of psychoanalysis is not taken it is a resistance directed towards the analyst. I prefer to allow the patient to wade in, assessing the situation, sizing up the analyst, and making a decision based on her feelings of safety and the match. During childhood, B had been repeatedly abandoned by one parent or the other and the idea of sustained contact was new and scared her. She had to test it out. Most striking was her need to be the good girl, to please and befriend everyone so the idea of accessing her rage was tremendously frightening.

Analytic Work with the Abused

To preserve confidentiality I have constructed Emma, a composite of patients I have seen over the years who have experienced some form of physical or emotional abuse in their childhoods.

Emma was the younger child. She had a brother 3 years older. According to her, and verified by relatives and friends, her mother was a difficult person, distant and moody. She had never wanted children, and often told Emma the story of how she tried to flush dolls brought to her as a child down the toilet. During her frequent rages she called Emma a piece of shit. She preferred Emma's older brother who abused Emma when she was 4.

Father, on the other hand, was quite the opposite. His warm, caring, adoring attitude towards Emma saved her life in many ways, yet also disturbed his wife, making her jealous. Father told Emma that she was special and could accomplish anything she set out to do. His positive attitude was experienced as seductive by Emma.

Emma grew up with a very conflicted pictures of herself. Piece of shit and very special. And with very conflicted pictures of her parents and brother who she feared and adored.

Emma's mother physically abused her until she was 6 by shaking her and slapping her face. The emotional abuse continued as Emma grew up. Mother would say "I love you but I don't like you". Emma's fear of her mother was manifest by the following memory. One day, her mother picked her up from kindergarten. Emma closed the car door on her thumb and rode home that way because she feared aggravating her mother. The thumbnail turned black but Emma never explained why for her mother never asked.

Emma began twice weekly psychotherapy during a depressive episode in her life. She felt alone, abandoned by her husband of one year, and blamed herself for the breakup of the marriage. She was bright, attractive and after six months in treatment she got a job in publishing. Her promiscuity was understood as yearning for affection and not being able to accept it. Romances lasted briefly as she could not trust or tolerate true intimacy. This played out in treatment by missing sessions and then calling the therapist over weekends.

Pushing people away and pulling them back was a clearly defined pattern. From age 20 to 25 she had three therapists/analysts. When I began seeing her we reconstructed how she would seduce her therapists into thinking she was a good patient, capable of in depth work, even analysis, and when they broached the topic Emma fled. Once this pattern was identified Emma and I began to trace its roots. Not surprisingly, the roots included the fear of trust, the attachment to the abusive mother, and the sado-masochistic reliving of her past. Her father's seductive style, teasing and loving, left Emma over-stimulated and always wanting more. Her lack of trust involved trusting others and herself with what she experienced as insatiable needs.

Emma came to me when I was a senior analyst and I will try to explain how my treatment might have been different if she had come while I was in training or recently graduated: my classical or orthodox period.

Treating Emma Then

The main difference would have been my analytic stance. How to assess Emma's analyzability would have been my first job. Was she 'so called borderline' thereby seeing her problems as externally caused? Did she blame the boyfriends or therapists, unable to see the role she played in her life? Did she use primitive defenses like splitting and projection exclusively? Could she recognize a person as separate and constant? Was she a suicidal, acting out person who could not bear the pain of separation? I would have seen the resistance and interpreted it rather than letting it build enough to understand and explore it. In other words, the influence of my training would have been in the front of my mind, still unmetabolized, unintegrated, and uninternalized. If I was in desperate need of a four times a week couch patient I may have lured her on to the couch. I may have seen her as unanalyzable. It would take somewhere around five more years after graduation and independent experience to find my own voice and to recognize the many shadings and levels of a patient.

During this time of assessment my ability to relate to Emma would have been compromised by what the requirements were—at least to some extent. I would have called her Ms. Smith and introduced myself as Mrs. Hall. My technique would have been somewhat rigid or distant as I strived for neutrality and abstinence. I would ask her to reflect on any questions she asked, would not reschedule appointments, and underneath all that I would have been sitting in sessions with my supervisor on my shoulder, worrying about being correct, yet also feeling supported and not alone. During the years of my training, relational theory was not on the map. The analyst was seen as a blank screen, an opaque mirror (not in the Kohution sense) reflecting back the patient's productions. Glover (1955), and Fenichel (1945) were main texts, with Greenson (1985) bringing a somewhat more human touch to technique. The idea of "not knowing" was not considered and we analysts were supposed to eventually know enough to recognize and resolve a transference neurosis, and to properly terminate a treatment. Of course, as candidates we idealized people like both Freuds, those just mentioned, Annie Reich, Phyllis Greenacre, Edith Jacobsen, Abraham, and others. I believe that one almost has to fall in love with their training in order to continue—at least in days of yore. Only after many years of listening to patients and reading the literature did I begin to think on my own. But after immersion in so much received wisdom the idea of thinking on my own was just a spark. It was only after graduating from the institute and turning supervision into consultation that I began exploring Melanie Klein, Fairbairn, the Middle English group and others. My foundation felt firm enough to permit me to explore other ways of conceptualizing, and most importantly each new patient challenged what I thought I knew with different variations and twists.

Treating Emma Now

As a graduate and then training analyst I would greet Emma with benevolent curiosity and the idea that internalization of a new internal and external picture of others (self and object representations), along with remembering the original caregiver with fewer projections (softening the self and object representations), would be useful. Also, permitting Emma to express the rage and needs at both parents with me as her object would eventually alleviate her need to distance others. Working with the negative transference as opposed to analyzing it too quickly, permits the patient to trust without fear of retaliation. Most importantly, I would not assume that every feeling and reference Emma makes is at base, transferential in the usual sense.

As I think about the case, I realize that the relationship Emma and I would develop was more than an alliance or a transference neurosis. There would be aspects of both, but there would be more. My realness would impress Emma. Emma was real and not just a product of her past For instance, in one session Emma, seemingly out of the blue, asked if I had seen a certain movie and if I liked it, saying she had not. Rather than asking her about her question, I answered that I had seen it and did not like it, going on to say why. Emma was relieved as her friends all liked it but my psychological interpretation of the movie impressed her and gave her "food for thought." My sharing was quite unplanned and I can only base it on an intuitive recognition that Emma needed a nurturing, intelligent person/mother-type—someone very different from her schizoid, shallow, out of touch, withholding, angry one. Interestingly the movie was *There Will Be Blood* (a story about an oil man filled with greed) and I had noticed the lack of a maternal figure in the story and the many references to milk. The lack of mother's milk and all that it stands for was very lacking in this patient's life. So, not only did I answer Emma's question readily, I give her my impression of why I thought the movie failed. Not realizing why I gave my opinion at the time, I look back on it as based on intuition. My unconscious had responded to hers. I do not consider this self-disclosure in the literal sense but I did feel free to share my perception without first exploring Emma's. Looking back, it seemed more authentic, spontaneous, and natural this way.

The question I pose here is whether the resolution of the transference neurosis (if indeed there is one) or the internalization of a new object in Loewald's sense is the goal of analytic work. Or, are they really the same thing.

Carol's Ending

If we speak of transference is it ever 'resolvable'? I do think that when patients are ready to end treatment, the lenses through which the world is seen have been changed in a major way. New people are seen without the burden of the past experiences and expectations. Self and object representations are softened. Brains develop new synapses and ways of connecting memories (Doidge, 2007).

Carol ended after a long analysis, five and then four times a week and although she still wanted me to be a real part of her life, she knew that I always would be in her mind—and gradually, less and less. "I've rewritten my past," said Carol in the last days of treatment. But, I think she also internalized me as a different kind of mother—one who could give her optimal attention and empathy, unlike her real mother who was depressive and had four others to care for. She also softened her image of her real mother and developed the empathy that a child can not always call on. I began analysis with Carol in 1982—and it was during her treatment that my voice became my own. However, Carol continued to call me Mrs. Hall and she and I did not alter the traditional frame in any way. We did discuss the name issue and she said that she preferred Mrs. Hall. She said "To me, you'll always be my Mrs. Hall even though I know others call you Jane. It feels special that way."

My answer to the question about transference resolution versus changed self and object representations or new object internalization is that as lenses change, vision expands and that new experiences with others become possible because others are experienced differently.

With a masochistic patient, seeking opportunities to be treated sadistically diminish measurably after analytic work. Why? My experience has shown that masochism is among other things a way to project one's anger on to another. In analysis, the anger is put into words, worked through, understood, analyzed if you will, and owned. Many papers (Coen, 1988; Hall, 2003) have addressed this difficult subject and the connection between the dyad must be strong enough to withstand often extreme pain. Sometimes no amount of work succeeds and a stalemate occurs. The original view that sadomasochism is a normal stage deserves study, as does the very bedrock of psychoanalytic theory: libido and aggression. All of these are constructs but there is a strong tendency to see them as concrete truisms which naturally affects the way we hear our patients. How far will the psychoanalysis we know today expand? This question depends on our comfort in not knowing; our comfort in being open-minded.

TRANSFERENCE YESTERDAY AND TODAY: HOW THE CONCEPT HAS CHANGED OVER THE YEARS

A transference neurosis, classically speaking, is based on the infantile neurosis, based on the way the child negotiates the Oedipus complex intrapsychically with ego and superego keeping the instincts in check. With many people in analysis, the superego or fear of punishment inhibits a full life with freedom to love and be loved. Supposedly this infantile neurosis reappears in psychoanalysis with the analyst as oedipal figure. A classically trained analyst, no matter how advanced, will buy into this view of psychoanalysis and its technique. This explains why the orthodox analysts remain distant enough to evoke what is called a transference neurosis. Onto this blank screen will be projected the oedipal parent imago. It is hoped that this constellation will be interpreted so that the adult can reorganize defenses and that guilt and anxiety will ebb.

I think that when one's early training goes well enough, the concepts learned are not easily thrown away—at least for me. I see transference manifestations in every case. The relationship that emerges between analyst and analysand contains remnants of unconscious fantasy from early development. However, in most of the cases I see, character issues as defensive styles defend against recognition of early precursors. In some cases more than others a reliving of the past clearly does occur in treatment and in life. In other cases such reliving, remembering, and working through occurs more outside of the dyad, at least at first. It often takes many years to delineate the transference neurosis in treatment with the analyst.

My personal explanation of transference is as follows: We all grow up with unique equipment and under unique conditions and these conditions are dealt with in unique ways. Some children have too much, others not enough, and so on. Their characters are formed accordingly. The way each of us experiences and defines his/her reality is due to the lenses formed by early experience, endowment, and inner conflict. The lenses (defenses if you will) distort or at least determine how the world and the people in it are experienced. We might say that people "transfer" expectations based on experience, endowment, and inner conflict, onto others. So I see transference as universal and natural.

As I write this, it seems quite seductive and reasonable on paper. But once you step into the consulting room with a person such conviction must be diminished by the whole theory of object relations, self psychology dealing with narcissistic libido and rage, child development with its separation/individuation tasks, attachment theory, paranoid and depressive positions with the question of a recognized separate object, early trauma, fixation and regression, and so many other tasks and calamities that resolving a transference neurosis, if in fact one exists, seems not to address the complexity of an individual.

How does minimizing the Oedipus complex as central to development affect technique? How does it affect the analyst? Does it make the analyst choose a different 'school of thought'? Must one call oneself a self-psychologist or a Kohutian, a Kleinian, a Mahlerian, or a Bionian?

I have found that for me, boxing myself in to one particular theory stifles my ability to relate to a patient on fair ground. If I bring preconceived notions to our meetings, do I not risk burdening a patient with these expectations? On the other hand, without some of this received wisdom, would I not flounder? How would I listen? What would I listen for?

What I do listen for—or feel for—is the connection that either forms or doesn't. My capacity for connection, for whatever reason, seems pretty good. I have worked with people that others might reject. (See Mr. Min Hall, 2003.) But, when the connection is missing, benign curiosity takes over. Why, I ask us (myself and the patient). Something seems to make us. uncomfortable here. Can you see what occurs to you about that? Maybe this approach works and if it doesn't, I search my own problems with relating to working with such a person. Also, maybe the match is not a good one. That happens sometimes.

When I meet with a patient, whether in the beginning or further on into treatment, my conscious mind is usually listening to every word and inflection the patient utters—and also to the silences and my thoughts about them. Theory, hardly ever, at least consciously, intrudes. It is as if the present is all that exists. It is not that we are even alone, as we both bring others into the conversations and thoughts. When, for instance, I told Emma about my reaction to *There Will Be Blood,* I was totally in the story—with the knowledge that I was siding with her dislike of the movie against her friends. As I see it now, I was allying myself with her purposely and that by feeding her I was hoping the treatment could deepen. I struggle with this decision now—as it sounds seductive—but then it seemed like reaching out my strong enough hand to encourage her to deepen the work. (But none of this was conscious at the time). Actually, the next session was filled with affect heretofore unexpressed. This reaction is not a typical one for me as the old classicist in me usually waits until I have more evidence about what is going on and for the patient to do some work on the question. However, I find myself much looser and relaxed about how I work—more natural and less rule bound. I still believe in a frame, end sessions on time, do not reveal much about myself though many patients google these days and know about my books and my musician husband. I have not found this problematic—just interesting.

A male patient in psychotherapy helped me learn to diminish my active interest in his feelings towards me. His transference feelings were very evident in the material but every time I tried to comment on his thoughts about me into the work—he balked. The classical me calmed down and I relaxed. He had already connected me with a "Mrs. Robinson" type woman in his childhood and although there was no sex involved, she had been extremely seductive. My response was to leave it alone until he made his ideas more experience near. He was eventually able to say that maybe I did look the seductress and the treatment deepened—but this took a long time.

As I approach the homestretch in this paper, I see that I am basically classical at heart. Yes, I have given up on orthodoxy but the unconscious is unconscious—so who knows? The real relationship with my patient feels more natural and comfortable now and I see us as partners—two rowers in the boat.

What a rich body of work Freud gave us to ponder! Even his mistakes taught and teach us. I am deeply impressed and respectful of the many theories that have evolved since Freud. The sincere attempts that have led psychoanalysts to understand their patients are truly mind boggling. So, instead of competing with each other, my wish is that we find some way to pool our ideas and to cooperate in helping each other to help our patients. Martin Bergmann gave his students the advice to see something helpful in every paper we read. I have taken that idea to heart.

IN SUM

Learning the chords to a piece of music gives structure on which to build melodies. I am a melodist at heart. Classical music is written by the composer, read by the performer, and. sedately listened to by the attentive audience. Jazz music is improvised by the performers, many of whom have studied scales, composition, and theory and who respond by listening to each others' improvisation using the chord structure of a composer, (or free form) and listened to by attentive audiences who often move or even dance as they listen. In this paper I have tried to explore the arc of my experience doing psychoanalysis in terms of how my analytic attitude has changed. My classical roots will always be part of me but the freedom to improvise with my partner as a co-worker has and is still evolving.

REFERENCES

COEN, S. (1988). In *Masochism: Current Psychoanalytic Perspectives,* ed. Glick and Meyers, pp. 43–59. Hillsdale, NJ: The Analytic Press.

DOIDGE, N. (2007). *The Brain That Changes Itself.* NY: Viking Books.

FAIRBAIRN, W.R.D. (1958). On the nature and aims of psychoanalytic treatment. *International Journal of Psychoanalysis* 39:374–385.

FENICHEL, O. (1945). *The Psychoanalytic Theory of Neurosis.* New York: W. W. Norton and Co., Inc.

FREUD, A., NAGERA, H., & FREUD, W.E. (1965). Metapsychological assessment of the adult personality. *Psychoanalytic Study of the Child* 20:9–41. New York, IUP.

GEDIMAN, H. (1991). On the transition from psychotherapy to psychoanalysis with the same analyst. In *Psychoanalytic Reflections on Current Issues,* ed. H.B. Siegel, L. Barbanel, I. Hirsch, et al. pp. 177–196. New York: New York University Press.

GREENBERG, J. & MITCHELL, S. (1983). *Object Relations in Psychoanalytic Theory.* Cambridge, MA: Harvard University Press.

GREENSON, R.R. (1985). *The Technique and Practice of Psycho-Analysis,* London, Hogarth Press.

HALL, J. (1998). *Deepening the Treatment.* New York & London: Jason Aronson.

———— (2003). *Roadblocks on the Journey of Psychotherapy.* New York & London: Jason Aronson.

GLOVER, E. (1955). *The technique of psycho-analysis.* London: Bailliere, Tindall and Cox

GROSS, H.S. (2008). Personal communication.

KULISH, N. (2008). *A Story of Her Own: The Female Oedipus Complex Reexamined and Renamed.* New York & London: Jason Aronson.

LOEWALD, H. (1960). The therapeutic action of psychoanalysis. *International Journal of Psychoanalysis,* 41:16–33.

MALCOLM, J. (1981) *The Impossible Profession.* New York, Random House.

Nass, M. (1974). Personal communication.

REEDER, J. (2003). *Hate and Love in Psychoanalytic Institutes: The Dilemma of the Profession.* NY: Other Press.

ROTHSTEIN, A. (1990). On beginning with a reluctant patient. In *On Beginning An Analysis,* ed. T. Jacobs and A. Rothstein, pp. 153–162. Madison, CT: International Universities Press.

SHARPE, E. (1950). *Collected Papers on Psychoanalysis.* London: Hogarth Press and The Institute of Psychoanalysis.

SHENGOLD, L. (1989). *Soul Murder.* New Haven: Yale University Press.

SHEVRIN, H. (2003). *The Dream Interpreters: A Psychoanalytic Novel in Verse.* International Universities Press.

STONE, L. (1954). The Widening Scope of Indications for Psychoanalysis. *Journal of the American Psychoanalytic Association* 2:567–594.

STRACHEY, J. (1934). The nature of the therapeutic action of psychoanalysis. *International Journal of Psychoanalysis* 15:127–115.

TURO, J.K. (2007). *Gold and its Alloys: The Role of Psychoanalysis in the Age of Psychotherapy.* Paper presented at Conference on the Future of Psychoanalytic Education, New York December 1, 2007.

MERGE OR PURGE: CHALLENGES OF TREATING AN IDENTICAL TWIN WITH AN EATING DISORDER

[Lawrence, L. S. (2006). *Psychoanalytic Social Work* 12(2):83–104.]

Treating an identical twin with an eating disorder poses special challenges highlighting separation-individuation and attachment issues. Where parenting is less than "good enough," twins become their own dyad using each other for self-regulation at the price of impaired relationships with others. When that bond is threatened, the eating disorder serves as a substitute "evoked companion." The paper draws on Stem's infant research and Bowlby's attachment theory.

INTRODUCTION

Anorexics and identical twins share similar treatment domains. Both can be difficult to engage in a treatment alliance. A twin is already involved in an exclusive dyad and can see the therapist as a threat, or intruder. Anorexics are struggling to maintain a rigid control over their bodies, and similarly do not easily let one "in." Both twins and anorexics have difficulty believing anyone can be interested in them for them-selves-for anorexics it's their body image and being perfect; for twins, it's the curiosity of their twinship. A sense of helplessness and power-lessness to be effective is common to both. In the last twenty years there has been an explosion in the literature about siblings, eating disorders, and more recently, with assisted technology, twins.

Literature Review: Twins

A 1988 issue of *Psychoanalytic Inquiry* was devoted to "Siblings." Among the featured authors, Graham sees the sibling as a developmental companion and transferential shaper. Parens highlights the sibling as a parental substitute. Shechter alerts us to the sibling relationships that come alive in the treatment, Agger to the quality of the attachment, e.g., predominantly anaclitic or narcissistic and how that influences ego development and identity formation.

Obviously twins are siblings, but they are unique siblings that transform the dyad into a triad. Ainslie (2003): "The mother-child dyad is altered by trying to raise two children who are going through the same developmental stages, engaged with the same issues at the same time. These all transform the climate of the mother's experience of mothering as much as they transform the child's experience of being parented" (p. 224).

Hartman et al. (1997) describe a case of a non-identical twin with concurrent diagnoses of hypertrophic cardiomyopathy and anorexia nervosa. When this twin, at age 28, suffers a heart attack while exercising, her twin, for the first time, develops anorexia nervosa. The authors conclude that the threat of mortality in her twin caused this twin to find regressive solutions in both cathecting her own body, and returning to the pre-pubertal relationship with her sister.

A psychoanalyst who is a twin writes about twins who are playwrights: Jules Glenn (1974) highlights twinning themes that appear in the work of the Shaeffer twins: "rivalry intertwined with intense libidinal attachment, lifelong identification with the other twin; the unconscious fantasy of being half a person, and the associated belief of being deprived of half his body in the womb; the desire for revenge toward both mother and sibling, the wish to make things even" (p. 271).

Lewin (1994) alerts therapists to be mindful of specific twin transference issues, e.g., splitting and projection, the reconstruction of a twin dyad, and the use of the therapist as a containing mother. Sheerin (1991) issues a caveat against treating an identical twin in psychoanalytic psychotherapy when the real drive is the "assassination" of the internal and external twin object as a means of liberation from the twinship. Miliora (2003) discusses the self object function of twinship, concluding that "the relationship can provide one or both with a sense of kinship and alikeness to each other, and can serve to compensate at least in part, for the self object failures of parents" (p. 263).

Arlow (1960) speaks of the mythology of twins and their impact on culture. "Since ancient times twins have aroused wonderment and awe, were ascribed magical symbols, were forecasts for good and evil." They were believed to have telepathic communication resulting in one twin being able to rescue the other. Peter Shaeffer (Hamilton, 1995), the playwright and a twin, writes, "The nightmare of being a twin is always being asked, 'which one are you?' "For him and others, the mirror has only one face.

Eating Disorders

Describing the etiology of anorexia, Rizzuto et al. (1981) conclude, "the beginning of the disturbance appears to be located at the mirroring phase within which the mother is unable to see and reflect the child as itself. A specific conflict emerges in the child's sense of self, between the body as a visible aspect of itself, and its feeling 'unseen' by the parent. The loss of body weight is a desperate appeal to the parents to make contact with the 'unseen' person" (p. 471).

Geist (1995) notes that the "anorexic girl peers into the mirror of the mother and perceives not the reflection of her whole body .self, but a prismatic image of isolated parts: her stomach protrudes, her thighs are fat. When eating, the anorexic girl does not sit down to a whole meal-dinner, she dawdles before isolated pieces of meat, vegetables and potatoes" (p. 272).

Sacksteder (1989) highlights the pathological split between an anorexic's psyche and soma. The split "creates a potential space between the mental self and the body self and the anorexic discovers she can displace interpersonal conflicts onto this field" (pp. 395–396).

Chassler (1997) links eating disorder behavior to attachment theory finding that a history of threats of separation was a consistent predictor in the development of anorexia nervosa. Deprived of a secure attachment base, eating disordered patients develop strategies to ensure proximity to elicit worry and concern from others.

Attachment Theory

The literature is replete with examples of attachment difficulties within families that have eating disordered children. Bowlby (1958) defines this as a way to conceptualize the way human beings make strong affectional bonds to others and of exploring the many forms of emotional distress and personality disturbances (anger, anxiety, depression, emotional detachment) to which unwilling separation and loss give rise. Bowlby (1973) introduced the, concept of "anxious attachment" to describe people who become apprehensive when attachment figures are unresponsive or not available.

Daniel Stern (1985) also highlights attachment theory: "The period of life from roughly nine months to eighteen months is not primarily devoted to the developmental tasks of independence or autonomy, or individuation—that is getting away and free from the primary care-giver. It is equally devoted to the seeking and creating of an intersubjective union with another, which becomes possible at this age" (p. 10).

A CLINICAL ILLUSTRATION

Alice, an identical twin, is a 27-year-old female with an MS degree in nutrition who works on a neonatal unit of a metropolitan hospital. Excluding her twin, there are three other sisters, all older, all married. She felt that I already knew her and she wouldn't have to "start over" because I had treated her immediately older sister many years before.

Model-thin, hair in a ponytail, wearing glasses and carrying an over-stuffed satchel, she appeared more schoolgirlish than her twenty-seven years. So soft-spoken as to be almost inaudible, she presented with long standing dysthymia, expressed feelings of low self-esteem, inability to make decisions, and being tortured by those decisions she did make.

Presenting Problem

Currently Alice is dating a man 14 years her senior, whom she's been seeing for one year and who wants to marry her. (His first name begins with the same initial as the patient's first name, so to avoid confusion, he will be known as "A," and the patient as Alice.) She is not sure she loves him, but is sure she is not ready to marry him. The age difference makes her feel she will lose a decade of her life and catapult her not only into marriage but also into childbearing. The boyfriend has just turned 40. She is ambivalent about the break-up of a prior relationship, which she pre-cipitously ended upon meeting the current boyfriend, who pursued her so vigorously that she was unable to say no to his pressure for increasing contact. As she put it: "I didn't leave myself any time to be single." As it turns out, this is the patient's pattern—she becomes involved with one relationship until it gets serious from the boyfriend's end and then she bolts. Now here is more pressure. The older sisters are all married. Only the twins remain "uncoupled." Her mother screams at her "you've been doing this for years now—how could you not want this—he's a great guy—what's wrong with you?"

Indeed, what is wrong? How does it come to this—that an attractive, young, bright woman is so tortured, depressed and miserable?

History of Present Illness

Since college, Alice has had an eating disorder. Anorectic, restrictor, fanatic exerciser, she purges up to five times daily. She does not cook for herself but eats well when her boyfriend takes her out to dinner. Often self-isolating during meal times at work, she is self-conscious, anticipating the critical stares of other nutritionists, when she eats only a bagel. In addition, she practices "rumination"—the capacity to call up digested portions of food and re-chew them. Rumination comes from the digestive system of cows. Cows have four parts to their stomachs. One part is called the rumen. In it, swallowed food that is not yet digested can be regurgitated and re-chewed (chewing their cud). Swallowed a second time, it goes now to another part of the stomach and is digested. What is the function of this for Alice? This will become apparent later in the case.

Alice is the elder identical twin. Both she and her sister have eating disorders, are on the same medications and, until a month ago, saw the same psychiatrist. They speak daily, often more than once a day, live two miles from one another and, until college, were never separated. As children, they ate together, slept in the same bed together, and went to the toilet together—literally on the bowl at the same time. When I questioned the patient about the practicalities of this, she steadfastly insisted it was that way, but I suspect it is more a screen memory representing being "dumped" together. Alice feels she and her sister are the only ones who really understand each other, even without speaking. Alice feels better when her sister is around, "more able, more alive." When together, they eat the same things at the same time and my patient wonders, "if sis isn't eating, should I be eating?" Or, "I'm hungry, why doesn't she want a bagel?" She and sis check everything out with one another, especially appearance and body image. Joyce McDougall, in an article aptly titled, One Body for Two, addresses the plight of a severely psychosomatic patient who was alternatively engulfed or obliterated by her mother. On return from vacation, McDougall was visibly sunburned. The patient asked, alarmed, "What have you done to my face?" (p. 150). McDougall refers to this as a "transference osmosis"—a primitive mirror transference. Alice feels only her twin will be honest with her about whether she looks too fat, or how an outfit looks. The psychology of the double or mirror image has been studied by Elkisch (1957) who concludes that patients tried to "retrieve in their mirrored images what they felt they had lost or might lose: their ego, their self, their boundaries." Orr (1941, citing Knight), noted the stunting effects on ego development by being confronted with a mirror image of oneself, namely that it is echoed in the society, which regards twins as reflections of one another.

Alice's job is a relatively new field, an area that requires special expertise: neonatal nutrition for at risk infants. She feels she did not earn the job, but was carried along by her supervisor, who moved into a position there and took Alice with her.

She complains of having no time for herself. She lives in her own apartment, but spends little time there, often staying at A.'s, which is across town. When she first began treatment, his 40th birthday party was imminent. Alice was planning a surprise party, but the concept was more in her head than in actuality, as she "ruminated" about it. She wasn't sending out invitations or calling people but rather relying on A's brother to come up with a plan. Similarly she had no air conditioning in her apartment because the unit was broken. Rather than do something active, such as getting it fixed, she elected to stay at her boyfriend's, living like a nomad with a huge satchel that seemed to grow by the week, which she lugged everywhere.

During our second session Alice confessed that she does something of which she's ashamed: "I steal money from A. He's disorganized too; he just leaves money on top of the bureau. I know it's wrong, but he makes a lot of money and sometimes I feel I need it. I know he never misses it and I don't take a lot." Not surprisingly, as we come to learn, this had its roots in stealing money from her mother in order to bribe two girls down the block to play with her and her sister. Now the money was used to pay her twin to do things with her, so she wouldn't be alone. On a more unconscious level, it has to do with her insatiable greed, and wanting the whole breast for herself. It represents an unconscious fantasy that the elder twin feels entitled to exclusive possession of the breast, but feels guilt for being a "thief' (Arlow, 1960).

Treatment

It seemed there were two outstanding issues in Alice's therapy as it began to unfold in terms of what she presented. First, the boyfriend: how to be with him when she was with him, how to be with herself when she wasn't. Second, her non-compliance—the way she said no to me in the treatment. In short, being able to say no was a precursor to separation-individuation. She was "on the way to." She told me she was on medication, and had been for quite a while. She was on a therapeutic amount but something was wrong. There was too much breakthrough of symptoms—

her constant sobbing and her paralysis by indecision. I began to question whether she needed an increase in her medication and I spoke with her about seeing her psychiatrist. Then it became apparent that her prescription had run out, so for quite some time she had been cutting her remaining tablets in half, or not taking them at all. Clearly, Alice needed to remain symptomatic. This coincided with another Event—she became engaged by default. How the engagement happened shed more light on patient's difficulties with separation-individuation. Alice reported she and A. were on vacation together and one morning she was looking through his drawers. Why was she looking in his drawers? Both wear Calvin Klein's unisex underpants and Alice, not finding her own, thought hers got mixed with his and, in the quest for Calvins, she found "the box" which she was sure housed "the ring." On another level, this represents the phallic twinship wishes for homosexuality. Unisex underpants neuter the phallus. Alice searches his drawers (literally) to find a box (womb) wherein is housed the ring jewels = vagina). She makes him into her twin sister. Arlow (1960): "Surveying the world of adults, twins observe other groups of two, a male and female pair who form a unit and share a bed. Accordingly, the already prephallic tendency of each twin consists of acting out the fantasy of being a heterosexual couple" (p. 189). Separation from the twin represents annihilation anxiety. The patient needs to castrate the boyfriend to defend against separation anxiety.

To return to the moment of engagement. She had been behaving with A. the way she was in treatment—one week "I think I can do this"; the next, "I can't do this" and in this cat and mouse game of teasing/approach/avoidance (the only way in her repertoire she can say "no"), hoped to both hold him and ward him off. As they were going to a romantic restaurant that night for dinner, Alice realized, from finding the box, that a proposal was likely and she provoked a fight to win a reprieve. The next week didn't go as she planned. A. took advantage of the positive side of her ambivalence, and in an "I-think-I-can" New York minute, said, "I can't do this anymore" and, without actually proposing, put the ring on her finger, silencing her, "forcing" her. The next week she had the two dreams which follow.

As we know, Alice is unable to "say" no. She felt she could not bear to lose A. because to be "single" would subject her to the recurring parade of obsessional thinking that categorized all prior relationships: "did I do the right thing, I'm so depressed, I'm so lonely, I want him back." And A. was so good to her: so patient, bright: he fed her, gave her money; he was turning 40; but he acted young; but all his friends were older, and so on.

When Alice was in the same room with him, she couldn't just "be single" (meaning do her own thing) even if both were working or occupied with their own projects. Unless he paid attention to her, something was wrong. "I love you" was the way they ended a sentence. Once again, Winnicott (1987) deconstructs how it comes to be that one can be alone, in a positive sense, in the presence of the other: "In the course of time the individual introjects the ego-supportive mother and in this way becomes able to be alone without frequent reference to the mother or mother symbol" (p. 32).

Annie Bergman (1978) also writes about this dilemma: "If the separation-individuation process fails, the space that both unites and separates is not available, and the individual is threatened by engulfment or unbearable isolation" (pp. 148–149). This was the crux of the matter.

The Dreams

Alice begins a session with nighttime on her mind:

> I had the most awful dream last night—two of them actually. I told you my grandfather was very sick before he died—he had bypass surgery that he never recovered from—he was a mess. My grandmother was angry with him for being sick. One day when he was in a lot of pain he asked me to do a "Kevorkian." Obviously I couldn't do that—kill my own grandfather. His birthday was last week—I guess that's what made me dream about him.

First dream: My grandfather is very sick and my father comes to tell me that he (grandfather) put his hand in his mouth to suffocate himself. I feel sick about this—it leaves me with such an awful feeling that he was all alone when he did this and I couldn't be there for him.

Second dream: It was the day of my wedding. It was at a house like a big country outdoor place. I'm on the second floor of the house overlooking the grounds. So many people are there. I'm so not into it. I'm in sloppy clothes—I didn't see A. (fiancé). I had no part in what was happening. My mother gave me this look—forcing me into it—she wasn't supportive at all. So many people were trying to move me into it and no one was listening to what I wanted. You were there—you were in the room with me. You played a mother figure role. You said, "You don't have to do this—who cares what they think."

In a few moments of embattled dreaming here it all is: the duel of the dual instinct theory fought between the plains of aggression (death) and libido (wedding). It is no accident of the unconscious that these dreams are reported in the same session. They are linked by the theme of suffocation. The patient feels no one is listening to her but the dream disguises that she has her own hand in her mouth, purging to expel feelings she cannot express, suffocating under the oppressive weight of her controlling mother. Close-mouthed, she refuses, heralding difficulties with taking nurturance in—food, relationships, a wedding, libido. Hand and mouth are instruments of death, highlighting oral sadism and aggression. The expression "don't bite the hand that feeds you" runs like a Jenny Holzer "word bite," framing the dream.

In the *Revision of the Theory of Dreams,* Freud (1933) cites Alexander's essay on pairs of dreams: "Two dreams which occur in the same night play separate parts in the fulfillment of the dream function, so that taken together they provide a wish-fulfillment in two steps, a thing which each alone does not do . . . One member of the pair of dreams represents the punishment, the other, the sinful wish fulfillment" (p. 43). In this pair, the grandfather in the first dream is a disguise for the mother in the second dream. Where there is smoke, there is fire. The patient, in the first dream, feels guilty for her wish fulfillment sin. In the second dream, the object of her wish-fulfillment appears: she feels guilty for the crime of wanting to suffocate her mother—she does want to bite the hand that fed her.

It is in the second dream that "no" dominates. Out of twelve sentences, "no" figures into all the object-related ones: "not into it"; "no wedding dress," "no A," "not supportive," "can't do this." Spitz (1957) speaks of withdrawal into sleep which annihilates the unwelcome intruder by excluding him first from visual perception and then from consciousness. Spitz is building his theory of how "no" develops: "Taking in and spitting out are consummatory behaviors. They cannot immediately be implemented when the hunger tension arises. They have to be and are preceded by a scanning and sending behavior, with the quality of 'striving toward' to make the 'taking in' possible. Avoidance is next on the negation food chain with the baby turning his head energetically side to side, away from the pursuing nipple. The patient in this second of the pair of dreams scans the crowd below. There is no A. It is her way of saying "no" to this wedding.

Some hint of the patient's difficulties with this psychic organizer and with food is also apparent. The mother is "forcing her into it with a look." On the manifest level, this refers to the wedding. On another level it is about the difficulties with taking in during the oral stage. Was the mother so overwhelmed with Alice and her twin sister that she fed them on her schedule, rather than theirs, "forcing" them? Were their "no"s ignored?

"Two's" are critical for Alice, as she is an identical twin. In this the "second" dream, she is on the "second" floor of the house. "I had no part in what was happening," she says. Her mother gives her a look "forcing" her into it. In this part of the dream, house equals womb: representing the patient s anger at being "forced" into the world as a twin. "I didn't see A." She is referring to her boyfriend whose name also begins with the letter A, but unconsciously she means she cannot see herself—she is the eclipsed twin in this duo. There are two mothers, the patient's and myself. I represent the "good-enough mother" who gives permission to let her voice her opinion. I also represent someone to twin with, who reads her mind and that other part secreted deep inside that, during the terrible twos, says a resounding "NO!"'

The Mirror

Winnicott beautifully describes the mother's role in mirroring the child's development. If all goes well enough, the mother sees the baby, and the baby, in looking at the mother, sees itself, its moods, its distress, its upset, reflected in her face. When this is not working well, the baby sees the mother, her moods, her upset. The mother's face, then is not a mirror.

> So perception takes the place of apperception, perception takes the place of that which may have been the beginning of a significant exchange with the world, a two-way process in which self-enrichment alternates with the discovery of meaning in the world of seen things . . . a baby so treated will grow up puzzled about mirrors and what the mirror has to offer. If a mother's face is unresponsive, then a mirror is a thing to be looked at, but not to be looked into. (1971, p. 113)

To return to the wedding dream: This is about looking, and scanning. It is about the mirror. The patient is looking for A. but, instead, finds her mother with a look "forcing her." She is being toilet trained, instead of getting married. Indeed elements and conflicts of the anal stage prevail—

she is in sloppy clothes, she is being "forced" and is not yet able to say "no." She cannot locate herself. Having unresponsive mothering and being an identical twin have severely compromised her autonomy. Like Narcissus running from his reflection, she is condemned to look for reflections of herself in others. Being an identical twin, she is a mirror not of individuation, but of replication.

Ken Wright (1991) in *Vision and Separation (Between Mother and Baby)* speaks about the notion of searching for a missing object. The object is based in the first visual space which opens between mother and child:

> It is the eyes and looking that hold dominance over all other sensory modalities; the mind is above all a visual space. It is the internalization of that visual space which first opened up between mother and child as the child became able to realize distance and separation and the possibility of the object being able to be lost, searched for and found again within that space. (p. 82)

> The baby searches for what will relieve its discomfort. What the mother could not "contain" was looked at in a way that banished and repudiated the self. (p. 290)

In Lacanian terms the dream is the equivalent of his "stade du miroir" (mirror stage). The child has an experience of not being encountered, where he expects the gleam in the mother's eye. "The pleasure at seeing one's wholeness is. countered by an experience of disintegration as the child feels a split between a self that is whole and external, and . . . its own sense of motor uncoordination" (p. 24). On the basis of the contrast between the baby's primordial jubilation when it encounters the mirror and the fantasies of dismemberment, Lacan explains how the human being constitutes his identity at the price of a fundamental split between a projected image of unity and an inner sense of fragmentation (the fantasy of the dismembered body, the body in pieces) (Gurewich, 1999, p. 25).

Thus, this patient has the experience of being "forced" .and controlled, rather than confirmed. So too, in the transference, I am both the good mother who helps her to separate (in the dream, she also sees me and I tell her she can say no), and the bad mother who "forces" her to take medication. She feels her only option is to be passive-aggressive: stop medication without telling me, turn her engagement ring around so that the diamond doesn't show and flirt with men at work. She is working on a different level of no—a precursor of attempting to fight off coercion. As Spitz says, "NO" is the child's first abstraction—it is the first sign of separateness from the object. This third organizer of the psyche develops hand-in-hand with anal stubbornness and negativism, with all the ensuing complexities in the field of object relations, defenses and character formation (Spitz, 1959, p. 49).

The History

Alice is not only a twin, she is one of five daughters, all born within five years of one another. The first-born is 31 and the product of a planned pregnancy. She had a congenital defect which resulted in her becoming legally blind. The next daughter, unplanned, born a year later, was the "apple of my mother's eye" and "spoiled rotten," according to Alice. Two years later came the third sister, the one regarded as "the mother-the one who really raised us." (This was also the patient I had treated years earlier.) Eighteen months later, unplanned, came the twins. Alice reports her mother was a horror: always yelling, with the kids hiding in closets to escape her wrath. The parents had a terrible marriage with much fighting, both verbal and physical; mother provoking; father retaliating. Her father was passive, aloof and ineffectual He lost the family business in a fire, not covered by insurance. Then he went to work for someone else. The mother was never home, earning extra money doing flea markets. Largely they were raised by the maternal grandparents, who were present but ill-equipped to deal with five little girls. Alice describes the grandfather (the one who died following open-heart surgery) as the only nurturing figure of her childhood. He stayed with her the night before her tonsillectomy, reassuring her that everything would be all right. He made sandwiches for the twins' lunch; unlike the mother, who was very disorganized and undisciplined. The house was always chaotic, with nothing ever in order. Alice remembers loving those times when her parents went away on vacation—an opportunity not to wreak havoc, but rather to clean up theirs. Like a troupe of Cinderellas, she and her sisters cleaned and scoured and put messes to order.

The twins were undifferentiated. They were the "twins." They wore the same clothes, had the same haircuts, and were lumped together for everything—including going to the toilet at the same time. In one poignant session recently, the following emerged:

Alice: I met a woman who is having twins but she's known all along she's having twins because of the sonogram. They didn't have sono then—when my mother delivered, she found out she was having twins. So she always thought she was carrying one child.

Therapist: So two became one.

Alice: I never thought of this before. I mean we were always just lumped together. The woman that's carrying twins said, "I always think of them as two separate people: one's here and one's here, they just both come out one after the other. When I see mothers of twins dressing them the same, I want to go up to them and tell them "you don't know what you're doing, this is awful." Yesterday I saw two 13-year-olds dressed alike to their same berets in the same place. I wanted to throw up.

Alice and her sister didn't separate until college, when Alice went to school in the Midwest, separating from home for the first time, too. Her twin also went to college also out of state, but attended the same school that her immediately older sister did. Alice fought to go her separate way, feeling she had to, painful as it was. Their relationship was not good. When they reached adolescence, they seemed to have no friends, went out only together, with each blaming the other for their miserable existence: "If you weren't here, I'd be different."

Alice describes herself as the caretaker of the two: she was the one who gave in and did what her sister wanted, or was subject to guilt-inflicting attacks of "you have a boyfriend, so I get the sweater." They both had trouble with relationships, feeling they were a curiosity and that people only befriended them because they were twins. Mostly Alice felt distant from girlfriends because they didn't understand her like her sister did and, with her sister, she didn't have to explain. This highlights Arlow's idea (1960) that twins "purchase" good relationships with each other at the expense of relationships with others.

Even recently, when her twin became very depressed, she stayed with Alice and her boyfriend. Alice wonders if she marries, will she still be able to do things like this, underscoring the unconscious fantasy that they will be able to live in a "manage a quatre" (Arlow, 1960).

When the first separation occurred: Alice dealt with it by having a "boyfriend back home," someone she met just prior to leaving for school.

They spoke occasionally, and saw each other on vacations. This "relationship" enabled her to avoid dating in college. She spoke to her twin sister up to five times a day, and by her freshman year had learned to purge, so that her whole college experience was one of avoidance, and not having to live her life. She made a few friends, but felt it was difficult to open up and "explain" herself, as opposed to the shared language of a twinship.

Separation-Individuation

How does separation-individuation occur under the unique circumstances of being an identical twin? Can it?

Much has been written about separation-individuation, but usually within the context of the dyad—the mother/child dyad. What happens when the "child" the mother carries, is in fact two? I would like to highlight some of the features of this process that shed some light on this case. Alice says:

> I can't sleep alone. It's not about sex. I never had to sleep alone, I always slept with V. (her twin). And sometimes we'd sleep with C. (the older sister who parented the twins) too. I always give A. Backrubs—I rub him all over. I used to do that to my mother to get her to fall asleep with me. I wish A. would rub me too, but he always falls asleep.

Mahler (1975) noted that, "The essential feature of symbiosis, forerunner to separation-individuation, is . . . the delusion of a common boundary between two physically separate individuals." He twins were put to toilet together, both to urinate and to defecate. Spitz (1959) and Mahler (1975) speak about the coenesthetic experience, with Mahler extending Spitz's concept to include "contact perceptual experiences of the total body, especially deep sensitivity of the total body surface. Mahler means this as the pressure that the holding mother exercises on the infant. If the capacity to turn the head toward the breast begins now, what is the impact on nursing twins, one at each breast, their faces turned toward mother at times, toward each other at times, during this moment of bliss? Given that these twins had conjoint toileting, feeding, and sleeping experiences, the question of another dyad is raised: twin to twin and their symbiosis with one another. Given Freud's bedrock that the "ego is first and foremost a body ego" (1923, p. 26), what are the implications when "two become one"?

Stern (1985) develops his concept of RIGS (representations of actions that have become generalized) from Mahler's coenesthetic phase: "cuddling or molding to a warm contoured body are events that regulate feelings of attachment" (p. 102). "The experience of being with a self-regulating other gradually forms RIGS. Whenever a RIG of being with someone is activated, the infant encounters an 'evoked companion' . . . Merger experiences at this age are simply a way of being with someone who acts as a self-regulatory other" (pp. 110–111).

Good enough mothering minimizes the frustration/discomfort level during drive differentiation. Not good enough mothering fosters excessive expelling experiences. Alice relies on purging to discharge bad feeling and whatever affects are on overload for her. In the second year of life during the rapprochement phase, the disappearance of the mother creates anxiety and an increase in motor activity, designed, according to Mahler, to avoid sadness. Sometimes a parent substitute may pacify the child. In this case, each twin relies on the other for self-soothing. For most of their childhood, while the mother was out working, the twins were left in the company of each other with nothing to do."

It is my contention that, due to the unavailability of reliable parenting, the twins functioned as self-regulating objects for one another and still do. Although not Siamese twins, they were psychically joined at the hip in terms of sleeping, eating and toileting and this merger experience of being together provided security in the face of overwhelming chaos. That Alice can, at will, summon up the rumination syndrome made reference to earlier, is about regressing to the coenesthetic "evoked companion" of childhood—the twin she fed at the breast with, spit up with, toileted with, and slept with. It is a versatile syndrome because it serves a dual function of merger and separation. She calls on it when alone to minimize separation anxiety; and calls on it with the boyfriend, to prevent what feels to her as engulfment.

Alice remains stuck in this rapprochement crisis. She is unable to be self-motivated or goal-directed. She relied on her twin to "push her." V. prodded her until the patient acted, crystalizing the unconscious fantasy Arlow (1960), that the elder twin opens the womb for the younger, literally paving the way for a passage into life. The patient feels enlivened by her twin. It is the bond and the bind between them. Each is depressed. Each is depressed without the other, and at times, fiercely resentful of the other. This intense ambivalence creates a pull toward merger, and with that, an intense need to flee. Togetherness fosters engulfment; aloneness, annihilation anxiety. Alice now enacts this in her relationship with the boyfriend.

Revisiting the Treatment in Light of These Dynamics

A recent session: Alice has just returned from a nutrition conference down south, where she has gone on her own. The last day there, under duress, she phoned her mother to ask about her father, who had some minor surgery the week before.

> So I called and my mother starts screaming at me, "why didn't you call before this?" and "if you don't come home with some news I don't know what I'll do." Like I'm in some kind of trouble. She didn't ask me how I was, or how the conference was, just, "How's A.?" and he's not even with me. I don't know. I wish she could be like R's mom. She calls and her mom says "I miss you, how's it going?" She was never there for us. I never told you this but V. and I used to sleep in our clothing because we were so scared we'd miss the bus. She'd never get up to give us breakfast. She was always sleeping and we'd have to wake her to get lunch money and then she'd get mad at us for waking her, but she would never think to give it to us in advance. I used to try to be so good to her. I'd give her a back rub and then fall asleep with her.

Largely, this poignant excerpt speaks for itself. Alice received inadequate parenting, longed for a close relationship with her mother, and could only achieve intimacy if she became the parentified child. The person she has this longed-for intimacy with is her twin—which in itself is a highly charged, competitive and ambivalent relationship. Alice "parents" her sister and allows her to depend on her to have money in the bank, so to speak, so that if needed, the tables could be turned. Each ensures the other will never be alone, but with each other, locked in a symbiotic orbit as they were in childhood.

We can conjecture that Alice's mother was clearly overwhelmed with five daughters, the first being born legally blind. It seems mother rejected this first-born daughter because she was unable to tolerate the narcissistic wound of a damaged child. Quickly and "unplanned" she had a replacement daughter, one year later. Two years later came the parenting daughter who mothered the twins. Then, the last children are born—

twins—and already there are three other daughters, ages: 4 years, 3 years, and 18 months. The eldest daughter, now 32, works in the Foundling Hospital with unwanted AIDS babies. The twins, unplanned as it was, arrived, and for the psychological sake of the mother, two were treated as one.

College represented a four-pronged separation experience: (1) from home, (2) from mother, (3) from twin sister and (4) from immediately older sister who parented her. Two things happened here. First, the development of an eating disorder where the body spoke, enacting the conflict. Alice felt out of control and the only thing she could control was her weight. Second, a fantasized "twin" relationship with, a boyfriend back home so she didn't have to feel alone, and which allowed her to avoid separation issues. She existed at college. She didn't date or pursue any interests, but she spoke with her twin daily.

Post-college, she returned to New York, earned a MS degree, got her own apartment and was involved in a series of relationships, all of which she ended when they turned serious. The current one is different. The man is 40, she 28. Of special significance, his aunts were twins, and his father died when he was very young. Due to his background, he has both abandonment issues and much tolerance for Alice and her twin. She is now enacting her twin relationship with this man, the problem being he does not magically understand her, so she must put her feelings (which she often doesn't know herself) into words. It is easier to purge, than to express upset, experience negative feelings, discharge anger, or to anesthetize herself against being alone. Her career choice, being a nutritionist with infants at risk, pinpoints the staging of her own distress and is her attempt at both re-enacting her own conflicts and attempting to master them.

A Shift in the Treatment

A turning point in treatment came several months after Alice became engaged. Because she was non-compliant with medication, I told her that she was trying to control her life by staying sick in order to avoid growing up and making decisions about her life; that she did not have to get married, and that she could work on separating in the context of this relationship. She states: "When I'm with him, I can't be single or myself and when I'm away from him either I feel bad that I'm all alone or guilty that I'm not with him."

In the last several months, the treatment gained traction. She has come twice a week and has been more verbal She has been to several nutrition conferences out of state and is spending more time in her own apartment. She bought a schedule book where she plans dates so she doesn't overbook herself. She is becoming more aware of what it has meant to be a twin and how she twins with significant others in her life to avoid separation-individuation. As the treatment intensified, so too did transference-countertransference issues. The wish to re-mother and provide her with a non-chaotic "house" was evident. The patient however, requested bringing her twin to a session so I could understand her better. Was I now becoming the intrusive mother that the patient needed to ward off by having her sibling present, or was it that she could not tolerate having me all to herself, in the same way that the only real dyad she experienced was with her twin? Counter-transference manifestations were multi-veined; the "good mother'' who wanted to lighten the load of her ever-expanding satchel by ultimately helping her to put the weight where it belonged; the bad mother who "forced" her when an issue was made of medication; the "phallic," effective, father who intervened between her and the mother to take the pressure off the marriage issue; "the twin," when the patient laughingly told me that my first and last initials were the same as the treating psychiatrist.

The rumination referred to earlier was also enacted between us. As the patient wrestled with the twin demons of yes and no, I felt I was being forced to watch her "chew her cud'' over and over. Herzog (2004) refers to the origins of narcissistic disturbances, which occur when paternal authority fails in combination with a demeaning, maternal presence. "The body as usable in what might be considered dialogue with another was present, the other was degraded, as self-with-body-part conversation went on, even as there appeared to be interaction with the other" (p. 896).

I also want to say something about the theme of starting over, which seems to be a pattern in her life: new man, a new therapist, returning to square one. On some level it is about avoidance: if she is always at the beginning, she can avoid getting into the nitty-gritty. On another level, it represents a deeper wish to start over from the very beginning of life as a single individual.

Quite recently, Alice told me of a conversation she had with a friend who envied her for being engaged. The friend said, "I wish I had that, I can't wait to share my life with someone." Alice then said to me, "I've already done that—I want to be single and find out who I am," dramatically confirming Arlow's (1960) idea of the unconscious fantasy of repudiating the twinship in preference to being born single. And so the work begins.

POSTSCRIPT

In his brilliant: encyclopedic book, *The Culture of the Copy,* Hillel Schwartz (1996) addresses our culture's mania for copying, replicating, twins, artifice and discernment (the "Real McCoy"). Twins have always and will always exert a fascination because on some level we are all searching for "our other half" to provide that elusive feeling of being complete.

Recently at an auction upstate, I saw a woman. across the room I was sure I recognized. My smiling and energetic waving went unrecognized by her. At some point, I went over to her, still sure it was Gail, Mailboxes Etc. down my block. I asked her if she had a sister. "No." The resemblance, the smile, the gestures were uncanny and I felt compelled to tell her she bad a double.

Doubling, facsimiles, cell replication, cloning—the multiples are multiplying at an exponential rate: witness that increased "success" with infertility drugs has most recently yielded octuplets. Ovum donation cannot guarantee that unrelated pairs of hopeful couples in the birth market won't produce children that are twins, giving a very science-fiction cast to "searching for one's other half." (In fact, this is now the subject of a current off-Broadway play, *A Number,* by Caryl Churchill. A father replicates his son's DNA. Without his knowledge, the lab makes "others." Somehow, this information, long a secret, gets leaked. The son, now "a number" among many, wants to know if he's an "original," or "a copy." "I don't feel like myself anymore," he laments.)

Assisted technology with its yet untold "advances" in these areas is sure to complicate and confound these issues, needing ethicists and parents with the wisdom of Job. Certainly, we will be treating more twins, triplets, etc., etc., etc., so it behooves us not to dismiss twins as the rare exception, but to continue to think about the implications for treatment.

EPILOGUE

This paper had a long birthing and began its journey before the millennium. After 9/11, I felt the paper to be irrelevant. I had no intention of doing anything with it. When I realized what my disconnect was about, it hit me like a thunderbolt, although it took me forever to make the connection. I was in mourning for the "real twins," the Twin Towers, and all that was lost in a world now divided by "before and after."

Of the thousands of lives lost on that day, 16 were twins. Of the 16, 5 were identical. The Hoffman brothers were identical twins, both had careers in finance, one worked at Cantor Fitzgerald. Gregory Hoffman, now a twinless twin, states, "I feel like a loose wire that can't be capped."

Dr. Louis Keith, a professor of obstetrics and gynecology, and himself an identical twin states, "one need only see a sonogram of twins in the womb, kissing or hitting each other to understand that this is a reality of a different sort, a relationship 'uncontemplatable' to those who have not experienced it."

Gregory confesses in a *New York Times* interview, titled "For Twins, a Lost Double and a Missing Half" (*NYT* 11/24/01), his envy of his widowed sister-in-law, who in time, he knows, will "start over," something he can never do. "Starting over," the recurrent theme enacted by my young patient, reflecting her unconscious feelings of being less than whole, here takes on the unrelenting sorrow of "searching for one's other half."

REFERENCES

AGGER, E.M. (1988). Psychoanalytic perspectives on sibling relationships. *Psychoanalytic Inquiry, 8*(1):3–29.

AINSLIE, R. (2003). Mothering twins. In D. Mendell & P. Turini (Eds.), *The Inner World of the Mother.* Madison, CT: Psychosocial Press, 209–226.

BERGMAN, A. (1978). From mother to the world outside: The use of space during the separation-individuation phase. In S.A. Grolnick & L. Barkin (Eds.), *Between Reality and Fantasy.* New York, Jacob Aronson, Inc., 145–165.

BOWLBY, J. (1958), The nature of the child's tie to his mother. *International Journal of Psychoanalysis, 39*:350–373.

——— (1973). *Attachment and Loss,* Volume 2, *Separation, Anxiety Anger.* New York: Basic Books.

CHASSLER, L. (1997). Understanding anorexia nervosa and bulimia from an attachment perspective. *Clinical Social Work Journal, 25*(4):407–423.

ELKISCH, P. (1957). The *psychological* significance of the mirror. *Journal of the American Psychoanalytic Association, 5:*235–244.

FREUD, S, (1923). *The ego and the id. Standard Edition, 19*:3–66.

——— (1933). Revision of the theory of dreams. *New Introductory Lectures on Psychoanalysis.* New York: W.W. Norton & Co.

GEIST. R.A. (1985). Therapeutic dilemmas in the treatment of anorexia nervosa. A self psychological perspective. In S. Emmet (Ed.), *Theory and Treatment of Anorexia Nervosa and Bulimia: Biomedical, Sociocultural and Psychological Perspectives.* New York: Brunner/Mazel, 268–288.

GLENN, J. (1974). Anthony and Peter Shaffer's plays: The influence of twin-ship on creativity. *American Imago, 31* (3):270–292.

GRAHAM, I. (1988). The sibling object and its transferences: Alternate organizer of the middle field. *Psychoanalytic Inquiry, 8*(1):88–107.

GUREWICH, J.F. (1999). Who's afraid of Jacques Lacan? In J. Gurewich & M. Tort (Eds.), *Lacan and the New Wave in American Psychoanalysis.* New York: Other Press, 1–30.

HAMILTON, J.W. (1995). Peter Shaffer's *Amadeus* as a further expression of twinship conflict. *The American Journal of Psychoanalysis, 55*(3):269–277.

HARTMAN, D., CRISP, A., & McCLELLAND, L. (1997). Two hearts beat as one. *Psychotherapy and Psychosomatics, 66*(4):222–226.

HERZOG, J. (2004). Father hunger and narcissistic deformation. *Psychoanalytic Quarterly, 73*(4):893–914.

LEWIN, V. (1994). Working with a twin: Implications for the transference, *British Journal of Psychotherapy, 10*(4):499–510.

MAHLER, M.S., PINE, F., & BERGMAN, A. (1975). *The Psychological Birth of the Human Infant: Symbiosis and Individuation.* New York: Basic Books.

McDOUGALL, J. (1989). *Theaters of the body.* New York: W.W. Norton & Co.

MILIORA, M. (2003). "Losers" and "winners within. an intertwined dyad. A case of twinship selfobject relationship of a twin. *Clinical Social Work Journal, 31*(3):263–274.

ORR, D.W. (1941). A psychoanalytic study of a fraternal twin. *Psychoanalytic Quarterly, 10:*284–296.

PARENS, H. (1988). Siblings in early childhood: Some direct observational findings. *Psychoanalytic Inquiry, 8*(1):31–50.

RIZZUTO, A. PETERSON, R.K., & REED, M. (1981). The pathological sense of self in anorexia nervosa. *Psychiatric Clinics of North America, 4*(3):471–487.

SACKSTEDER, J. (1989). Personalization as an aspect of the process of change in anorexia nervosa. In G. Fromm & B. Lazar (Eds.), *The Facilitating Environment: Clinical Applications of Winicott's Theory.* CT: International University Press, 394–423.

SCHWARTZ, H. (1996). *The Culture of the Copy.* New York: Zone Books.

SHECHTER, R.A. (1999). The meaning and interpretation of sibling-trans-ference in the clinical situation. *Issues in Psychoanalytic Psychology,*

21(1/2):1–10.

SHEERIN, D.F. (1991). Fundamental considerations in the psychotherapy of an identical twin. *British Journal of Psychotherapy, 8*(1):13–25.

SPITZ, R. (1957). *No and yes.* New York: International Universities Press.

———— (1959). *A Genetic Field Theory of Ego Formation.* New York: International Universities Press, Inc.

STERN, D.N. (1985). *The Interpersonal World of the Infant: a View from Psychoanalysis and Developmental Psychology.* New York: Basic Books.

WINNICOTT, D.W. (1971). *Playing and reality.* London: Tavistock.

———— (1987). The capacity to be alone [1958] in *The Maturational Processes and the Facilitating Environment.* Madison, CT: International Universities Press.

WRIGHT, K. (1991). *Vision and Separation.* Northvale, NJ: Jason Aronson, Inc.

SEVERE POSTPARTUM DEPRESSION AFTER THE SEPTEMBER 11 WORLD TRADE CENTER TERRORIST ATTACKS

[Pierce, M. (2004). *Journal of infant, Child, & Adolescent Psychotherapy* 3(4):466–479, 2004.]

Ms. A was referred for a severe postpartum depression. She had given birth four weeks earlier, shortly after the September 11 attacks on the World Trade Center. She reported that she had not been able to sleep for several weeks and feared she would descend further into the nightmares that kept her awake and in despair. She had been nursing her healthy baby girl but experienced fantasies of being devoured by her. The psychiatric consultant who had referred her recommended medication with the possibility of hospitalization if the severity of the depression did not abate. Dyadic infant-parent treatment as well as individual treatment for the mother were used to prevent the development of an attachment disorder in the child and to promote the mother's recovery from her severe depression. These interventions prevented the hospitalization that the referring psychiatrist had believed might become necessary.

IT WAS THE MORNING OF SEPTEMBER 11, AND THE FIRST PLANE HAD HIT THE World Trade Center. Ms. A, a young woman in her eighth month of pregnancy, was on her way to work in New York City when the subway halted in the tunnel. The train was held up for a long while. There was no information about what had happened. The woman panicked and felt faint and trapped. Terror overtook her; she was certain that she and her baby were going to die.

Ms. A worked close to the World Trade Center. Her psychiatrist had recommended that she not return and that she avoid the site of the disaster. As she anticipated labor and delivery, she had nightmares about bombs exploding and the hospital being attacked. When she arrived at the hospital, it was surrounded by barricades, pictures of missing people were posted all over the neighborhood, and police were stationed nearby. She felt as if she were entering a war zone. She kept thinking she shouldn't be having a baby now. Although minor complications occurred during the delivery, she and the baby were fine, and she felt relieved that they had survived. But her nightmares continued, and she felt alone and isolated, experiencing only sadness and no joy. It felt all wrong to her; this wasn't the way it was supposed to be. Her sleep deprivation intensified, and finding herself unable to care for her baby, she hired a nanny. Once she was ordered to wean her baby from the breast to the bottle, Ms. A withdrew further and further from mothering her infant, either remaining in bed or leaving her home to walk, all the while struggling with the impulse actually to walk away, to vanish.

SUMMARY OF PRESENTING SYMPTOMS

Ms. A was referred for a severe postpartum depression. She had given birth four weeks earlier, shortly after the September 11 attacks on the World Trade Center. She reported that she had not been able to sleep for several weeks and feared she would descend further into the nightmares that kept her awake and in despair. She had been nursing her healthy baby girl but experienced fantasies of being devoured by her. The psychiatric consultant who had referred her recommended medication with the possibility of hospitalization if the severity of the depression did not abate. The pediatrician recommended that Ms. A gradually stop breast-feeding and introduce formula in preparation for the introduction of her medication.

The immediate impact of the September 11 trauma before the baby's birth left this mother in a state of *primary maternal persecution.* No doubt this condition was linked to the earliest states of mind, which intensified her survival anxieties. In the clinical material presented here, I summarize the first six months of the treatment of a traumatized mother to highlight the levels of approach I chose in my work with her.

Benedek's (1970) early contributions on pregnancy and parenthood have expanded our understanding of the issues relevant to those experiences. She has inspired psychoanalytic clinicians and researchers to examine the perinatal period as a time of heightened vulnerability and potential disturbance. Researchers have examined the impact of maternal assets and deficits on the developing baby. Recent literature has focused on the impact the baby has on its caregivers (Fonagy et al., 2002). Guided by this work in my treatment of this mother, I arranged and designed home visits to promote holding and containment of her terrors. Individual treatment offered the vehicle for deepening the work via the transference. Both approaches, I believe, helped to prevent hospitalization at a critical time in this mother's life.

FIRST CONSULTATION

Ms. A looked younger than her 30 years. She was quite thin, with deep, dark circles under her very large eyes. She spoke in a soft, halting voice and became tearful as she expressed feelings of being a failure arising from her inability to continue breast-feeding and to feel comfortable holding and caring for her baby. Above all, she felt incompetent to protect her baby from terrorist attacks, fears of which were plaguing her. She experienced her internal psychic world as dangerous; fantasies of Nazi invaders would enter her nightmares. She wanted to escape, to disappear from the internal chaos that she experienced after the September 11 attacks. She felt she had "lost herself." She felt unable to connect to her baby, to connect to the mothering self she had expected to be.

She was also tearful as she talked about how devoted her colleagues had been subsequent to the World Trade Center attacks. She described how she could not even consider returning to work, because she felt unable to focus or concentrate. She was ashamed that she had deserted her colleagues and now felt as if she were deserting her baby. Her own mother lived a great distance away. Her mother, who had nursed Ms. A's father during a long terminal illness until his death three years earlier, was also ill. Ms. A's husband's family lived in Canada, and his father had died the year before. Her husband's family members were lobbying for them to return to Mr. A's home, given the terrorist threat. Ms. A was ashamed of her current state of mind and had avoided visits with either family.

She described her husband as supportive but at a loss as to how to help her. She thought she might be relieved once the baby was weaned from her breast, but felt that she was a bad mother for even thinking that. She feared that without medication she would find herself so depressed and sleep deprived that she would have to be hospitalized. This possibility terrified her, and she was sure she would die if hospitalized.

I recommended that I make a home visit, since this would give me an opportunity to meet Mr. A and the baby and to spend time with the family as a unit. Ms. A was most receptive to this suggestion. Her affect lightened as she talked about the baby, wanting me to see how pretty she was. Later in the session, she was again saddened and worried that she was having a negative impact on her baby because her depression was so profound. She had been reading many books about early infant development, and the more she read, the more despairing she became. I suggested she put her books aside. I noted that each baby was different and unique and that the "one size fits all" notion does not apply to babies. I was encouraged that there was again such a marked affective shift in this mother. As before, when she talked about her baby her eyes brightened, and she smiled. Her expression of concern and worry was an important indication that early intervention could benefit and include the baby.

TREATMENT APPROACH

I believed that home visits would advance my understanding of the home environment and benefit the family unit (Bergman, 1999). The Tavistock model of infant observation was an integral part of my training at the New York Freudian Society Infant Toddler Program. As a graduate of that pro~ gram and a current participant in the training of its new students, I have come to appreciate this naturalistic method of observation. Hirsch, Smith, and Pierce (2003) describe the therapeutic potential of establishing *not knowing bonds* with new parents. This approach provides the opportunity for the observer to help create the space needed for the infant to be known. Ms. A was beset with persecutory anxieties that prevented the establishment of that critical space—a *primary maternal preoccupation* state of mind—that allows for partnering with the baby. I hoped that home visits would provide a holding and containing function, allowing Mr. and Ms. A to express their concerns as new parents and about the intensifying impact of September 11 on their uncertainty' and survival anxieties.

Winnicott's (1965) concept of the holding environment includes "mother, father, baby, and home environment. Father, mother, and infant all three living together. The term *holding* is used here to denote not only the actual physical holding of the infant, but also the total environmental provision prior to the concept of living with" (p. 43). Winnicott's (1975) concept of primary maternal preoccupation, which he describes as a state of mind in which the mother can become absorbed and imaginatively identified with her infant, is essential for a "basic ration of environmental provision that facilitates the very important maturational developments of the earliest weeks and months, and any failure of early adaptation is a traumatic factor interfering with these processes" (p. 302).

Ms. A was suffering from primary maternal persecution rather than primary maternal preoccupation. Hospitalization, which her psychiatrist had recommended if necessary, would prevent healthy bonding with her baby. Bion (1962) refers to the mother's state of calm receptiveness to taking the infant's own feelings and give them meaning as reverie. His idea is that the infant will, through projective identification, insert into the mother's mind the state of anxiety and terror that he is unable to make sense of and that he experiences as intolerable. The mother's reverie is a process of making some sense of it for the infant. Because of the trauma of the World Trade Center attacks, Ms. A's capacity for reverie was undermined by destructive thoughts. Providing containment for her state of mind might then facilitate reverie.

FIRST HOME VISIT

Mr. and Ms. A live in a comfortable, warm environment. The baby has a bright, lovely room, and the parents have arranged sleeping so that they are nearby. Mr. A was most receptive to the visit. Ms. A was happy to show me the baby's room and the baby's toys and supplies, which were very present in the living space. The baby was sleeping soundly in a baby carrier and placed near the mother on the couch. Mr. A offered tea and talked about how difficult it was for Ms. A to sleep. Mr. A was up at night with the baby in an effort to allow his wife to sleep, but sleep did not come. Both were resigned to her taking medication for her sleeplessness as well as for her depression.

Feeding and sleeping are topics that preoccupy new parents, as are the adjustments that each family member must make to accommodate to the newborn. Our discussion revealed that Mr. A was very sad that Ms. A would be giving up the breast~ feeding. The baby appeared to be adapting by sleeping longer at night, perhaps because a substitute bottle was given at night or perhaps because this baby was sensitive to her mother's needs. Although alert and fussy during the day, she slept more than most four-week-olds at night. I commented on the baby's adaptive "fitting in," an observation that interested both parents. They described the different ways the baby, whom I call Zoë here, seemed to adapt. When focused on Zoë, the parents made various comments about her, her movements, the way she looked, and the way she nursed and gazed at Ms. A. Zoë was a beautiful baby girl, with healthy coloring and wide eyes, who looked very much like her mother. Her cries were no more than whimpers.

Ms. A asked many questions that expressed a new mother's anxieties about her baby's development. Was she doing things in the right way? Was the baby developing properly? Was she sleeping too much at night and fussing too much during the day? Because Mr. and Ms. A were asking many questions and expressing many concerns, we agreed that it would be helpful for me to visit with the family at home twice a week for the next few weeks. Zoë would be weaned from the breast and fed formula. Ms. A would begin medication. At this visit, I chose not to address the trauma of the World Trade Center experience, waiting for that to emerge gradually.

I left feeling reassured about Zoë's development. I had had an opportunity to observe her in both a drowsy state and an alert state and watch her nursing. The baby's color was good, her tone was good, and she was able to hold herself upright quite well during the time her mother was burping her. She molded well to the mother's body, sucked vigorously from the breast, from time to time looking around as the father and I spoke. When there was some difficulty with burping, father took her from mother, held her upright, and walked about. The father was gentle and softly spoke to her when she was distressed. When the baby was put down in her little sleeper, she whimpered, but found a way to comfort herself, an indicator of a good capacity to habituate (Brazelton and Nugent, 1995). During the visit the parent's voices modulated when they spoke directly to Zoë, and Zoë's cries were also modulated.

I was struck by the fact that this baby was already adapting to her mother's requirements, which might signal a potential for some future difficulty. Beebe, Jaffe, and Lachmann's (1997) research considers patterns of mutual regulation in analysis of face-to-face mother-baby pairs and demonstrates early evolution of patterns of self and interactive regulation. In studying mothers who are depressed, Beebe and colleagues have found that some infants of depressed mothers become what they call "high trackers"—that is, infants who work hard to engage with their mothers. I was concerned that Zoë, a baby with good alert capacities, might experience less than optimal self and interactive regulation unless the mother could be engaged. In fact, Ms. A had expressed concern that in some way she might be interfering with or harming her baby's development.

In contrast, Mr. A was actively engaged in play. He laughed at Zoë, and she smiled at him. She imitated his tongue movements, which indicated this baby's ability to be responsive. In subsequent individual sessions, Ms. A expressed concern that Zoë would "like her father better because she seemed to be able to play with him more." Beebe et al. (1997) view the origin of mind as dyadic and dialogical and believe the organization of experience begins as dyadic. This is a systems point of view of the infant's agency. This understanding is shared by Stern (1995). It has implications for early intervention and has been the basis for contemporary parent-infant treatment. I believe that the home environment offered an optimal opportunity for early interventions with Zoë and both her parents.

SECOND HOME VISIT

I made my second home visit the next week. Ms. A had begun to take sleep medication and an antidepressant. Zoë had been weaned to the bottle, and the nanny was now sleeping with the baby at night. As before, I found Zoë in her little sleeper on the couch with her mother next to her and her father in a chair across from them. Classical music was playing. Ms. A explained that Zoë enjoys music; it helps her sleep. She reported that Zoë was having some difficulty during the day, when she was more fussy. Ms. A, who was suffering with sore breasts and infected nipples, felt that Zoë was having a hard time adjusting to the bottle, and to help Zoë with transition stress, had introduced a pacifier.

There was sadness in the room as Mr. and Ms. A talked about the weaning process; they were in mourning. Mr. A felt that his wife was suffering because she had given up the breast-feeding. They both described a visit with friends who have a baby Zoë's age and the experience of observing that mother breast-feeding; Ms. A had been unable to remain in the room. She felt saddened that she and her baby could not enjoy that closeness. Mr. A noted that the other baby cried much more than Zoë and was a more difficult and fussier baby. Ms. A continued to talk about how ashamed she was in the presence of other mothers who breast-fed. She said she was avoiding spending time with those mothers and babies because she could not bear the terrible feelings of humiliation.

The nanny entered the room to speak with Ms. A, and I was introduced. She said hi to Zoë, who looked up at her and smiled. When the nanny asked if she could take Zoë with her, I suggested that it would be fine to keep Zoë with us. I noted that being together gives us an opportunity to see and learn. Zoë was now peacefully sleeping while sucking vigorously on the pacifier. I asked about the pregnancy and delivery. Both parents described the events before Zoë's birth; clearly there was much to talk about. It was agreed that I would, with their permission, arrange a conference with Ms. A's psychiatrist. They would not consider hospitalization and were upset that it had been recommended. They were feeling somewhat more optimistic about Ms. A being able to remain at home, though limiting the time that she would spend with Zoë, as Ms. A explained, to catch up on her sleep. I suggested that this would be a time for Ms. A to heal from her trauma. At some future point, she could think about visits to my office for individual sessions. She concurred. In conference with the referring psychiatrist, he agreed that, though he was very concerned that this mother not do her baby or herself any harm, my regular home visits and individual sessions would be stabilizing, and hospitalization did not appear necessary.

SUBSEQUENT HOME VISITS AND TREATMENT

During the home visits, we talked about the trauma before Zoë's birth. Mr. A had telephoned Ms. A's office on September 11. She had not arrived, and the office personnel were concerned. He made his way home to find her unable to speak. She had been watching television and seemed to be in a state of shock for several hours. He was very anxious about her and the baby. Issues of safety were paramount in his mind. When she was able to speak, she reported being trapped in the subway and helped by transit police to find her way home. The paternal family was very concerned, felt it was unsafe for them to continue to live in New York City, and were arguing for their return home. The couple decided they would give themselves some time before making any decision.

They were supposed to visit both parents' homes for Christmas to introduce Zoë to her grandmothers. Mr. and Ms. A were very anxious about flying or even driving. They felt any change would be unsettling. Ms. A felt safer in her own home with the support system that was in place. She seemed not to want to be separated from Zoë, even though she was not able to be alone with her. She felt safer when someone else was with her.

Nonetheless, I found her alone with Zoë during a visit when the baby was eight weeks old. I surmised that Ms. A had designed that time to be alone with me. Together we watched Zoë, who looked at me with some hesitancy. When Ms. A suggested that I hold her and gave her to me, Zoë protested. I said, "Zoë certainly does have her preferences" and then directed some comments of this nature directly to Zoë. She looked at me and smiled. Ms. A expressed concern that Zoë would like the nanny more than she would like her own mother because she spent so much time with the nanny. I believed that her bringing up this issue indicated that Ms. A wanted to spend time alone with me, and we arranged for individual sessions.

In the family sessions, I learned about the couple's respective families. Mr. A described his own father as a man who provided financially and was responsible in his parenting. Mr. A talked about his sadness at his father's death. His childhood and family life were in sharp contrast to those of Ms. A, who had experienced less stability. It seemed that Ms. A had found a mate who could provide the sense of stability that she felt had been lacking in her childhood. Ms. A described her family home as dark and dreary. Her mother had been depressed for years. While she had fantasies of bringing Zoë to meet her mother, and of bringing happiness and light into her life, she also anticipated that it would be very difficult for her to face the gloominess of her mother's home. Her father's death had been very trying, and she did not want to revisit it.

Ms. A was ashamed of the severity of her own depression. She and her husband delayed the baptism they had anticipated and planned. They decided to wait until Ms. A could handle this public event because seeing family and friends in her present state of mind would be overwhelming. I thought about the significance of the baby's name and of the baby naming. Zoë's name was derived from the maternal line. Naming is a ritual to acknowledge and celebrate the baby's birth and life. Hardy (1997) describes various birth-naming rituals from a historical and anthropological perspective. She believes that baby naming distinguishes between a new baby and a new baby that will be kept. I believed that Ms. A did not feel she was adequate or able to be mother to her baby and could not claim her or allow her to be claimed. This supposition was verified in subsequent individual sessions as she talked about wanting to vanish or of wanting Zoë to vanish.

Home visits focused on the family system. Zoë was a beautiful baby and very easy to fall in love with. Her self-regulating capacities were impressive, and she had been able to make the adjustment from the breast to the bottle in a short period of time. She seemed to use her endowments to great advantage. She was a calming influence on her parents, who were gentle and nonintrusive. The father described how they both enjoyed watching Zoë and talked about all the things she was now learning to do, the discoveries she was making. They are a musical family, and the parents delighted in seeing her move in response to the sounds of music. Ms. A gradually began to engage with and gaze back at Zoë and to take more pride and pleasure as she watched her baby develop and grow.

I was influenced and helped by the work of Raphael-Leff (2000), a British analyst whose work is informed by psychoanalytic thinkers from both sides of the Atlantic. The research on infant development emphasizes how the baby is interpersonally motivated and self-regulating, and this idea has influenced her thinking and work. She has written on postpartum depression and distress; it is she who coined the term *primary maternal persecution.* She describes the varying causes for maternal distress or postpartum depression and offers treatment approaches. She writes that having a baby can be so disturbing that it provokes inchoate memories in the adult. To quote her, "In some caregivers, its unmediated impact burst an internal dam, with eruption of inexplicable feelings—of wild passions, poignant yearnings, inarticulate dread and despair in an attempt to cope with the threat of breakthrough anxieties as correspondingly primitive defenses are mobilized to shore up internal barriers" (2000, p. 60). In my patient, the trauma that she experienced on September 11 had broken down those internal barriers, and the dam waters came flooding through. Ms. A talked about her experience of Nazi fears and terrors and her terror of harming her baby. At times she felt that she would like to walk in front of a car wheeling the baby carriage, and in this way she and Zoë would die together. She could not bear to leave the baby behind. She talked about her fantasies of being devoured by her baby during breast-feeding, expressing her shame that she could have negative responses to such a tiny creature. Her sense of her baby's helplessness only increased her guilt feelings. She was identifying with her internal baby's helplessness and powerlessness.

Stem (1995) notes that keeping the baby alive is a life-growth theme in the initial phases of motherhood. I contained Ms. A's anxieties and, by keeping her internal baby alive, contained the "alone" fears that flooded her and that she might have experienced in light of her own mother's early depressive history (Fraiberg, Adelson, and Shapiro, 1975). Ms. A described her reversal of roles with her mother. Part of her developing a musical ability was a way of fulfilling her own mother's unfulfilled musical promise. She basically had been a conforming child who did well in school but chose a career path following in her father's footsteps. Finding herself a new mother, she experienced an inability to be the good mother that she had wanted to be. She asked questions about my being a mother and how I might have handled her situation. Did I work or did I remain at home? Stern writes how important it is for a grandmother to be a presence for her own daughter in this beginning mothering experience. Ms. A's mother was not available to fill this role. I was to fulfill that aspect of the motherhood constellation that emphasized keeping her baby alive—the life-growth theme—that was ever present in Ms. A's concerns.

As treatment progressed, Ms. A expressed ambivalence about her dependency on me and her relief at feeling safe enough with me to reveal her hostility and rage at her mother, whom she felt had denied her the rite of passage into motherhood. As Zoë progressed in her development, Ms. A's survival fears and terrors diminished. The threat of hospitalization passed. Ms. A was sleeping better, was less panicked, and was no longer plagued by persecutory fantasies. She made plans to visit her mother at Christmas, though she expressed much anxiety about being separated from me. She felt that any change would destabilize her. Yet she felt the desire to show her baby to her mother. She wanted to show her that she had accomplished having a beautiful, healthy baby girl, that she had survived, and that she could offer her mother the gift of being a grandmother. She made the trip, but she needed to maintain regular telephone contact with me to manage that visit.

When Ms. A returned, she described her mother's frailty, depressed state, dark home, and inability to appreciate her and Zoë. Although Ms. A felt guilty, she was also disillusioned and disappointed. She described how it was as if she had been visiting a "dead mother" whom Zoë's presence could not revive. In her sessions we addressed the repetitive patterns in her own life that involved reviving her mother. She revisited the times as a child when she had made efforts to make her mother happy, to please her, to bring light into her life, and how those efforts had failed. Ms. A remembered that as a child she had loved her mother, and this discussion put her in touch with her wish to make her mother happy as a way of expressing that love.

Stern (1995) characterizes a component of his motherhood constellation as *primary relativeness,* which includes human ties of attachment, security, affection, and regulation. In helping herself to overcome some distress, Ms. A would frequently sit Zoë on her lap and read to her, which felt calming and soothing. She found herself reading books to Zoë that were similar to the ones that she recalled her mother had read to her, and she found she treasured reading those books to her own daughter. This reliving of her early mothering experiences was also reflected in the way in which she dressed Zoë and made clothes for her. She had learned from her mother and had recaptured these experiences during the course of her treatment.

Ms. A continues in twice-weekly treatment and from time to time brings Zoë to her sessions. She was able to resume full-time care for Zoë when Zoë was approximately six months old and Ms. A's depression had lifted. She recognizes that there are many unresolved issues arising from her early life experiences. The turning point in her confidence as a mother came in an unexpected visit from her and Zoë. That morning Ms. A decided that she would take Zoë on the subway—something she had not done or felt comfortable doing in the prior months. She entered my office beaming with pleasure. She described how Zoë had made a tremendous hit on the train and had had many admirers. She was feeling proud. I looked at Zoë, who was in her mother's backpack and said to her as she smiled at me, "So you made a hit, you've had your debut." (I was thinking, this is truly a "hatched" baby.) It seemed that this little baby girl was just laughing at the entire experience.

We sat on the floor watching Zoë play with her toys. Her mother had brought toys that would challenge her dexterity and cognitive abilities. Zoë worked hard while Ms. A noted the ways in which she was able to manipulate her toys, noting her fine motor control. Zoë was sitting, but not yet crawling, and made her needs known to her mother. She would point to a toy that was too hard to reach, asking her mother for help. At times her mother would place the toy just outside her grasp to challenge her to move, and Zoë complied. I kept enough distance from Zoë so she could engage with me at her own pace. She made noises that were inviting, and I began to babble at her; she babbled back to me. She was a social baby who was beginning to demonstrate initiative. Ms. A noted that they have been spending time with mothers with babies of Zoë's age. Although she feels deficient because she is not breast-feeding, she has decided that it is more important for Zoë to have playmates. The mothers are accepting and have become a source of support. Zoë's baptism was held soon after this visit. The paternal grandmother traveled to New York to attend. She fell in love with Zoë, and Zoë fell in love with her. That family continues to lobby for the family's return to Mr. A's home. Mr. A is not sure that he cares to leave his place of employment. Ms. A is clear she is not ready to leave treatment.

POSTSCRIPT

On the first anniversary of September 11, Ms. A visited Ground Zero, taking that opportunity to also visit with colleagues at her former job. This was her first visit since the attacks on the towers. She observed that the gaping hole was like the gaping hole she felt was inside of her. Although the persecutory anxieties had abated, she continued to mourn the profound losses she had experienced—being unable to continue to breast-feed Zoë, her inability to face going back to work, and the loss of being the mother she wanted to be for both Zoë and for her internal baby self. The themes of loss reverberate with recovered memories of the traumas of her own childhood. Current reparative experiences involve the good connection she enjoys with Zoë, who has managed to seduce her mother into playful exchanges. They share the love of music and reading Zoë's books. Ms. A did achieve a rapprochement experience with her mother, with Zoë having had the effect of bringing life to her depressed grandmother.

A major focus of Ms. A's second year of treatment was her wish to have another child, coupled with her fear that the severe postpartum depression would return. Ms. A became pregnant when Zoë was 18 months old. Mr. A took a job near his family of origin to provide a support system for his own growing family. They moved to their new home when she was in her last trimester, and we arranged telephone sessions. The leave-taking was difficult. Ms. A came to the last session with Zoë. I had a gift for Zoë, and Zoë left me a drawing she made during the session.

We understood that Ms. A needed to have the opportunity to be like the other mothers in her peer group. She had expressed this need when she decided to get pregnant again. She talked about wanting to be able to enjoy her newborn child. She delivered two weeks early, and I received a telephone call soon afterward. She said, "While I was in the shower this morning I began to cry, tears were washing down, washing away all the doubts and fears, and the terrors were not there and the breast milk was beginning and I was unable to stop crying." She continued, "This must be what women talk about when they feel those powerful mixed emotions, and when I look at my baby girl, it is a miracle, I am so very present with her, I felt the pain of labor and delivery and at the same time felt the joy of being present to see her born."

REFERENCES

BEEBE, B., JAFFE, J. & LACHMANN, F. (1997). Mother-infant interaction structures and presymbolic self and object representations. *Psychoanalytic Dialogues* 7:133–182.

BENEDEK, T. (1970). The psychology of pregnancy. In: *Parenthood: Its Psychology and Psychopathology,* ed. A.J. Anthony & T. Benedek. London: Little Brown.

BERGMAN, A. (1999). *Ours, Yours, Mine: Mutuality and the Emergence of the Separate Self.* Northvale, NJ: Aronson.

BION, W.R. (1962). *Learning from Experience.* London: Karnac Books.

BRAZELTON, T. & NUGENT, K.J. (1995). *Neonatal Assessment Scales.* London: MacKeith Press.

FONAGY, P., GYORGY, G., JURIST, E. & TARGET, M. (2002). *Affect Regulation, Mentalization and the Development of the Self.* New York: Other Press.

FRAIBERG, S., ADELSON, E. & SHAPIRO, V. (1975). Ghosts in the nursery: A psychoanalytic approach to the problems of impaired infant-mother relationships. *Journal of the American Psychoanalytic Association* 14:387–421.

HARDY, S. (1997). *Mother Nature: A History of Mothers, Infants and Natural Selection.* New York: Pantheon Books.

HIRSCH, E., SMITH, D. R. & PIERCE, M. (2003). The bond of not knowing: The importance of early anxiety in self and mutual regulation. *International Journal of Infant Observation* 6:25–42.

RAPHAEL-LEFF, J. (2000). *Spilt Milk: Prenatal Loss and Breakdown.* London: Institute of Psychoanalysis.

STERN, D. (1995). *The Motherhood Constellation: A Unified View of Parent-Infant Psychotherapy.* New York: Basic Books.

WINNICOTT, D.W. (1965). *The Maturational Processes and the Facilitating Environment.* New York: International Universities Press.

——— (1975). Primary maternal preoccupation. In: *Through Pediatrics to Psycho-Analysis: Collected Papers.* New York: Basic Books, pp. 300–305.

I BELONG

[Razavi-Newman, M. (2008). *Psychoanalytic Social Work* 15(1):53–59.]

This essay focuses on the experience of an immigrant returning for a visit to her home country after forty years. She
describes her surprise at finding herself "at home," her
changed relationship to her family, and her desire to be buried in
her ancestors' crypt. She alludes to the immigrant's fate of not
belonging to either country.

As I stepped off the plane and stood on the platform at the top of the
stairs, took my first breath of the polluted and petroleum smelling air of
Teheran, the thought "I am home" astounded me with its unexpectedness.
"I belong."

After forty years in the United States, I had resolved to go to Iran for
a visit. In the days following my decision, I was doubled over with anxiety
and nausea. A million things worried me: Islamic garb and expected
behavior; possible problems with two citizenships; competency in Farsi;
and, mostly, my relationship with my family.

That relationship was an extremely ambivalent one. We are the-
atrical people given to emotional ups and downs. We express our caring
through bickering, criticizing, and needling. The family fights, with their
accusations, complaints, and threats, (followed by making up, joking,
and laughing) had reverberated in my head for years, and I did not want
ever again to be in that atmosphere. Only an abstract kind of affection
tied me to them.

In my mind everything was settled: I would talk to them in a
friendly fashion, mail them a package from time to time, but never see
them again, not even at funerals. And yet my brother's diagnosis
of emphysema threw me into a panic. I could not tell, from halfway
around the world, how sick he was, and I wanted to see him before
his possible death. That desire was also odd. Emotions are rarely what
they seem.

I had come to the United States as a student, married an American,
given birth to a daughter, absorbed the culture, and integrated into the

society. I had thought forty years was long enough to run roots in one country and sever them from another. But I was wrong.

On the day of my departure, I was extremely anxious. My husband guided me through the ticket counter, checked my baggage, and walked me to the security line. I wanted to go back home with him.

On the plane, I relaxed a little. But throughout the flight, the eight-hour wait in Amsterdam, and particularly, the final leg to Teheran, I could not think clearly, could not read, did not sleep. I kept wondering what it was like to live under Islamic rules and how awkward meeting my family would be. When the plane began its descent, I promptly spilled the contents of my handbag and lost a contact lens.

We landed in Teheran airport. Dark scarves and black smocks came out of bags, and we transformed ourselves into Islamic women. I watched how other women wrapped the scarves around their heads and necks and imitated them. Heart palpitating, I joined the line to the exit and stepped onto the platform. Instantly all my anxieties vanished. A big internal smile lit up my soul. Thus began my month in Teheran.

My mother, who had shrunk, my older brother, who had aged dramatically, and his family—whom I had never met—came to the airport to welcome me. Surprisingly not only was the introduction tension free, but an immediate flow of affection went both ways.

My mother and I went to her house which was on a residential street in the center of town. She lives on the second floor, enough stairs for exercise, but not so many as to be an obstacle for a ninety-year-old lady. There, my younger brother was waiting for us. In his pictures he looked very aged, but in person, except for his white hair, he was his old self. His beautiful blue eyes were, as always, breathtaking.

In the following days I met many people, talked, laughed, and joked. My rusted Farsi was barely noticed.

Why such ease? Perhaps because in the United States the moment I speak, I am identified as a foreigner. There are many words I cannot pronounce correctly and others I can barely pronounce. I don't understand most of the jokes and have no idea who the characters are in the comic books. In Iran, when I make a mistake, I am considered an Iranian who has been away for years. The background chatter of Farsi and its rhythm energizes me. I had not realized how fatiguing speaking and listening to English has been, with my constant stumbling over proverbs and struggling with metaphors. In Teheran, I was delighted to hear old idioms. For example, when I ask a taxi driver for the fare, he answers

"It is not worthy of you." I respond with, "I beg of you," and after he tells me the fee, I hand it to him, saying, "May your hands not be tired," and then we call for a benediction on each other: "May God give you life" or a plea "don't take your shadow away from me." When I was a child, it puzzled me to hear my father say, "May you grow old." I was well into my adulthood when I finally understood that it meant, "Have a long life." These idioms cannot be translated smoothly into English and the sentiments they reflect belong to another land.

In Iran, I am a fish *in* water . . . swimming, flowing with the culture. In the United States, I am a hyphenated person, one facet of multiculturalism, and it confuses me. For the last forty years, whenever I meet someone, I am invariably asked, "Where are you from?" I am not one of the Americans.

When I was a sophomore in the sixties, the era of folk songs and hippydom, Pete Seeger was popular, and I saw him live in concert. Automatically falling into the group spirit, I sang along with the audience about social justice and the poor, but I heard a muffled voice in my guts wondering what all that had to do with me. The poor they were singing about were not my poor, the ones who lived in the vacant lot behind our house in Teheran. One day a fire broke out in one of the mud and straw huts and scarred a young woman. The neighborhood was concerned that she would not be able to find a husband and joyous when she became engaged, and we all contributed to her dowry. Then we worried that she would not be able to bear a child and were particularly happy when she did. My mother and I went to visit her, taking food, money, and baby clothes. We sat on the floor in her humble room and drank tea. I imagine other neighbors did the same. The people in the huts were poor, the women washed our laundry, and the men did our gardening. Nevertheless, they were our neighbors and part of the community.

And then there were the working poor, the adults with faces ravaged by the weather and life's harshness and the children with their big dark eyes and olive skin. I would see them at noon, sitting in a bit of shade or sun depending on the season, and eating their lunch of feta cheese, sesame bread and grapes.

One day, walking home from school, I saw a door slammed by an uncaring person on the hand of a beggar who had rung the bell in the hope of being given food and who had extended his hand across the opened door. Blood flowed from the wound. I was less than ten years old and timid, but I asked him to come with me and knew that my mother would be kind to him. She bandaged his hand, gave him tea, bread, cheese and money. He came back once more to have his wound cleaned, and for a cup of tea, bread, cheese and money. Having been healed, he did not return again. He did not want to take advantage.

These were the faces of my poor. The American poor were some neb- ulous abstract mass somewhere in Appalachia. Had anyone offered them tea, bread, and cheese?

Many years later, on a cold night, I began talking to a couple of homeless men, Alex and Don, who slept behind the wall of the church across from our apartment building in New York and offered them cof- fee. I went up to the apartment and made them coffee with espresso beans and took it to them with cinnamon and raisin bread. We talked, joked, and empathized. Forty years into my stay in America, the poor acquired a face and we became acquainted with mutual gestures of kindness. After a couple of days, they moved away. They had told me that, for safety rea- sons, they changed their "home" frequently. I miss them.

Back in Teheran, relatives I had not seen in four decades welcomed me with open arms. I was one of them. The older generation had known my father, my mother, my brothers and me since forever. The younger generation had perhaps met my brothers, knew my mother, and knew of me. I was the daughter of so-and-so, the sister of so-and-so and the cousin of so-and-so. I was a known entity, and there was a place in their hearts for me, just as there was a place in my heart for them. The fact that we had not met and did not know each other's personality, habits, likes or dislikes was irrelevant. I might become good friends with some and not with others, but we are each other's clan, and have a preferential spot. The matriarch of the family gave a luncheon in honor of my return. The men sat in a row on one end of the room while the women in their beau- tiful veils gathered at the other side of the room where they sat graceful- ly in a group on the floor. Their veils, made of luxurious printed fabrics, flowed into each other forming a colorful tableau. They reminded me of butterfly wings. When they stood, their veils draped like Grecian togas. My veil, made out of ordinary cotton, fell from my head to the floor in a stiff fashion. I had difficulties keeping it on my head and when I sat, I pulled on the fabric, and the veil almost fell to my shoulders and uncov- ered my hair. The responses to my embarrassment and awkwardness were amused, but affectionate, smiles.

After lunch, in the hallway, with peals of laughter, my cousins demonstrated how they wrapped their veils. Even the little girls took part in this Islamic fashion show. Like women everywhere in the world, playing with clothes led to intimate conversations about marriages, husbands, and children. There was affectionate gossip, and I wondered what they would say about me after my departure. But whatever they said, there would still be a place for me.

Accompanied by my brother and mother, I went to a cemetery located around the shrine of some holy person. My family owns a mausoleum there. It is a well-proportioned, well-lit, medium-size room. The floor is marble, and the names of those buried in the room are written in gold, either on the floor or on the walls. The large mirror over the mantel and framed family pictures hanging on the walls created a welcoming atmosphere. As soon as I entered this room, I felt comfortable and at ease. Dying became anxiety-free. I was with my family, and for eternity we would remain together. It was the same feeling that I had when I stepped out of the plane.

My father is buried in Père Lachaise in Paris. There, the families set up the grave according to their own artistic taste. The amalgam is beautiful and individualized. For several years, I have talked of acquiring a cemetery plot for my husband and me. But I can't imagine myself in Queens, or Westchester in some sterile cemetery with all kinds of rules. The thought that, even after death, I will be regulated, makes me angry and claustrophobic. Of course I know it will not matter, but thinking of it while alive is unpleasant. The mausoleum was inviting. We sat around, drank tea, and shared incidents and memories. The thought that the other world will be pleasant is silly, but comforting.

And now I am back in the United States. Yesterday in my home I felt lonely and homesick. A negative of my mother's kitchen firmly adhered to my eyes and became superimposed on whatever I looked at. I am making the bed and glancing out at the golden fall foliage, but what I see is a window giving into a Teheran street; my mother and I are sitting at her kitchen table playing backgammon. I move into my kitchen, but my eyes take me to the living room where she reads Hafez. My eyes tear and the film becomes more opaque. I put Mozart on the CD player, but the melodious sound of the Persian tar echoes in my ear, and I switch CDs.

For the next forty years, I will not belong to one land, nor be able to let go of another. For the immigrant, this is a fact of life.

And now I am in my office listening to my patient. Parvine is a twenty-three-year-old young woman from the eastern part of Turkey, and she is in the second trimester of her pregnancy. She and her twenty-eight-year-old student husband are Muslim and come from a small, culturally conservative town. They have been in the United States for six months, and her English is adequate enough to allow her to express her feelings. The counselor of the small school her husband attended referred her to me. He was concerned that she might sink into depression as many of the spouses did. He had noticed that she was not socializing, looked tired, and generally ill-at-ease. She does not know much about psychotherapy and comes to see me regularly, I suspect, out of loneliness.

In this session Parvine walked in very somber, and began to cry. She recounted the following incident:

"My next door neighbor is a very nice and helpful lady. She is very excited by the baby and is always asking me questions about my health and what the doctor said."

"Two days ago, she invited me to her apartment for a "surprise." When I arrived, a dozen nicely dressed women greeted me. I felt very awkward not knowing who they were or why I had been invited. My hostess introduced me and then said her "club" had organized a shower for me. I was totally lost. Then they sat me down and put all kinds of packages around me. My neighbor was very excited. She said, "Open them." I did. They were baby things. I felt horrible and started crying. The ladies looked happy. I think they thought we could not afford to buy baby things. We have become their charity. We are not poor, we are students. We have our families who will send us many things for the baby. I am so ashamed! How can I face my neighbor again! She sees us as a charity case."

She continued crying for some time as though she had lost someone.

My experience as an immigrant, revived by my recent visit home, reminded me of situations when I had misunderstood the culture and, worse, the culture had misunderstood me. She had experienced both. She had been taken for a poor person and did not know what a shower was.

I explained that a baby shower is an American tradition not related to income level, and that the ladies meant to be kind and not hurtful. As she continued to cry and mention her shame, I saw that a trail had to be followed that would add another layer to the narrative. Her shame was triggered by being treated as an object of pity. But what was it related to in her psyche? One of the difficulties in working with Muslim immigrants is the intertwining of Islamic culture and an individual's neurosis. Although developmental stages and psychic structures are universal, the way they manifest themselves is culturally bound. Unless the therapist is able to separate the two strands, culture itself becomes a defense mechanism.

It was much further into our therapy that I understood some of the cause of her shame. While engaged to be married, she had broken the virginity taboo and slept with her fiancé and immediately regretted it. She had been ashamed to look at her parents' face and worried that her fiancé would lose respect for her. In her self-punitive fantasy world, she would be abandoned by everyone and become an object of pity.

The baby shower had rekindled the shame. Immigrants are particularly vulnerable to their own cultural misunderstandings, but when the emotions attached to the incidents become traumatic and not resolved by educational explanations, they reflect a psychic conflict.

As a therapist who is an immigrant, I understood that a faulty compromise formation had become wrapped in a typical cultural misunderstanding. We have a lot of work ahead of us to understand why an infraction of her own cultural norms which had no apparent consequence in her present life was so tenacious.

Another layer of the onion has to be peeled.

LOSS TO LEGACY: THE WORK OF MOURNING EARLY PARENTAL DEATH

[Schlesinger, N.J. (2014). *Psychoanalytic Social Work* 21:75–89.]

This article proposes that an important aspect in treating adults with early parental loss is helping them retrieve a positive inner sense of the deceased parent. Not having an inner representation of the parent is experienced as a double loss: the actual loss due to death, and additionally, the loss due to a lack of memory and inner connection to the deceased. Access to memories and inner representations are often lost in the process of defending against layers of pain experienced at the death of the parent. This article first discusses salient issues to be dealt with when treating such adults and then speaks to the value of therapeutic work which encourages retrieving memories and positive identifications with the deceased parent.

The first day that Mrs. A., age 48, came to my office, she would not sit in the chair I pointed out to her. She explained that she was too "nervous" to sit and instead paced the room, turning to look at me occasionally as she politely and dispassionately answered my questions. She proceeded to do this for the remainder of our first session. In response to my asking what had brought her and how I might be of help to her, she described having recently returned from a longed for vacation on the West Coast. The trip had been cut short because she was unable to stop shaking, unable to sleep, and unable to enjoy the beauty of her surroundings. When she returned home, the trembling continued, as it now did in my office. In the course of telling me about herself, she spoke rapidly and unemotionally in staccato-like manner, describing being happily married, having three children, working as a school librarian, having two older sisters, having grown up in Connecticut, loving nature and arts and crafts. Casually, in the midst of this description, almost in a whisper, and in response to my having asked about her parents, she told me that her father had died 6 years ago and that her mother had died when she was

10 years old. I took note of the stilted manner of her speech as she mentioned the death of her mother. As the weeks and months of Mrs. A.'s treatment ensued, I carefully and gently returned to the subject of her mother's early death. Years later, she told me that she had initially found my pursuance of the topic torturous and had vowed to stop seeing me except for the fact that each time she had left a session she felt less anxious and noted that she was shaking less and sleeping more. Somehow I had not followed one of her unspoken rules: No one was to ever, ever speak about her mother. Through the years she had acquired an ever-expanding island of avoidance of the unspeakable topic. Everyone who knew her soon learned that she would not see a film that dealt with death or with mothers nor would she discuss mothers, read a book that entailed loss, watch a television show that focused on mothers, participate in Mother's Day, and so on. What was wrong with her therapist, she wondered, that she kept "harping" on the subject?

Mrs. A. exhibited symptoms I have found to be typical of adults who experienced the death of a parent in childhood. Access to memories and inner representations of her mother seemed lost in the process of defending against layers of pain. She had no understanding of any connection between her early trauma and her current anxiety as she had isolated all affect connected to her mother's death and minimized, avoided, and denied any meaningful importance to it.

I propose that one of the most important aspects in treating adults with early parental loss is helping them retrieve an inner sense of the deceased parent. By doing so one can begin to repair the self-representation of a poor lost child or an angry child or a child who holds the unconscious belief that there never will be any recovery from the loss he has suffered. I also propose that whenever possible, retrieving positive identifications and inner representations is particularly beneficial. In this paper I focus on those individuals for whom the exploration of positive experiences leads to enriching inner connections. I begin with theoretical foundations which have enabled me to better understand my patients and help these individuals who have lost a parent in childhood to do reparative work, giving them more inner capacity to live life more fully. Coupled with theoretical concepts I present clinical material which speaks to the theory and exemplifies my belief in the importance of garnering positive object representations and identifications. I am not suggesting that it is always possible to come upon affirming memories and identifications. For example, children who have experienced the death of a parent at a very young age, especially if the loss occurred prior to the acquisition of language, have few or no memories to work with other than the stories they may have been told about the deceased parent. In other situations, the parent may have been neglectful or perhaps cruel and abusive, and the child's reaction to the death will likely be ambivalent at best. It is beyond the scope of this paper to deal with the work involved in such cases. Clearly, psychoanalytic work promotes the emergence of a wide range of emotions, not just positive ones, all of which pave the way toward inner growth and understanding. I believe, however, as I have learned from my patients, that whenever it is possible to promote positively valenced identifications and object representations, it serves well to do so.

I discuss salient issues in the treatment of adults with early parental loss including work with identifying and dealing with defenses, taking note of the ongoing impact of early loss, acquiring a broad picture of the experience of the parent's death and focusing on common reactions to early loss. Such core understanding lays the groundwork for exploring and retrieving parental object representations and identifications.

RECOGNIZING DEFENSES

Like Mrs. A., many adults I have worked with initially avoid talking about the death and its impact and wonder why I "dwell" on it. They tend to deny the meaning of this major event in their lives, frequently treat it as if it were not important, and find it painful to focus upon it, just as they did in childhood. As children, they defended against the pain of loss and have lived under a cloud of unresolved mourning and closeted grief. McDougall (1986) has written that "traumatized children tend to develop ways of mental functioning designed to prevent the return of a helpless or hopeless state . . ." (p. 138). I have observed that what began in childhood as a specific defense against feeling flooded and overwhelmed about the death radiates out to other areas of their lives. This attempt to avoid pain continues into adulthood and I believe it is crucial not to join these adults in their denial and avoidance but rather to persist in empathically exploring with them the intrapsychic meaning and impact of the early loss. They need help to put into words both facts and feelings that have long been denied and disbelieved (Furman, 1964a; Karan, 1961; McDonald, 1964). Generally, when my patients were children or adolescents they were unable to absorb and integrate the reality of the death and the feelings generated by it. With care, tact, and empathy, and a feeling of safety within the therapeutic relationship, treatment helps these adults who avoided grief in childhood to deal with the mourning that was averted. I would suggest that the path of recovery from the trauma of early loss begins with feeling previously shunted pain.

THE CONTINUING IMPACT OF EARLY LOSS

Experiencing the death of a parent at a young age is a life-altering event and may make the world seem as if it has turned upside down, as if the universe has fallen apart. Losing a parent at this time poses ongoing challenges because the child has to deal not only with the immediate loss but also with the impact of the loss on subsequent stages of development. Many who have written about this subject emphasize that the death of a parent constitutes a developmental interference, developmental stress, as the child is forced to continue psychological growth in the absence of a vital person (Nágera, 1970; Pollock, 1961; Sekar & Katz, 1986). They further explain that this tends to complicate the resolution of many typical and normal developmental conflicts of childhood and adolescence such as separation/individuation and the oedipus complex (Barnes, 1964; Nágera, 1970; Sekar & Katz, 1986). Knowing the particular phase of development of the bereaved child is important since children adapt to the death of a parent in ways that are compatible with their stage of development (Altschul, 1988). One has to take into account such variables as the innate endowment of the child; the level of drive development; the quality of object relationships; the influence of antecedent and later developmental phases, experiences and fantasies upon each other; the impact of the event on other people in the child's life; and the degree of ego maturity achieved prior to the death (Abend, 1986; Blum, 1986; Furman, 1986; Laufer, 1966). There is no uniform agreement as to which children will maintain a memory of the deceased parent and which will not. For example, Stewart (1993, p. 241), writing of his 30 years of working with patients who experienced the death of a parent between 3 and 10 years of age, states: ". . . I have found that the image and memory of the lost object is not represented but repudiated and wiped from memory. The immature ego is not capable of the working through of mourning. Depression results and this painful condition forces the immature ego to find the solution of denial and renunciation of all existence of the object." Others, like Gaensbauer (1995, pp. 123–124), hold a different view: ". . . developmental researchers have generally found that . . . with the onset of language, children are able to verbally communicate fragments of memories for events that took place over previous months, with much cueing required." In my opinion, this latter view speaks to the importance of providing immediate opportunity to a child whose parent has died to speak of her memories of the mother or father. Barnes (1964, pp. 356–357) states that the younger the child, the more likely the:

> regression to somatic symptoms in stressful situations, particularly those involving long separations. . . . For a long period of time certain life situations, memories and events will reactivate feelings of loss: separations, illness in the child herself or in others, quarrels, and the deaths of both animals and people. All will continue to produce a surplus of anxiety, sorrow, and at times, some temporary regressions.

RECAPTURING THE STORY OF THE PARENT'S DEATH FROM THE CHILD'S PERSPECTIVE

Before in-depth work begins to assist the patient in retrieving memories of the deceased parent, careful attention needs to be paid to obtaining a history of the original trauma since the circumstances surrounding the loss are significant. For example, one reacts to death following extended severe illness differently than to sudden, unexpected death. When death is expected, mourning may have begun prior to the actual death. When the death of a loved one is unanticipated, the griever is stunned and unprepared. The experience may feel surreal, the reaction is immediate, and feelings of overwhelming panic are felt. A shock response is experienced both when the death is anticipated and when it is sudden, but the intensity of the initial reaction may differ (Jozefowski, 1999; Pollock, 1961; Volkan & Zintl, 1994).

When seeing an adult who has experienced early loss, I find it important to inquire about how the death was explained, what traditions and rituals were practiced, what memories, if any, remain of the mourning period. I explore how religious beliefs and cultural influences affected the child and his or her family. I ask whether there were supportive adults to help the child through the grieving process. Frequently, the surviving parent is so bereft as to be unable to attend optimally to the child's needs and the child is alone with his grief and despair. Were there cultural prohibitions against the expression of grief? Did the child attend the funeral? If so, was the casket open so the body was seen? Was anyone available to help the child deal with the loss not only of the deceased parent but also with the "loss" of the grieving one? The widowed parent is not only mourning the death of a spouse but is typically overwhelmed with the responsibilities of caring for the child or children.

> Mrs. A. (whose mother died when she was 10) did not attend her mother's funeral. She was whisked away to the home of a friend while her entire family went to church and then to the cemetery. Mrs. A. knew her mother had been very ill for years with a serious liver disorder but, upon her death, no one explained anything further to the child about the death nor did it occur to anyone to ask her if she wanted to participate in observed ritual. In addition to feeling excluded and isolated, not being able to participate in the funeral and the burial contributed to a sense of her mother's death as not being real. All she recalled was being sent away and then being brought back to the house and told not to cry, that she had to "grow up and deal with it." Her two sisters, many years older than she, expected a stoic response from the despondent 10-year-old and had little visible compassion. Her father was silent, her siblings were absent. Part of Mrs. A.'s therapy experience involved giving herself permission to sob, to grieve, and this led to her going to her mother's grave, saying a prayer, bringing flowers, and creating a ceremonial ritual of her own which she honored each year on the anniversary of her mother's birthday.

Sometimes the child whose parent has died is expected to fulfill the needs of the bereaved, surviving parent. He thus suffers a double loss and is angry about this (Pollock, 1961, p. 350).

> Mrs. B.'s father died when she was three years old. He had been a strong, handsome, healthy man whom she vaguely remembered. He had died suddenly from endocarditis at the age of 36. Shortly after his death, Mrs. B. was sent off to her maternal grandmother's house while her sister (15 months younger) stayed with an aunt. The mother was described as unable to cope with the two children because she was so overwhelmed by and preoccupied with her own grief. No one spoke to Mrs. B. of her

father; no one ever spoke about emotions; no one acknowledged that she had lost a father. The initial focus was on her "poor mother" who was sadly widowed at a young age. Mrs. B.'s sense of her mother as a weak, dependent woman upon whom she could not ever rely was manifest in an early therapy session when she described her mother as a woman she would have to pick up from the floor were she ever to speak of her own need. Clearly, the three-year-old child's images of her mother as unavailable and needy were etched in her memory as was Mrs. B.'s anger toward her.

SADNESS AND RAGE IN THE MOURNING PROCESS

There is general consensus among those who have studied and written about early parental loss that although children mourn, they mourn differently from adults because feelings of prolonged grief are avoided and the finality of the loss is denied (A. Freud, 1965; Lampl-De Groot, 1976; Perman, 1979; Wolfenstein, 1973). There is little doubt that children feel sadness, distress, and longing, but the work of mourning, when understood as . . . "the acceptance of a fact in the external world (the loss of the cathected object) . . . and the effecting of the corresponding changes in the inner world (withdrawal of libido from the lost object) . . .)" are difficult for a child or adolescent (S. Freud, 1917; A. Freud, 1960, p. 58). Most agree that for mourning to occur, the child must have achieved a coherent mental representation of important attachment figures as well as object constancy (Worden, 1996, p. 10).

I have found that generally my patients, as children, were unable to manage the staggering flooding of painful feelings they experienced with loss. In addition, the denial of the reality of the death was frequently reinforced by the surviving parent's refraining from speaking of the deceased spouse. Usually, to defend against facing the finality of death and feeling overwhelming despair, the bereaved child initially has fantasies that the deceased parent will return, yet at the same time she superficially acknowledges the reality of the death. The child thus has a paradoxical mind-set regarding the reality of this major loss. Wolfenstein (1969, 1973) describes this process as ego splitting since the two opposing views of the lost parent (as both alive and dead) are not confronted. She also states, "Instead of grief, the most common reaction to the loss of a parent which we find in children and adolescents is rage . . . a . . .

sense of having suffered an injustice may develop, with a vindictive need to prove how mistreated the child is" (1969, pp. 432–433).

Children who have suffered the death of a parent are angry at the parent for dying, feel guilty about their rage, and are frightened by it. Some children express rage against the surviving parent or other care-takers, some against God, some against peers fortunate enough to have a mother or father. In addition, I have repeatedly noted my patients' har-boring a sense of helplessness and a longing to be taken care of. On some unconscious level there are fantasies that the deceased parent will return to take care of them.

> Mrs. B. (whose father died when she was 3) held a sense of having suffered an injustice because her father died so young (at 36). Feeling bereft, she had the unconscious fantasy that because she suffered so, her father should and would return to care for her, save her, and protect her. From childhood through adult-hood, if something occurred that differed from what she yearned for, even if she seemed to acknowledge what really happened, on a deeper, feeling level, she did not. She denied the failure of her marriage, including the likelihood that her husband was involved in an affair while they were still married; denied difficulties with her son, who was displaying serious acting-out behavior; and denied financial problems, including her avoidance of paying income taxes and her need for a job. Her avoidance of reality reflected the original denial of the reality and impact of her father's death. She seemed to initially acknowledge potential indications of trouble and difficulties but soon ignored them. Although a brilliant, highly functional adult in many ways, she often seemed naive and childlike.

> Mrs. C., a patient whose mother died when she was three, vivid-ly recalled a time when she was about six years old, playing on the street in front of the apartment house where she lived. Nearby, a young mother sat on a folding chair as she attended to her baby, who was sitting up in a carriage. Mrs. C. walked over to the carriage and stared at the baby, who was wearing a pink sweater and hat, surrounded by several stuffed animals, smiling, looking out at her mother. In a short while, Mrs. C. drew closer to the baby and pinched her face very hard, making it "red." She

was severely reprimanded by the baby's mother. Mrs. C. described feeling strong anger and jealousy at this fortunate baby who had beautiful clothes, a warm blanket, a handsome carriage, and most importantly, a mother!

A SENSE OF GUILT

Sometimes there is regret at not having spent more time with the deceased parent, not having expressed enough loving feelings, or not having been more physically affectionate. Due to a magic belief in the causality of death, the child may retain a guilt-laden fear that his anger has caused the death of the parent and thus may have a sense of "badness" (Furman, 1964b). The belief that his "badness" was responsible for the parent's death creates guilt, which in turn seeks punishment. He may fear that his anger has the capacity to "kill" again. Blum has written that "the trauma-tized child is often convinced of his own badness, with heightened tendencies toward guilt, self-reproach, and loss of self esteem" (1986, p. 24). The more likely that previous feelings held toward the deceased parent were ambivalent, the more probable is the child's being certain his badness caused the death and the more difficult is the course of mourning. Pollock has stated that " . . . any previous ambivalent feelings, conflicts, or hostilities with death wishes can play an important part in the mourning process. The magical belief in the causality of the death with great guilt may be the major contributor to subsequent severe psychopathology" (1961, p. 349).

> At the age of 16, Miss D.'s alcoholic mother committed suicide. Previously, Miss D. had come home from school numerous times to find her mother had attempted to kill herself by taking large numbers of pills. On those occasions, she had managed to "save" her mother by calling an ambulance to take her to the hospital. One beautiful spring day, Miss D. chose to go out with some friends after school rather than going directly home, as she did customarily. By the time she arrived home, her mother was dead, having successfully overdosed, evidenced by the empty bottle of pills beside her. Miss D. felt great guilt over not having arrived home in time to rescue her, guilt over having wished her dead many times, and guilt over having chosen to be with friends that day. Viewing herself as selfish and vile, she was convinced

she was responsible for her mother's death. In adulthood, she repeatedly was involved in relationships with men who mistreated her, men whom she tried to woo with devotion and care, however unrequited. With unrealistic expectations and a denial of how they truly regarded her combined with her feeling deserving of punishment for her mother's death, Miss D. unconsciously repeated one failed romance after another, always with the hope that the current relationship with a new beau would have a happy ending. She repeatedly longed for a good outcome while disregarding the unlikelihood of such possibility.

NARCISSISTIC INJURY

Sometimes a child may experience the death of a parent as a blow to his healthy narcissism. He may feel stigmatized, less worthy, and different because he does not have two parents. To be motherless, fatherless, or an orphan, is felt to be degrading (Jacobson, 1965, p. 209; Leon, 1999). In addition, losing a parent evokes feelings of powerlessness and helplessness, feelings which contribute to a narcissistic injury.

Mrs. E.'s father died when she was 10. She had vivid memories of being the only child she knew who did not have a father. She described painful memories of attending synagogue during the day of memorial services for the dead, feeling mortified when all other children left the sanctuary as memorial prayers were to begin. It felt to her that everyone's eyes were drawn to her, the "poor fatherless girl," and her sense of being pitied filled her with shame and humiliation. She hated being different. Her father's death was also a stunning testament to the fragility of life. It was frightening to have to acknowledge the reality of mortality at so young an age. She now had to face the sense of helplessness in being unable to control life and death. If her young father could die, so could her mother; so could she. The world seemed unsafe.

FACILITATING POSITIVE OBJECT
INTERNALIZATIONS AND IDENTIFICATIONS

Over time, as the death of the parent is discussed in treatment and the understanding of its impact is deepened, layers of defense against acknowledging the reality of the death are worked through. As the grief that has lain underground and dormant is felt and memories of the deceased parent are retrieved or discovered, mental pictures of the parent are created or restored. This enables the largely unconscious process of selective identification, as described by Jacobson (1964), in which various functions, values, and attitudes of the deceased parent are integrated and become part of the self, thereby providing an inner connection to the mother or father. Identifications can be felt as internal keepsakes, providing comfort and consolation as positive aspects of the deceased parent are internalized. With this process one can take in what was good about the relationship with the parent and make it part of one's identity (Volkan & Zintl, 1994).

Sometimes, the process of identification with the deceased parent is difficult. Wolfenstein (1969, p. 457) explicated this point when she stated, "The image of the parent's illness and death may in its terrifying impressiveness blot out the image of the parent in his living and constructive aspects. There is then a fearful avoidance of identifying with the lost parent . . ." I would suggest that work to retrieve pleasant prior-to-death memories enables the focus to return to positive experiences and I have found that this promotes an internal sense of a good, loving parent, which, in turn, furthers a better feeling of one's self as a good, loving person and facilitates parenting oneself in a loving, protective way.

When patients who have lost a parent during childhood and adolescence are able to retrieve the object representation of the deceased parent, the pain of the loss is eased as recollecting memories, especially positive ones (in order to maintain a positively cathected inner image of the parent), promotes a sense of having the deceased parent within. An inner presence of that parent enables one to maintain an ongoing internal relationship with the mother or father. Some adults, like Mrs. A., initially report either not remembering anything about their deceased parent or remembering very little. Not having an inner representation of the parent is a double loss: the actual loss due to death, and in addition, the loss clue to a lack of memory and inner connection to the deceased. Helping Mrs. A. and others to regain a sense of who this parent was, what role the parent played in her life, and fostering positive identifications with this parent all help to heal the wounds of the early loss. Whatever the age of the adult sitting in my office, I have in mind the child she was at the time her mother or father died.

Toward the end of her fifth year of treatment, Mrs. C., age 49 (whose mother had died when she was 3), had a strong reaction to my 10-day absence. When I returned she appeared quite visibly relieved to see that I was all right and spoke of being upset when she did not see my car in the parking lot as she arrived at my office. I indicated that I had been in an automobile accident, had fractured some ribs, but was on the mend. She spoke of how anxious she had been about me and how her fear had turned to anger: "I was so frightened because I didn't know what was wrong and if you'd be back, and I was worried about myself; then I felt selfish; then I felt angry. How could you do this to me; how could you *do* this to me . . . like my mother!" She spoke of feeling abandoned and frightened, and yet realizing that in reality what happened had happened to me and was not something I had done to her. She had experienced panic about the possibility of my not returning and was aware of how much she needed me, how important I was to her and how frightened she was to face that. As a result of our work with this material, a major shift took place during subsequent weeks: she began to get in touch with a longing and need for her mother: "I've never been able to consider that she loved me . . . that she really, really loved me and did nurture me and take care of me, and was delighted with me, and held me and rocked me, and wanted to . . . ." This was the beginning of work toward retrieving a lost sense of her mother as having loved her.

Miss F. was beginning her senior year of high school when she began therapy with me. She sought treatment to deal with feeling depressed and anxious, particularly in anticipation of leaving home in one year to attend college. She casually mentioned that her mother had died when Miss F. was nine, after a two-year battle with cancer, and that her father had remarried three years later. Initially, Miss F. described not having been close to her deceased mother who had worked throughout her childhood as an editor of scientific books and was not often home. There were few memories of her and even fewer that were warm and comforting. Miss F. longed to know more about her mother but past requests for information were regarded by her father as being disloyal to her stepmother. Generally, her father and stepmother spoke ill of her mother, giving Miss F. little that was positive about her to hold onto. Her father repeatedly told her how fortunate she was to have her stepmother, that she was a better mother than her birth mother had been.

Work focused on retrieving information and memories of Miss F.'s mother and gaining a realistic picture of her. Early on, in response to Miss F's persistently requesting stories about her mother, she described being told by her father that her mother was beautiful and intelligent, a woman who always had a book in her hands, who had an extraordinary vocabulary and always knew "exactly the right word to use." Miss F.'s only fond personal memory was that of her mother reading to her when she was a little girl, especially when she was sick and home from school. She recalled her mother reading children's literature, stories such as *Charlotte's Web* and *Heidi*. During the last year of her mother's life, her mother had isolated herself, deciding that it would be easier for everyone to deal with her death if she withdrew from them. At the time, this was experienced by Miss F. as grave rejection, convincing her that she was unloved and unlovable. Since her mother had not let Miss F. see her without her wig, and had kept contact to a minimum, Miss F. spoke of having the sense that she was unable to remember early good things about her mother and their relationship because she primarily remembered the bad ending. As work progressed she recalled that while her mother was alive, she had arranged for Miss F. to see a therapist to help prepare her for the impending death and to continue to see the therapist after she died. Although Miss F. did not remember anything about the therapist or what they talked about, she began to consider that her mother's having arranged for the therapy experience was evidence of her having loved her and having cared about her. The more Miss F. and I spoke about her mother, the more memories of her mother returned. She began to recollect her mother taking her to museums, driving her to religion classes, attending her soccer games, delighting in watching her play. Most striking was taking note that her own love of books and reading was connected to the pleasurable hours spent with her mother reading to her when she was a child and her identification with her mother as a reader. She smiled one day, commenting that she, like her mother, was a bibliophile.

When Mr. G. was five years old, his father died while serving in the army during World War II. In the early years of treatment, his most vivid memory was that of seeing his mother sobbing as she read the telegram informing her of her husband's death. At the end of May in the fifth year of our working together, he came into his weekly session reporting that he had begun to cry in church that past Sunday of Memorial Day weekend. The sermon had dealt with the importance of honoring those who had served in war to protect our country and its values. Sitting in church, he began to think about his father, how sad it was that he had died so young and had not had the opportunity to be with his family. Mr. G. said it was the first time he recalled thinking about his father's death from his father's perspective, rather than from his own. Previously, his sadness and pain focused on how difficult life had been for him and his mother. He had been left unprotected and, from a young age, had had to work hard to "get where I am." He planned to go to France the next year to visit his father's gravesite. He recalled his father taking him to the park to play ball with him and took hold of their mutual love of sports and described feeling "closer to him."

Mrs. B. (whose father died when she was three) also turned to relatives to learn more about her father. She discovered that her father used to sing to her at night; that his face beamed with pleasure as she greeted him at the door when he came home from work; and that she squealed with delight as he put her on his shoulders and walked about the house making believe he did not know where she was. Looking at photographs, she studied his facial expressions and was pleased to see that he looked content and relaxed. She had always experienced herself as the "outsider" of the family since she was the only one who delighted in books, culture, and learning. As a child, reading had provided a socially accepted way to retreat from the reality of her surroundings, but it had distanced her from other family members who were not intellectually oriented. Upon discovering that her father was considered highly intelligent, she delighted in saying, "I must have gotten his genes."

Mrs. A. (whose mother had died when she was 10) retrieved forgotten memories of long walks on the beach with her mother, of talks about nature and beauty. She planted petunias in her garden, recalling them as her mother's favorite flowers. She sought out old photographs from relatives and asked them to talk about her mother, laughing at amusing stories of her mother as a young woman who loved to sing about the house, who had a sunny disposition, loved to read, and adored being a mother. Going through old boxes in the attic, she discovered some items that previously had been put out of sight because she could not bear to have any visible reminder of her mother. She now took pleasure in displaying a lace doily, a small jewelry box, a doll, an antique cup and saucer, all of which had belonged to her mother and now helped Mrs. A. feel connected to her. She proudly admired the physical resemblance to her mother and delighted in other shared characteristics such as liking to sing and to read. As joyful memories returned, she began to feel enveloped in a blanket of warmth and love.

CONCLUSION

These examples speak to helping the now-adult, but in many ways still bereaved child, feel less bereft, to have a sense of a loving parent within and to identify with the parent in constructive ways. There is less a sense of inner emptiness as selected traits, values, interests, and other aspects of the parental object representation are internalized and become part of the self-representation. So, Mrs. A. can now see herself as a loving mother; Mrs. B. takes pleasure in her good mind; Mrs. C. feels loved and lovable; Miss F. takes pride in her love of books and learning; Mr. G. delights in his love of sports. Each has mourned in a way that was not possible in childhood; each has accepted the reality of the parent's death; each is able to speak of his or her deceased parent with a range of feelings. Each has experienced some measure of healing and a more cohesive sense of self with the recapture of affirming memories and identifications.

ADDENDUM

I would suggest that as therapists our awareness of the importance of promoting memories and identifications inform our work when we have the opportunity to help families who are currently dealing with the death of a parent of young children. Providing the widowed parent with as much support as possible is a good place to start. The surviving parent needs assistance with the ordinary tasks of daily living, creature comforts, help with child care, an empathic ear, and time to grieve privately. By supporting and taking care of the parent who is mourning, we enable that parent to be better attuned to the pain and needs of his or her bereaved children. We need to promote the importance of speaking about the deceased parent. This is fostered by encouraging the expression of feelings and by encouraging the perpetuation of positive and realistic images of that parent. We live in a technological culture which enables us to provide digital photographs, videos and tape recordings to help keep the memories of the deceased parent alive. The viewing of videos, hearing stories about the deceased, perusing personal writings at age-appropriate stages, examining photographs, being surrounded with familiar trinkets and treasured objects connected to the mother or father—all of these assist in maintaining a rich and textured sense of the parent. In addition, children saddened at being deprived by death of a mother or father need the support, care, and love of grandparents, aunts, uncles, cousins, and good friends, both adults and peers. The more loving people there are to attend to the child, the better. The more the child can retain a sense of a loving mother or father within, the better. Positive parental object representations will enable the child to have positive feelings about himself or herself and others.

REFERENCES

ABEND, S.M. (1986). Sibling loss. In A. Rothstein (Ed.), *the Reconstruction of Trauma: its Significance in Clinical Work* (pp. 95–104). Madison, CT: International Universities Press.

ALTSCHUL, S. (1988). Summary and conclusions. In S. Altschul (Ed.), *Childhood Bereavement and its Aftermath: Emotions and Behavior.* Monograph 8. *Psychoanalytic Quarterly* 59:305—309.

BARNES, M. (1964). Reactions to the death of a mother. In *Psychoanalytic Study of the Child* 19:334–357.

BLUM, H. (1986). The concept of the reconstruction of trauma. In A. Rothstein (Ed.), *The Reconstruction of Trauma: Its Significance in Clinical Work* (pp. 7–27). Madison, CT: International Universities Press.

FREUD, A. (1960). Discussion of John Bowlby's paper. In *Psychoanalytic Study of the Child* 15:53–62.

—— (1965). *Normality and pathology in childhood: Assessments of development.* New York, NY: International Universities Press.

FREUD, S. (1917). Mourning and melancholia. *Standard Edition* 14:237–260.

FURMAN, E. (1986). On trauma: When is the death of a parent traumatic? In *Psychoanalytic Study of the Child* 41:191–208.

FURMAN, R. (1964a). Death and the young child: Some preliminary considerations. In *Psychoanalytic Study of the Child* 19:321–333.

—— (1964). Death of a six-year-old's mother during his analysis. In *Psychoanalytic Study of the Child* 19:377–397

GAENSBAUER, T. (1995). Trauma in the preverbal period: Symptoms, memories, and developmental impact. In *Psychoanalytic Study of the Child* 50:122–149.

JACOBSON, E. (1964). *The Self and the Object World.* New York, NY: International Universities Press.

—— (1965). The return of the lost parent. In M. Schur (Ed.), *Drives, Affects and Behavior* (Vol. 2, pp. 193–211). New York, NY: International Universities Press.

JOZEFOWSKI, J.T. (1999). *The Phoenix Phenomenon: Rising from the Ashes of Grief.* Northvale, NJ: Jason Aronson.

KARAN, A. (1961). Some thoughts about the role of verbalization in early childhood. In *Psychoanalytic Study of the Child* 16:184–188).

LAMPL-DE GROOT, J. (1976). Mourning in a six-year-old girl. In *Psychoanalytic Study of the Child* 31:275–281).

LAUFER, M. (1966). Object loss and mourning during adolescence. In *Psychoanalytic Study of the Child* 21:269–293.

LEON, I.G. (1999). Bereavement and repair of the self: Poetic confrontations with death. *The Psychoanalytic Review* 86:383–401.

MCDONALD, M. (1964). A study of the reactions of nursery school children to the death of a child's mother. In *Psychoanalytic Study of the Child* 19:358–376.

MCDOUGALL, J. (1986). Parent loss. In A. Rothstein (Ed.), *the Reconstruction a Trauma: its Significance in Clinical Work* (pp. 135–151). Madison, CT: International Universities Press.

NÁGERA, H. (1970). Children's reactions to the death of important objects: A developmental approach. In *Psychoanalytic Study of the Child* 25:360–400.

PERMAN, J. (1979). The search for the mother: Narcissistic regression as a pathway of mourning in childhood. *Psychoanalytic Quarterly* 48:448–464.

POLLOCK, G. (1961). Mourning and adaptation. *International Journal of Psychoanalysis* 42:341–361.

SEKAR. C., & KATZ, S. (1986). On the concept of mourning in childhood: Reactions of a 2 1/2-year-old girl to the death of her father. *Psychoanalytic Study of the Child* 41:287–314).

STEWART, S. (1993). Some reflections on trauma and psychic reality. *Journal of Clinical Psychoanalysis* 2:219–243.

VOLKAN, V., & ZINTL, E. (1994). *Life after Loss: The Lessons of Grief.* New York, NY: Scribner and Sons.

WOLFENSTEIN, M. (1969). Loss, rage, and repetition. In *Psychoanalytic Study of the Child* 24:432–460.

——— (1973). The image of the lost parent. In *Psychoanalytic Study of the Child* 28:433–455.

WORDEN, J.W. (1996). *Children and Grief: When a Parent Dies.* New York: Guilford Press.

SOME COMMENTS ON LONELINESS AND WIDOWHOOD AS DEPICTED IN *VISITORS* BY ANITA BROOKNER

[Spira, L. (2003). *The Round Robin* (Newsletter of Divsn. of Psychoanalysis (39), APA), Vol. XVIII.]

How do lonely people mitigate the sense of being alone? Psychoanalysts, psychotherapists, social scientists and novelists all address this question, as does Anita Brookner in *Visitors;* and the different perspectives complement and enrich one another.

Weiss (1973), a social scientist, found that loneliness was caused by the loss of an intimate attachment or by the lack of a social group. As psychoanalysts, we understand this intuitively and are not surprised when a woman who has lost a loving husband takes a long time to recover from her grief or is enduringly lonely as a result of her loss. The presence of loneliness, or in some instances depression and anxiety, may be exacerbated if the woman has neither a passionate interest nor a career. For the widow or widower, being without the support of a loving family can contribute to what is already a tenuous situation.

Lonely people are often ashamed of their loneliness (Satran, 1978) and when they come to psychotherapy may not complain of such feelings. Some others do not or cannot allow themselves to be aware of being lonely, and the defenses, necessary to mitigate longing, are maintained by a delicate balance.

Dorothea May, or Thea, as she is called in Anita Brookner's *Visitors* is a character in whom we can consider some of ideas, questions and concerns that are relevant to a psychoanalyst or psychotherapist in treating a socially isolated person. Thea, a childless widow in her seventies, wears aloneness like a suit, so well-tailored that no one senses her loneliness underneath. Her elegant apartment, bought with an inheritance, protects like a cocoon. Though she has almost no friends or intimate relationships, she does not appear to be lonely. Perhaps, Brookner has decided not to focus on the loneliness often associated with widowhood, but has chosen instead to explore how a more chronically isolated person might resolve her aloneness as she nears the end of her life.

Thea seems never to have had any real intimate connections. Her relationship with her deceased husband, although described as comfortable, was likely not an intimate one; he knew very little about her thoughts and feelings. We are not given much basis for speculation about why Thea seems emotionally unconnected to any of her objects; and, since she is not a real person in treatment, we do not have the opportunity to explore her history and her fantasies in order to develop a hypothesis that might explain the state of her current emotional life.

Thea's social isolation is presented in the novel as if she had chosen it. She is portrayed as the architect of her solitary life, and therefore, not pitiable, in contrast to Lieberman's (1991) findings: many women without families of their own are often thought to be pitiable. In this novel, that role is assigned to another female character, Thea's sister-in-law, a woman who never married, never had a career, and remained childless and reclusive. We know that Thea did not choose to be a widow. She experienced enforced singleness as do many women as a result of death or divorce. This happens more frequently to women than to men; men not only have shorter life spans than women, thus often leave their mates behind, but also frequently leave older spouses to marry younger women.

We are told that in Thea's adolescence and young adulthood, Jane Austen's Anne Elliot was her ego ideal. Like Anne, she believed if she waited passively she would be claimed by the "right" man. This is a familiar fantasy of many chronically lonely women. But, Thea's fantasy, unlike those of most of our single and lonely patients, becomes an actuality in the form of Henry May, who helps her up from a fall on the sidewalk and marries her.

Being rescued by a man and living happily ever after has been a core fantasy for several of my conflictedly-single women patients. Interestingly, two of my lonely women patients, though not familiar with this novel, have expressed the same fantasy of falling on a sidewalk and being rescued by "Mr. Right."

Henry is a courtly gentleman, who appears in Thea's life when she is thinking of herself as an old maid, and years after she has taken what she judged to have been an uncharacteristic wrong turn. She once had, she tells us, an exciting, and to her mind forbidden, sexual affair with a man whom she considered unsuitable and unlikeable. Her secret encounters with the lover, which never went beyond the confines of his bedroom, ended when he committed suicide, a fact that Thea learned from a newspaper.

The news of her lover's death, and the shame about how the relationship ended, left her resolved to ignore her sexual instincts, even, to some degree, after she married. She had also felt guilty about deceiving her parents after the affair. Here, her parents could be understood as standing in for her superego, allowing an external solution as a way to mitigate guilt. Henry, as Thea saw it, gave her back her respectability when he married her. She could then think of herself as a wife, not as I understand her self-perception, as a "fallen" woman. This is neat rendering of the reparation and penance themes and fantasies that are the stuff of both life and fiction; acceptance by an idealized other brings about redemption. Marriage allows Thea to feel less ashamed, enabling her to regain some of her self-esteem, as Kohut believed was necessary throughout life.

Together Thea and Henry establish a balance between responsibility and quiet pleasure that generally suits them. They spend many weekends socializing with Henry's cousins and his reclusive sister. Yet Thea, though physically present at the gatherings, never reveals much about her inner self and certainly nothing about the negative feelings she has toward these relatives. She asks little from the environment, and she gives little back. Her interactions with Henry's family seem to have a quality of reparation; she suffers quietly as she is quietly present. Brookner seems to imply that the mask of psychic blunting hat Thea wore for years became the real self. This blunted person is the one we meet at the outset of the novel. Aware how constricted most of her adult life has been, Thea recognizes how others might be critical of her lack of worldliness. This idea hurts her. In her marriage, Thea appears to have been a passive, rather than a full, partner.

In her widowhood, Thea holds her self together in the daytime with her gardening, and at night with her reveries, particularly the reveries of her youth. This was the time when she was happiest since she took comfort in being her parents' daughter. We gradually learn that Thea is longing for her dead mother, the person she misses most. Does this suggest an unresolved negative oedipal? If that were the case, we might hypothesize that Thea is allowing herself pleasure only in small doses to resolve unconscious guilt connected not only to her having had a tragic sexual affair, but also to loving her mother more than Henry.

Alternatively, a Kleinian view would suggest that Thea's longing for her mother is about the wish for an idealized early object, an object who could understand one without words (Klein, 1963), and with whom, therefore, aggression could be avoided. In this novel, as in life, there are no perfect objects. Perhaps Thea relied on the avoidance of others to control aggressive feelings. She may even be warding off love hunger to protect her objects as Guntrip (1961) suggested in his description of the schizoid personality. As mentioned earlier, we do know that her partner in her early sexual affair committed suicide.

Through Thea's narrative, the reader is allowed to get closer to her than to any of the other characters in the book. With them Thea is contained and perhaps withholding, a style found with patients who are conflicted about their solitary state (A.K. Richards and L. Spira, 2003). For Thea, as for many lonely people, relationships are seen as intrusions, to be politely tolerated, until she can flee to the solitude of her home and possibly her fantasies. Henry was not viewed as an intruder since each needed him to regain her self-esteem; this was true for him as well.

Thea's equilibrium is threatened when she is asked by Henry's cousin Kitty to put up a visitor, the "best" man, at the wedding of Kitty's grand-daughter, Ann. This Ann, is no Anne Elliot. Pregnant and almost a stranger to Thea, Ann goes after what she wants. Since Thea's polite refusal is ignored, Thea must either risk losing the tenuous connections to her late husband's relatives, her substitute family, or suffer the anxiety she anticipates if she allows a stranger into her home.

An analyst might say about Thea's situation that the environment is making the symptom less syntonic. Certainly, an analyst would understand that there might be many reasons why a person might not want to take a stranger into her home. Confronted by this fear on the part of a patient, we might point out that the person is fearful both of taking the person in and of saying, "no." And as the patient comes to understand the source of her conflict, she might become less fearful about either of the options she sees, or might realize that new options or compromises are available to her. Thea, for example, could have decided to put the visitor up in a hotel. But, in the novel, taking the visitor into her home and engaging with him was used as a device to allow Thea to reconnect with the affects that a relationship can bring. As Thea sees it she can no longer maintain any connection to her "family" and be fully in control of her space, actual and psychological. She chooses to maintain their love, or respect, as she reluctantly opens her home to Steve, the boarder, who is awkward, and ungracious, and Ann and her fiancé.

Thea comes to realize, however, that these three young people are lost and at risk of not finding a place in life, they need each other as an anchor. Perhaps, she sees aspects of herself in them. Their comings and goings, and her concerns about their future, begin to preoccupy her. Is Brookner suggesting that youth, or relationships in general, enrich us by infusing life into our psychic space, even when it is apparently empty or filled with the ghosts of dead objects? Again, if Thea were a patient in treatment, an analyst might play the role the young people did, helping the patient to consider that our internal world needs nourishment and a little help from the environment; that is a view held by many analysts who believe that growth takes place in the context of a relationship.

The three bring Thea in touch with her longings—for something young—we are told, leading her secretly to make Ann her heir. We learn that once Thea had wanted a daughter but missed the chance to have one, and now Ann will inherit the elegant apartment that has provided Thea with a respite from the world. By taking this definitive step of deciding who will get what she has nurtured, and allowing herself to be a more active participant in her life, she comes to find that it is she who must make attachments, and recognizes that the ones she has made although not ideal, are, for her, more sustaining than solitude. This recognition implies that real inner peace and the lessening of aloneness come not from avoiding one's instincts, but rather from actively following oneself to love—not only an other but also, one's self. Seeing herself as a person with something to give may allow Thea to love herself in a way that she could not do before. Also, it may connect her with her deceased mother, making her feel less alone. Perhaps, the awareness that one can be a libidinal person despite aggressive wishes, is some of what therapy can give the lonely isolated patient. How Thea undoes her sense of aloneness seems to encompass Klein's (1963) view of reparations as key in mitigating loneliness.

In summary, this novel focuses on a woman mostly alone who seems not to have understood how lonely she was. She had become so used to her loneliness that it was almost invisible to her until her appetite for a relationship became quickened by an outsider. It is not only the visitors, but also Thea's awareness of her aging, her growing fragility, and her place in the life cycle, that positively impacts her as they influence her to make solutions that take into account a wider range of her feelings. The anticipation of death can seem a very lonely place. To anticipate it, as Thea did, without any heirs, may make it even more lonely, especially when there are compounding feelings of being unable to love one's self or anyone else. This recalls a question raised by A. K. Richards and me in a study of loneliness, singleness, and social isolation: is emotional loneliness the obverse of love (2003)?

REFERENCES

GUNTRIP, H. (1961). *Personality Structure and Human Interaction: The Developing Synthesis of Psycho-dynamic Theory.* New York: International Press.

KLEIN, M. (1963). *On the Sense of Loneliness. Writings of Melanie Klein. 1946–1963.* New York: The New Library of Psychoanalysis 1984: pp. 300–313.

LIEBERMAN, J.S. (1991). Issues in the psychoanalytic treatment of single females over thirty. *Psychonalytic Review* 78(2):176–198.

RICHARDS, A.K. & SPIRA, L. (2003). On being lonely: fear of one's own aggression as an impediment to intimacy. *Psychoanalytic Quarterly* 72:357–374.

——— ——— (2003). On being lonely, socially isolated and single: A multiple-perspective approach. *Psychoanalysis and Psychotherapy* 20:3–21.

SATRAN, G. Notes on loneliness. *Journal American Academy of Psychoanalysis* 6(3):281–300.

WEISS, R.S. (1973). *Loneliness: The Experience of Social and Emotional Isolation.* Cambridge, MA: M.I.T. Press.

THE WOMAN WHO COULD NOT GRIEVE: A CONTEMPORARY LOOK AT THE JOURNEY TOWARD MOURNING

[Sugarman, I. (2006). *Clinical Social Work Journal* 34(2):201–213.]

The inability to mourn is a common but not sufficiently recognized theme underlying various forms of psychopathology. The paper will demonstrate how a patient has defended against the pain of loss by turning away from the external object in reality and creating a maternal object in fantasy over which she has omnipotent control. Focus is on a contemporary understanding of the inability to mourn as a "disease of narcissism." Aspects of transference distortion, annihilation fantasies, and merger with the maternal object will be highlighted. Through treatment the patient has begun to relinquish the fantasied object, have moments of experiencing real loss of others, and connect more realistically with others.

In a recent paper, Ogden revisits Freud's "Mourning and Melancholia" and contributes a new understanding to the patients Freud was writing about who were unable to mourn. Ogden suggests the usual reading of this paper is accurate but not sufficient to explain this phenomenon. Inability to mourn does, as Freud said, involve an identification with the hated aspect of the ambivalently loved object that has been lost. Ogden suggests, however, that the central point of Freud's thesis is that, ". . . what differentiates the melancholic from the mourner is the fact that the melancholic *all along* has been able to engage only m narcissistic forms of object relatedness." In other words, such patients have not surrendered their omnipotence. They have not been able to modify their narcissistic delusions or their hold on their oneness fantasies. Freud's shadow metaphor—the shadow of the object fell upon the Ego—can be understood as the patient's destroying the object to possess it—to be one with the shadow (Ogden, 2002, pp. 773–775, emphasis mine).

Some challenge to this internal relationship is often what brings patients into treatment. The problem for the clinician is not that the patient has experienced this threat, but rather that the individual has needed to avoid the threat of separation from the beginning through this shadow attachment. The pain of subsequent disappointments or real losses are avoided through the lens of this attachment. These early and later efforts to defend against loss interfere with the process of mourning (Schlesinger, 2001, pp. 27–28). In the case presentation that is to follow, I will be highlighting how the patient's creation of an omnipotent object in fantasy has been her primary defense against mourning. Through this magical thinking the patient, Mrs. A., does not experience me and others as real and denies limitations. She has been unable to bear the necessary pain of depression connected with relinquishing her fantasy and thereby experience actual loss in reality.

WORK WITH MRS. A.

Mrs. A.'s avoidance of the mourning process was evident in her reaction.to her brother's death when he was twenty-six. She expressed no sadness or missing feelings. Rather, she experienced dread that her childhood wishes to get rid of him had come true. A variation of this fantasy was that her mother had gotten rid of him to be exclusively joined with the patient. The patient's dread, with accompanying panic attacks, propelled her to move, back home after having moved out the year before her brother's death. She experienced envy and jealously observing the depths of her parent's grief. She remembers thinking, "Why are they still so concerned about him." It was as if the real relationship with her brother was absent. He mattered because he was a rival. to Mrs. A.'s, wish to be "the only one with mother."

The majority of the treatment has been a preparation to enable the patient to face her dread of separating from the hated internal maternal object. This has been possible through the deepening of the loving transference. It has enabled Mrs. A to let me into the previously closed self-object unit. Increasingly she has moments of experiencing me as separate from her. This has enabled her to challenge her oneness fantasy and consider relinquishing it. The patient's journey in treatment could be considered "on the way to mourning."

Mrs. A. entered treatment at age twenty-five because of severe anxiety over getting married. She grew up in an intact family and had one sibling—a brother three years older who died of cancer when she was 23. The patient works as a bookkeeper and her husband is in the computer field. She is in twice weekly psychotherapy.

One of the patient's earliest memories is of lying in her crib and dreading the approach of her mother. In later infancy, the patient recalls vomiting when her mother forced cereal on her. She reports suffering from severe constipation. The patient said she knew she could have had regular bowel movements, but chose not to. She recalled her mother and aunt carrying her into the bathroom and forcing enemas on her. She also remembers scalding her foot under the hot water faucet when her mother was drawing her bath. Mother was enraged and said, "that will teach you."

The patient recalls a "disturbing" scene when she was three, a scene around which much of her fantasy life is organized. She saw her mother towel drying her brother after his bath and saw his penis. She experienced profound pain and humiliation.

Mrs. A. had fond memories of her father, brother, and maternal grandmother. Her father was affectionate and played with her. She was hurt when he turned away from her in her adolescence. Her brother was protective and loving toward her until his teen years when he became more involved with his friends. The grandmother lived upstairs and adored the patient. The patient cherished those visits except when her mother was present. She then felt painfully excluded.

Mrs. A. describes her mother as unpredictable, depressed, and attacking. She dominated the household with her rages and moods. The patient recalled the father giving up fights and telling his wife, ". . . What's the use; you are always right." After her arguments with her mother, Mrs. A.'s father would plead with the patient to make up with her mother even though he acknowledged the patient had done no wrong.

School was a source of great anxiety for Mrs. A. Mother was often in rages before Mrs. A. left for school, and once in school the patient worried about mother's mood and wondered if she would let the patient in at the end of the day. If her mother did not like one of her friends, Mrs. A. dropped them. Later, she concealed her accomplishments and gave up the lead in the school play because these activities, in the patient's mind, would meet with her mother's disapproval.

The patient moved out in her early twenties, but returned home after her brother's death, fearing that her annihilation fantasies had come true. She married at twenty-five, to a man she experiences as nurturing and supportive. Early in the marriage she was troubled about her rages toward her husband—experiencing herself as behaving like her mother. Her overt rages have diminished, but today she feels them, nonetheless, in response to her husband's recent financial reversals or anything else which diminishes his power in her eyes. At the same time, she can be supportive when he is feeling vulnerable. Mrs. A. has been able to experience pleasure in taking care of her home, entertaining, reading, playing sports, and attending the theater.

The patient is an attractive woman who ·presented in a lively, warm manner which belied her troubled internal world. She was feeling conflict about leaving home and was saddened and furious that her parents were not giving her a wedding. She felt troubled over her mother's competitiveness and jealously about her upcoming marriage. The patient introduced me to her troubled thinking early on, telling me that by choosing her husband, her father would have to die, and that she was taking revenge on him for having chosen mother over her. Further, Mrs. A. thought mother would take revenge on her for leaving home. The patient was also worried that she was treating her fiance like her mother treated her—like, "a piece of shit." Mrs. A. initially experienced great relief in having me to talk to. She often felt like singing when she left her sessions. At the same time, within sessions she would have rapid mood swings, experiencing anger and disappointment when the sessions ended or the telephone rang.

In the first months of treatment, Mrs. A. shared her worry that she was "going crazy" over thoughts about her brother's death. She had gone into a trance on the subway with the thought, "I didn't do it. I am going to be punished. If he came back he'd be so angry." When I asked her how her murderous fantasies worked, she said she could make her brother disappear and then her mother could not love him anymore. This was the beginning of a long, arduous process in treatment of addressing how her infantile idea of murder was a magical solution to all childhood disappointments.

As Mrs. A. continued to share her story, she spoke about how intimidating it was to hear mother telling people to drop dead. The patient cried for the first time saying she had never been able to cry at home. It was considered "stupid to cry." She said she felt unsafe getting close to mother and never felt hugged. She recalled being in her crib and dreading her mother· coming into the room. "I would rather die than have her come near me."

Mrs. A. had a cataclysmic reaction to my vacation at the end of the second year of treatment. She hated me for leaving her. "How can I know who to be with. I chose you over my father and now you left." Upon my return, she felt humiliated and resented having "to crawl back to me." She saw me as "King Tut." I have everything—a penis, breast and vagina—and she has nothing. In other words, in the transference she is turning to me because I am so powerful. Love and tenderness are absent. The mention of her father here informed me how early on she turned from one parent then to the other, and back and forth in response to disappointment. She alternately endowed each with omnipotence. Her fantasized safety was in being with only one parent at a time (Jacobson, 1946).

In the fourth year of treatment when she was telling me further about her wish to get rid of people, Mrs. A.'s. thoughts turned to her brother's death. She had the fantasy that her mother could have saved him from dying, but was punishing him for growing up, getting married, and having a child. She said the same thing was in store for her if she became a woman. She better understood now why she had had such anxiety about getting married. She also understood why she gave up the lead in the school play and other accomplishments. She recalled her mother threatening her with abandonment when she had ideas different from her own. She expected I too would abandon her if she had her own ideas. When I asked why, she said because I had everything and she was nothing. As I continued to underscore that it was hard for her to believe I would be interested in her having her own ideas, Mrs. A was able to question her notion that I would use my strength to humiliate her. I talked with her about children needing to know they can think for themselves and know when they crawl and walk away they can look over their shoulders and know mother was still there (Mahler, 1975). This sounded wonderful to Mrs. A. Such interventions, over time impacted the patient, helping to convince her that I would not retaliate or abandon.

In subsequent sessions, Mrs. A. acquainted me with the other side of her submissive position. In this solution, she will possess the object through her specialness. This was most apparent in her relationship with me and her sister-in-law, Carol. The mere mention by the latter that she was with anyone else evoked painful feelings of exclusion and envy. Toward me she said, "And you, you go away with your husband and you have other patients and a family. I can't bear it. I want you all to myself." She would then turn this wish around and try to attack me. She would want to rub it in my face that she had the best husband, was the most attractive, read the best books, saw the best plays. Her hope at these times was to evoke envy so we would see her power and never leave her (Kohut, 1972).

Toward the end of the 7th year of treatment, Mrs. A. was beginning to have more moments in which she could think more realistically about me. She would talk about wanting to come to the sessions without her anger. She said, "My thought about this is that you are not just someone to be angry at or to keep close to out of my desperation." She reflected on her reactions to my vacations. "I know you have a separate life and you need to get away, I wish I could be glad for you that you would be going on vacation." She said she was seeing me for the first time in all these years and listening for longer periods of time before tuning me out. This awareness of her oscillation and her ability to experience my presence and value for longer periods of time signaled a growing capacity of her ego to sustain separateness (Asseyer, 2002).

As Mrs. A. continued to reflect on her anger, she became aware of her need to experience me as disappointing. She said that if she felt encouraged by me that meant I hated her and did not want her anymore. She wanted me to disappear—to re-unite us—thereby undoing the threat of separation. She referred to a previous session in which she experienced, "... your caring and sweetness." She said she wanted to wipe me out, and added, "This is crazy thinking; I know it is." Mrs. A. is questioning here her belief that her anger and wish for disappointment is what keeps us together. She has needed to defend against the loving transference by turning me into a disappointing figure. For her, pain and disappointment are more predictable than love (Valenstein, 1973).

At this time, Mrs. A. retrieved a memory from her third year of life. This memory has been pivotal in helping the patient gain insight into her object world. In this memory, she is watching her mother towel her brother after his bath. She saw his penis. She felt shock and excruciating pain over being excluded. She spoke abou.t her fear that if her mother and brother saw her they would leave her permanently. Her further response to this scene was to want to tear off her mother's breasts and take her brother's penis. Then she would have everything and her mother would never leave her. (Shengold, 1994). This was followed by an inner response of spiteful self sufficiency with these words to herself, "I don't need you either." Here she is denying her need for a relationship because it is fraught with too much pain. As she has heard herself repeating this refrain over time, she has reflected on how quickly she responds with "not needing" when she experiences the presence of a third person.

"Look how I always add 'either'." She has become aware she projects her wishes to "get rid of" onto the third person.

A few months after this session, in the eighth year, Mrs. A.'s father was diagnosed with lung cancer and died within months. She thought her wishes to have her mother all to herself brought about his death. These wishes, however, did not evoke the anxiety she had experienced over her brother's death. While she could not mourn her father, she did seem better able to tolerate her murderous wishes without being overwhelmed. She had a dream in which everyone in her family was dead. Her association was relief that now she would no longer have to deal with any of them. When I tried to talk about her father and the good memories she had shared with me, she was unresponsive and showed no signs of missing him. In subsequent sessions she talked about now it was just her and her mother. "But that's always been my whole world. No one else really existed."

While she was unable to experience any real feelings over her father's death, Mrs. A. was moving closer to me. "I am seeing you. I want you. to get to know me, after all these years. But after I saw you in the last session, seeing how you care about me, I wanted to wipe you out. But I don't want to feel that way anymore. Then I get scared. Now what?" When I asked her what she thought would happen, she said she felt it would be our last session—that I would be rushing her to grow up. "My upbringing in treatment makes me want to work this out. Now I'm not so sure. Maybe because the session is ending. I wish you could always be in the next room." I said, "I can't be in the next room, but I can be here." She said, "I know and that's what makes me feel strong."

Her loving feelings toward me reminded her of her warm relationship with her grandmother. She loved to spend time alone with her upstairs. She recalled the painful feelings of exclusion when her mother would be present. She spoke about wanting. to feel less angry about leaving her sessions., "Or, in being angry that I can talk about it and I can learn to say good-bye."

During the 10th year, Mrs. A.'s mother died of a heart attack. Mrs. A. experienced some sadness in thinking about her mother's life. She talked about her mother being an infantile woman who was to be pitied. She felt badly when she came across a card from her mother asking the patient why she hated her so. When I asked if she would miss the pleasant visits she had begun having with her mother, she denied any missing. For a time after the death, Mrs. A. would have thoughts of dying as a way of being one with mother. She had a dream in which she is walking with her mother. "A big wave is about to crash." She felt both dread and comfort that she would be buried with her mother.

In the last year and a half of treatment, Mrs. A has been able to tolerate moments of mourning her fantasy life. Increasingly, I have been able to help her return to the pain and tolerate the vulnerability she fears and work through her loss. (Schlesinger, 2001). I have found myself wanting to rush the process now that she has done so much work. I experience impatience particularly in response to the patient's regressions.

Mrs. A. is increasingly able to express her yearning for love, along side the need for disappointing experiences. While sobbing and with great sadness; she spoke about her mother,

> Pt. I always felt she'd forget about me. It felt like she never touched me. If she would have I would have lingered with it. I know I would have. Instead, I built this wall. (Sobbing more). I was so afraid of being alone. I would do anything to keep her. When I was angry she'd say, 'I hope you don't wake up in the morning.' She attacked me for my feelings. Is that what is going to happening here? What will I do?
>
> I.S. We know how painful that would be. And yet you do assign me that role. When I go on vacation or you hear another patient come in, you feel the humiliation of me getting rid of you.
>
> Pt. You've said this to me so often. Now I'm seeing it. I hope for disappointment. Any disappointment justifies clinging to my facata ideas. If you say 'good luck', then I'd say 'fuck you.' I've stunted my growth. This is the bottom line—holding on to my feelings of net being wanted . . . I'm in total make believe—a world of rage. I want to make someone one with me. I'm bringing this to the table more, but I still feel the pain.
>
> I.S. Why wouldn't you have pain. You are wanting to have real relationships but also feeling the pain of letting go of the make believe relationship.
>
> Pt. But I don't want it anymore. I don't want to be attacked. I want to be soothed . . . I see there has been nothing genuine in my relationships.

Following this, she spoke further about feeling sad and depressed to be in reality. She said if all this had happened later in life, she could have, "Ironed it out." She questioned why she should let herself endure the pain in our work, yet at the same time said, "I'm feeling there is room for growth—to call on reality—so I can take in the love, you, Allen [her husband] and Carol have for me. I've missed out on so much with all of you."

Soon after this, Mrs. A. began to evidence humor as her thinking was becoming more dystonic. She was talking again about her dread of being alone. When I said, "But I'm here, and have been all along," she said, "But you have a separate life, a family and you don't care about me. You have it all." At this point she started to laugh at herself, "Oh my God, get a life." In a further moment of reflection and humor, she was able to take a more realistic view of her mother. "If I say I can't function without my mother, it throws all my work with you out the window. If I recognize her behavior as infantile; if I see her as she truly was—depressed, childlike—then I can no longer turn to her as a powerful mother, to be one with." She paused and laughed, "This is such *bubba mises.* It doesn't have to be this way."

This move forward was followed by Mrs. A. feeling depressed. She said she was "hitting bottom" and sleeping all the time.

Pt. I don't want to be real and I don't want you to be real. Am I depressed because I'm putting this on the table? What would I do if I lost you?

I.S. You believe your power has kept me with you all these years.

Pt. *Crying.* For anyone to be real devastates me.

I.S. You are depressed. because you are thinking about letting go of your fantasies. Part of you doesn't want to settle for reality.

Pt. *Crying.* Yes, Yes, I yearn for her. I wish I had my mother here.

As Mrs. A. continued to experience the conflict between reality and fantasy, she said it was the worst time in her life. She had a dream in which she gets me to change my mind about making her real. She associated to the bathroom scene. She said all she thinks about is someone hurting her. I said we had come to understand it was she who wanted to do the hurting. She responded with tears. "I can't get past the two of them being together. You are right. I do want to hurt them. They hurt me by being together. I'll get my mother to change her mind and get rid of Michael. I'll get her to kill him . . . I will kill them."

I said I wondered if her wish to have me change my mind in the dream indicated she felt I was forcing her to be in reality—as if I was taking away her fantasy life. She denied this. I underscored that she had assigned me that role in her dream as well as getting her mother to change her mind in her associations. While she continued to deny this had meaning, her dramatic regression in the next session with a reliving of an enema scene, confirmed the transference experience of me forcing her.

She was feeling anger toward me. She did not want me to be with anyone else and said no one would want me. "You have shit on your face. Yet, I feel like I want to eat shit, drink urine. Maybe I want to throw shit on your face to destroy you . . . How dare you leave."

She stopped here and was perplexed. "I don't understand this." She then recalled the enema memory: "My aunt and mother are carrying me into the bathroom to give me an enema. How could you do this to me. Someone is trying to kill me. I won't look at my mother. I swore I wished my mother dead."

> When I wondered about eating shit, she said, "eating it—getting it back from my mother who forced it out of me. (*Crying*). She stuck that that enema in me in anger. Her touch was in anger. I feel like I have no one to turn to. I don't want anyone near me. No one will ever see me. I'm not giving anyone a chance to do right by me. The next person will buzz and I'll turn you into my mother wanting to get rid of me."

I experienced both impatience and concern with this level of regression. I wondered if our work on helping her relinquish her fantasy life was more than her ego could tolerate. My awareness of my own feelings and the patient's reflective question about what was going on with her helped to create some therapeutic space (Ganzer & Ornstein, 2002). I asked Mrs. A. again if she was feeling forced in our relationship to be more realistic; did she feel it was not really her own wishes. She thought about this and said she got scared after the last session. "I tried to make it feel like you were forcing me so I could be angry with you. It's all in my head. Look how my rage has taken such a toll on me. If only my mother could have shown some gentleness."

Shortly after this session, Mrs. A. was able to. express feelings of mourning for the 'first time. She began the session reporting a violent

dream in which a cat is attacking a huge snake and eating it. In her association, Mrs. A. realized she was the cat and the snake represented her
father and brother. She experienced herself as having great power—
being bigger than life. I had no power and no life, She then mentioned
she has been to a family gathering and seen a home video of herself
at two-years and her brother at five-years-old. Her cousin wept when
she saw the patient's late brother with whom she had grown up. When
I asked the patient how she felt seeing the pictures of her brother
she said she also felt weepy. She said, "There are moments, more
moments of crying over his loss than my usual 'Good, look what I
can. do.'" Further, she said she missed her mother. "If my mother were
here, I would have felt her pain over her unhappy life. And sometimes
I ache for her." Mrs. A. felt sad that she had to cover up the loving and
missing feelings with her rage and revenge. In response to my curiosity
about her postponing telling me of these new feelings, Mrs. A. said that
to share them with me means I'll take advantage of her. I'll be bigger
than life.

The patient is now beginning to tolerate the pain over her past losses.
Her further resistance to these issues, including her need to be bigger
than life in relation to me signals the direction of our future work.

CONCLUDING REMARKS

So in the conclusion is the beginning for the patient who could not
mourn. Her case illustrates what Ogden refers to as a "disease of narcissism" (p. 775) This means in the case of Mrs. A that prior to the actual
deaths of her family members she never experienced the object as sufficiently separate from her. Separation, pain, and loss were denied through
her belief in her omnipotence. She has denied the object in external reality and has been obsessed with possessing the maternal object through
her power. She has attempted, through this thinking, to reassure herself
that no one will ever leave her. Her reaction to her brother's death
was cataclysmic anxiety, not one of mourning. She felt no sadness or
missing feelings. Rather, she was experiencing panic as her murderous
wishes became a "reality." This degree of aggression caused ego regression that left her feeling overwhelmed. Her response to her parents' deaths
was not one of panic; but her feelings did reflect a similar absence of
sadness and missing. Only after a lengthy treatment did she begin to tolerate mourning her fantasy life and thereby experience the actual loss of

family members. This case presentation has been an attempt to illustrate how this has come about.

In the beginning of treatment, Mrs. A felt reassured to have someone to talk to. These positive feelings were accompanied with her expectation that I could easily get rid of her. This was a projection of her wishes to get rid of anyone who came between us or between her and another on the outside. As treatment progressed the initial unrequited need to have someone to care about her and to listen, came more to the forefront. This was instrumental, over time, in loosening the calcified self-object unit.

Mrs. A.'s dependence on her omnipotent solutions arose from her early unbearable emotional experience with her mother. Mother's rageful, unpredictable nature made contact with her dangerous and something to avoid. In her failure to have "good enough" experiences with her mother, Mrs. A. turned her feelings of helpless rage into omnipotent solutions to avoid the pain of loss and disappointment (Novick & Novick, 1991). Her reactions to anything about me that suggested I was separate from her elicited feelings of rage and hurt. If I wore something new, this was evidence that I had gone shopping without her. Her rageful response of "I don't need you either" has run like a red thread through the treatment. She has taken refuge in the state of "spiteful self sufficiency" (Jacobson, 1946), which of course, is a short-lived solution since Mrs. A. does seek object connections.

At the same time, this object hunger masked her need to avoid real contact. Her description of her dread of her mother's approach when she was in the crib, while a possible condensation from later feelings, is reminiscent of Fraiberg's (1982) work in which her researchers observed infants as early as three months turning away from their unattuned nursing mothers. When in distress, these infants did not even signal their mothers for comfort.

In the transference, Mrs. A. avoids me by turning me into an object she incorporated omnipotently for her own purposes. She has freed herself from the necessity of depending on me and making real contact (Asseyer, 2002, p. 1305). One of the reasons vacations and the telephone ringing were so difficult for the patient is that they were evidence that I was real. 1 could leave her and have other people in my life. It shattered her belief that she could control my every move.

A salient feature of Mrs. A.'s tie to the fantasied object has been her attachment to pain. This has been a major resistance allowing the patient to defend against more constant loving feelings in the transference. No sooner does she have positive feelings toward me than she has needed to cast me in the role as the humiliator. This has prevented the process of further separation since she searches out painful experiences real or imaginary—to justify this type of tie to the object. Early on, Mrs. A. turned her painful experiences into signs of her magical powers. Recall the incident with her mother over the scalding water. The patient's response was "Look how I am able to make my mother so angry." While Mrs. A. dreaded separations and threesomes, she used the experiences to justify her belief that "It doesn't .pay to be real" (Novick & Novick, 1991; Valenstein, 1973). The coupling of her attachment to pain and her belief that she was not real, contributed markedly to her early inability to accomplish the developmental task of mourning.

Hatred has fueled much of Mrs. A.'s thinking. When love predominates in the early relationship with the mother, it promotes separation and growth. Hatred and revenge bind one to the object, resulting in a static relationship that precludes alternative ways of thinking .and experiencing oneself. The intensity and pervasiveness of Mrs. A.'s rage suggest the murderous, oral cannibalistic rage Shengold writes about. "There will be no other but me." Such thinking precludes experiencing, "the dearness of the other." Mrs. A. must get rid of any third person. In her last dream, Mrs. A. is the cat attacking, tearing, and eating the snake. Earlier she has wanted to tear off her mother's breasts and her brother's penis. These wishes are characteristic of the oral period when the other is not seen as a total person—only as a sexual organ the child wishes to possess.

Another aspect of Mrs. A.'s hatred is her wish to obliterate the other with her specialness so that the other will stay with her. This is most apparent in her relationship with me and her sister-in-law. Anytime her sister-in-law mentioned a family member or a friend, or the patient thought about me being with anybody else, she would experience rage and immediately want to impress one of us with her specialness. She would want to blind one of us with her grandeur so we would give up everyone else in our lives to only be with her. This type of narcissistic rage has been a powerful resistance (Kohut, 1972). It has predominated over loving feelings since it reinforces her sense of power. Her wish to have everything, to be both male and female, is inherent in this rage. In her wish to be the best, she resembles the Queen who wants to destroy Snow White when the mirror tells her that the latter is the fairest of them all.

In the past one and half years, as the patient has become more reflective about how her mind works, I have begun to encourage her to keep returning to the pain of relinquishing her fantasy world. I have indicated that I think she can tolerate her vulnerable feelings and that she will not be left with nothing (Schlesinger, 2001). While she resists, she has come to believe that having people in her life who she loves and who love her is a more mature, realistic solution for her. This new understanding has allowed her to further question her thinking and hatred.

In conclusion, Mrs. A is beginning to feel depressed as she experiences this shift in her thinking and emotional life. Her ability to feel depressed has allowed her to have hope for the future. While she still worries she will have nothing, she also observes that this beginning mourning offers her "room for growth." She felt sadness realizing how much she had missed out on with other people. Most recently, her capacity to weep over the deaths of her brother and mother was a hallmark experience for her. While she still has to defend against these moments by omitting them from the sessions, she nevertheless, is on her way toward tolerating the task of mourning.

REFERENCES

ASSEYER, H. (2002). The exclusion of the other. *International Journal of Psychoanalysis* 83(6):1291–1309.

FRAIBERG, S. (1982). Pathological defenses in infancy. *Psychoanalytic Quarterly* 51(40):612–641.

FREUD, S. (1917). Mourning and melancholia. *Standard Edition:* 14:237–258.

GANZER, C., & ORNSTEIN, E.D. (2002). A sea of trouble: a relational approach to the culturally sensitive treatment of a severely disturbed client. *Clinical Social Work Journal* 30(2):127–144.

JACOBSON, E. (1946) The effect of disappointment on ego and superego formation in normal and depressive development. *Psychoanalytic Review* 33(2):129–147.

KOHUT, H. (1972). Thoughts on narcissism and narcissistic rage. *Psychoanalytic Study of the Child* 27:360–400.

MAHLER, M . (1975). *The Psychological Birth of the Human Infant.* Basic Books.

NOVICK, J.K.K. (1991). Some comments on masochism and the delusion of omnipotence from a developmental perspective. *Journal of the American Psychoanalytic Association* 39:307–332.

OGDEN, T. (2002). A new reading of the origins of object relations theory.

International Journal of Psychoanalysis 83(6):767–782.

SCHLESINGER, H. (April 2001). The unrecognized prevalence of mourning in the analytic situation. An earlier version presented at the 32nd Annual Margaret S. Mahler Symposium.

SHENGOLD, L. (1994). Envy and malignant envy. *Psychoanalytic Quarterly* 63:(4):615-640.

VALENSTEIN, A. (1973). On the attachment to painful feelings and the negative therapeutic relation. *Psychoanalytic Study of the Child* 28:365–392.

TRAUMA, TRANSFERENCE, AND HEALING: A CASE PRESENTATION

[Thompson, T.C. (1999). In: *The Social Work Psychoanalyst's Casebook: Clinical Voices in Honor of Jean Sanville*. Hillsdale, NJ: Analytic Press.]

The concept of trauma encompasses those disorganizing forces, internal and external, which interfere with stable ego functioning and render the ego helpless and vulnerable. Forced into a state of regression, the person resorts to more archaic means of self-protection in order to reestablish and maintain some level of personal intactness and control. In the case of the patient considered here, Miss W, a comingling of strain and shock trauma (Kris, 1956) had interfered with forward movement in her development, causing serious alterations and compromises in ego functioning and self-esteem regulation.

Strain trauma is a longstanding external noxious force that continuously stretches the defensive and adaptive capacities of the child, and shock trauma is a trauma caused by a single event, such as a seduction, that overwhelms the ego, flooding it with anxiety (Kris, 1956).

Trauma always initially involves interaction with the external environment and is thus associated with reality and the effects of reality on the person's development. One's affective reactions to the trauma and the meanings one ascribes to the traumatic interactions or events become an integral aspect of one's psychic reality. Psychic reality encompasses elements of actual reality, perception, fantasy, affect, and belief (Good, 1996).

The powerful tool that both patient and analyst have at their disposal for grappling with trauma, albeit each with differing tasks, is the medium of transference. Psychic reality fuels the transference. The compulsion to reenact aspects of the trauma, in defensive ways as well as literal ways, is very powerful. The defenses that a traumatized patient uses to help reestablish some necessary degree of control often serve adaptive purposes as well. When these defenses, including regression, are repeated in the transference, they need to be interpreted for both their defensive and their adaptive aims. When the defense of regression is employed, the "as if" quality of the transference may be affected. At these moments, the analyst's clarity about herself or himself is critical to the interpretative work and to aiding the patient's return to reality. Often, during regression, interventions other than those considered strictly interpretive are the only ones the patient can assimilate.

The importance of the transference in treating traumatized patients was highlighted by Loewald (1955). Noting the creative and adaptive aspects of transference work, he stressed their importance in organizing past traumatic events (which might have existed only as body memory) into secondary process. He proposed that the transference experience for the patient may be initially a passive reproduction. With help from the analyst and the analyst's belief in the patient's adaptive capacities, passivity can be transformed into active aims for the patient's mastery and ownership of his or her needs and wishes.

The patient, according to Viederman (1995) possesses the capacity to be an active participant in the discovery and understanding of the trauma. Through the transference as well as through dreams and memories, the patient can be helped to reconstruct the past. The transference also provides a medium for the patient's growth. Along with the patient's capacity to integrate interpretations, the patient's self-righting tendency can provide the impetus for selective identifications with the analyst and, in some instances, the creation of identifications with the more benign aspects of the primary object (Sanville, 1991).

MISS W

Miss W, a high school graduate who was 34 years of age at the outset of treatment, sought treatment because of her social isolation and career disappointment. Prior therapies had not helped alleviate her concerns. She had few friends, kept mainly to herself, and seemed uninterested in men. Miss W never felt properly understood. She was easily hurt by, and disappointed in, others and withdrew from them. Preoccupied with thoughts about each of the individuals in her life who had emotionally injured her, she often constructed a fantasy wherein she was intensely connected to that person and assumed the bad qualities, real or imagined, that the person had attributed to her.

After a brief period of psychotherapy, during which her interactions with people continued to be painfully disappointing, Miss W entered a four-times-a-week psychoanalysis, which is currently in its seventh year.

As the intrapsychic meanings of her interpersonal difficulties emerged in the transference, Miss W recalled a childhood trauma of sexual abuse inflicted on her by her mother, unpredictably and repeatedly over a period of one to two years.

The patient's rediscovery of this early trauma was an essential part of her treatment. The childhood shock trauma had occurred within the context of chronic emotional neglect (strain trauma). The effects of both traumas had become internalized and had colored and given distorted meaning to her current object relationships and had compromised her ability to regulate her impulses and her affects. For example, Miss W felt unable to cry. The effects of Miss W's traumatic experiences on her current anxieties and her capacity to form relationships became manifest in, and were dealt with through, the transference. The overall therapeutic work led to an understanding of the way in which the sexual abuse and the emotional neglect (strain trauma) she had experienced had become unconsciously organized into a pattern of defenses and internal object relations that had a regressive impact on her ego and self-esteem.

At the same time, certain of her defensive efforts contained seeds of progressive development that helped to serve adaptive purposes. One such seed, and a positive aspect of her inner life, was a detailed childhood conscious fantasy of a substitute mother, an adoptive mother who was an idealized good, loving, firm object. This fantasy had played an important developmental and adaptive transitional function in Miss W's childhood life. Once worked through in the treatment process, it served as a positive foundation for and eventuated in the creation of the analyst as a realistic, useful, and good object who could be trusted and with whom a therapeutic alliance could be formed.

Miss W was originally from Europe, where her parents continue to live. Both were high school teachers. The family had inherited money on her mother's side and lived in a very large home, but, according to Miss W, they behaved above their station. She has a brother nine years older than she, who now resides in South America. She has had little or no contact with him over the years.

Miss W felt unwanted and unloved by her parents. Her father was a distant presence whom she experienced as deadened and morose. He appeared emotionally alive only when fighting with his wife or arguing with his son. Her strongest memory of him was seeing him from the back as he entered his study and closed the door. The father of her childhood memories rarely, if ever, spoke with her and is still uninvolved with her.

It was her mother who raised the children. She also was experienced as self-absorbed. However, Miss W has remained in constant contact with her mother over the telephone. She mainly has taken the role of listener; she sees her role as that of mother's caretaker.

When Miss W was growing up, her mother worked part time. When she was at home, she compulsively cleaned the house and rarely talked to her daughter or responded to her approaches. Miss W felt alone. She would often overhear her mother talking to herself. This behavior frightened her and caused per to feel that she didn't really exist for her mother. She became preoccupied with what her mother was thinking. As an illustration of the loneliness of these times and the longing for a connection, Miss W remembers lying on the kitchen floor, next to the dryer, loving the rhythm of the machine's movements and the feel of its warmth against her body.

Despite her chronic anxiety, Miss W tried to have some life in school but found it painfully frustrating. She longed to play with other children but felt odd and awkward. Learning was sometimes difficult because of the interference of pleasurable adoption daydreams as well as her preoccupation with thoughts of her mother. Miss W persevered, though and, using her intelligence and Jove of reading, achieved good grades. She was an A student, but neither parent seemed to pay much attention to her accomplishment. She had to come right home after school, brought no friends with her, and alone with her mother, always silently wanted, but often was afraid of, interaction with her.

Miss W gave the impression of having felt emotionally abandoned, understimulated and yet trapped by her mother. When there was interaction, she felt invaded by her mother's controlling criticism. The emotional climate was bleak and dark, as Miss W rattled around the large house, forbidden to go out and play because "bad people could hurt her."

When Miss W related her history or shared her memories in one or another session at the start of our work, she frequently seemed to be watching me in a cool, aloof manner, as if she were being careful not to give too much of herself away. Her language was often vague and elusive. Later in the treatment, she told me that, even though I had not said much to her during the initial phase of treatment, she had thought of me as a Nazi and that was good because it meant that I could handle her. Yet throughout the early period of the treatment, I sensed that Miss W was trying to reach out to me.

Miss W manifested certain ego strengths in spite of her childhood traumas. She was a very intelligent woman and, when not overwhelmed by infantile needs and conflicts, evidenced curiosity and a capacity to think and act appropriately. With the help of her therapy, these ego strengths aided her both in developing a therapeutic alliance and in understanding that her internal world was the center of her difficulties. Her perseverance in the work and her capacity to contain transferential regressive needs and wishes, without severe acting out, were most impressive. Her motivating need to love and be loved (object hunger) and her self-preservative needs facilitated her investment in our work throughout the treatment.

Miss W's need for a positive connection and her capacity for idealization seemed only partially diminished by her early disruptive experiences. Her adoptive-mother fantasy suggested to me that there might have been some positive early experiences, meager as they might have been, that she was drawing on. This fantasy, which did not seem to hamper Miss W's ability to function in reality, helped her to maintain ego integration. It served an anxiety regulating (preventing continuous panic) function and a self-esteem regulating function (preventing a decompensating depression). As she struggled with premature psychological separation it had helped her through a myriad of narcissistic disappointments and traumatic experiences, including her father's unapproachability, his failure to facilitate separation from her mother, and his unavailability as a clear oedipal presence.

Certain events that Miss W reported did suggest that there had been at least some positive experiences with her mother. For example, Miss W recalled her mother's occasional nostalgic references to other women's babies. She had also discovered her own baby clothes and toys neatly packed away. She mused that maybe, just maybe she had been her mother's good baby. She reported a fantasy of purchasing a baby bottle, taking it home and using it, and then bringing it to her session. At one of the sessions when Miss W brought this fantasy up, I interpreted that she believed that her "bad behaviors" (of her own invention) had disrupted a togetherness she once had had and longed for. I suggested that she satisfied this longing through her adoptive-mother fantasy and her tendency to use vague and global communication in our sessions, with its underlying wish that we could read each other's mind.

Throughout Miss W's life and during the early part of her treatment, she was unable to organize her feelings into words or to find the words to express what was going on inside of her. In the transference, she recreated, through somber, dark, often wordless moods, the silent and depressed family atmosphere in which she was raised. These moods, often accompanied by vague speech, reflected childlike behavior that served a defensive function and conveyed the belief that thoughts transformed into words would be ignored or harshly criticized. This regressive behavior also indicated the disruption of ego functioning that the strain trauma had had on her.

Although anxiety producing, Miss W's attempt to put thoughts and feelings into words, locate and organize memories, and find and rediscover fantasies began to lead her to greater self-expression and to discover the pleasure of speaking to me as a real person. This newfound ability to verbalize slowly reduced her reliance on projective identification (Klein, 1946) and furthered the process of ego expansion and integration. The gratification she derived from experiencing a sense of real power, based on the acquisition of new skills, enabled her to cope better with the frustration of not actualizing the adoptive-mother fantasy in the transference.

The adoptive-mother fantasy was expressed as wishes for closeness with me. Miss W spoke of her longing that she and I would stare up at the moon together and not have to speak about what we saw because we would both know what the other was thinking. It would be warm and close. This longing for an imaginary mother felt dangerous, though, in the present because she wanted to make it real and had to grapple with the pain and frustration of not being able to do so. She had felt this longing to be dangerous in her past as well, because it had become connected with a memory of walking into the kitchen and finding her mother playing with a big knife. She said that it looked as if her mother was cutting into the tips of her fingers, digging deeper and deeper. This memory fitted with Miss W's unconscious fantasy that her mother wanted to kill her because of her very existence and because of Miss W's longings for the fantasy adoptive mother.

This terrifying childhood belief that her mother would kill her and the corresponding, intensely conflictual wish to kill the much needed mother constituted a powerful organizing unconscious fantasy (Arlow, 1969). This fantasy further influenced and was reorganized by the acute sexual trauma, which was reconstructed by us to have occurred sometime between her third and fifth year.

When the negative transference became manifest in the treatment, it sometimes lost its illusory quality. At such times, Miss W was compelled to relive and make real certain aspects of the abusive relationship with her mother. As emotionally difficult as this transference was for both of us, it was imperative that the unconscious hatred my patient felt toward her mother, and the conflict surrounding it, be culled from her sullen-toned moods, be made specific, and be directed toward me if it was to find its original target and meaning. It was equally important that, within the negative transference, her hatred not remain in its projected form, with Miss W as its victim. Miss W painfully came to realize that she possessed profound hostility to her mother as a result of her own conflictual, frustrated desires. The degree of fear and guilt associated with her hostility was found to be due to, among other things, the omnipotence with which she had endowed her feelings and wishes and the overpowering intensity of the emotions she experienced. Under the sway of such strong feelings, she would become dizzy and feel the emotion as if it were physically moving through her body. In addition, she was overwhelmed with the fear of her capacity to do real harm to herself or me, and most important was the fear of the destruction of her loving self.

As we worked on Miss W's positive and negative transference fantasies, she was exquisitely sensitive to rejection and frequently turned interventions into criticisms. This state of affairs permeated the treatment off and on for some time. I initially interpreted this phenomenon from an adaptive standpoint. I spoke with her about her need to establish control over both of us and influence the pace of the treatment process in order to feel more powerful and worthwhile. Such adaptive-oriented interventions seemed to diminish the controlling superego influence on our work. Specific homosexual and sadistic features, which were unconscious and were being defended against by her concern about being criticized, were brought out and interpreted later in the treatment.

CLINICAL PROCESS

A session from the third year of the analysis afforded an opportunity to see how powerful the patient's fantasy was about her mother's negative feelings toward her. In this hour, Miss W expressed anxiety about not being able to see me. She wasn't sure of my presence. She wasn't sure where I really was, or where she really was. She said this with a mixture of detachment mingled with a bit of anxiety. Then there was a long silence. I said to her that the feeling about us seemed to suggest her experience of her mother when Miss W did not know where her mother really was and where she herself was. They were both present and yet absent, lost in some twilight of daydreaming. She responded that it felt as if her words were coming out of her and she was disappearing, yet she was worried for my mental well-being. In the midst of this confusing regressive feeling-state, she suddenly reported that she couldn't breathe. She grew more anxious and asked what she should do. She abruptly sat up, breathed in deeply, and slowly turned to look at me. Feeling a little anxious myself and concerned for her, I asked her if she was all right and if she felt that she could continue? She calmed down and went on, describing that the feeling she had was one of drowning, of being held down, of having something heavy on her chest, and of time going on forever.

This led to a memory of a childhood boating accident, when she and her mother, while standing to change seats in a canoe, had capsized it. They were pulled from the lake by relatives who were canoeing close by. Following the incident, her mother would not look at her and did not offer solace. Miss W's screen memory of the incident was of going under the water, sensing light and darkness, experiencing terrible pressure, and having a feeling, which she recaptured on the couch, of being lost to her mother forever.

For many sessions following the memory of the boating accident, Miss W consciously cooperated and worked on the meaning it held for her. However, she appeared distant from me and cold in her manner, as she had been at the beginning of the treatment. This way of being was so subtle that I did not always recognize it in the moment.

Soon after relating the boating incident, during a session when I was jotting down some thoughts, Miss W exclaimed, in alarm and anger, "What are you doing to me?" She then became frightened that she had expressed anger in my presence and could only explain that the sound of the pen on the paper really upset her. I asked her to work on what had frightened her so, but she became guarded and silent and turned to reality events and conflicts with coworkers who she felt were wronging her. She also cancelled some sessions.

In the overall context of feeling wronged, Miss W began to play with the idea of telling me more of what was on her mind about my taking notes and the sound of the pen on paper that had previously upset her. There occurred a rapid oscillation between Miss W's passively experiencing me as if I were her mother, too invasive or too distant, and then her unconsciously and actively, in an identification with the aggressor

(A. Freud, 1936), taking on her mother's role and placing me in the passive, often bewildered state she had experienced. It is difficult to describe the quickness in the switch and flow of associations and transference-countertransference feelings that transpired.

I consciously tried to place myself in just the right place within her orbit, to stay engaged and to move the therapeutic work along. I did this by trying both to be quiet and to interpret her spoken content at a certain ·pace and rhythm. This use of regulated intervention is usually discussed under the technical concepts of tact and timing. I believe, however, that when a therapist has to be so careful about what she says and how she says it, she is usually responding to an unconscious communication from the patient. In Miss W's case, I believe that I was responding to her unconscious invitation to be aggressive and invasive with her. I had to be careful not to withhold my ideas and questions to counter her offering, but to interpret this invitation at the right moment.

During this period of the treatment Miss W was consciously acting as if she were being coerced to talk; at the same time, by withholding her associations, she unconsciously was trying to coerce me to reassure her, to promise her that I would not criticize her or make any interpretations or ask any questions. Yet my silence was also unacceptable to her. My interpretive efforts here were fruitless for something more powerful was going on, something beyond my wish to understand the material. The here-and-now action between us, organized on a preconscious level was the real work to which Miss W was drawing our attention. This enactment taught me the value of being able to move flexibly from content interventions to process interventions and to pay interpretive attention to the function of a piece of behavior or attitude.

My eventual refusal to perfectly locate myself within her prescribed orbit, as Miss W had done with her mother as a child, played itself out by my charging her for her missed. hours. Once I realized the meaning of my behavior, I interpreted the totality of the action in terms of her projective identification (Porder, 1987). In essence, I said to her, over time, that I was meeting with her mother, that she had disconnected from her little-girl self because it made her feel weak and frightened, and that she wanted to put me in her childhood shoes. In addition, I said that she wanted me to know the depth of her tie to her mother, both its importance and how bad it made her feel and that she was doing all this out of a need to have some control over the bad, helpless feelings. My interpretive movements got her attention and moved her sufficiently out of the regressive transference so that she could reestablish reality contact and a therapeutic alliance. In this state of mind, Miss W expressed relief in the knowledge that I was strong and in control, in the best sense of the word, and, further, that I was me, a confident me, not her or her mother, and that she was safe and could trust me.

Using this growing sense of trust, the memory of sharing the experience of the boating incident, and the immediate trigger of my sitting behind her and taking notes, she revealed that her mother had repeatedly, and in secret from the rest of the family, sexually abused her. In a halting, sometimes whispering, sometimes fragmented narrative, Miss W related the memory of the abuse. She had been made to lie on her bed while her mother inspected her rectum. She thought that she was very little, which made her think that this abuse had begun before she had started the first grade. The rectal inspection had started out feeling good. Looking at her intently, her mother would gently wipe her anus with vaseline. Her mother's look and my patient's good feeling blended together. Her mother would then begin to poke and probe, sticking the vaseline and maybe other things way up inside. As MissW began to squirm, her mother held her down by putting her arm across her chest and by covering her mouth with her other hand. Miss W had trouble breathing and felt tremendous pressure down there inside her body while watching her mother's excited or angry face, she wasn't sure. Pleasurable sensations turned into painful sensations and ultimately made it difficult and fearsome for her, even as an adult, to go to the bathroom.

Later in the analysis, Miss W revealed a masturbation fantasy in conjunction with her current bathroom difficulties. The fantasy involved her and a female nurse tending to a man with diarrhea. As he struggled not to let go, she became aroused, her orgasm connected with his release of explosive diarrhea.

Returning to her revelation of the abuse, Miss W related that, while her mother was hurting her, she felt that she both did not exist and keenly existed as she succeeded in having her mother's full, excited attention. She felt weak, as though she wanted to surrender to the mother, and at the same time she felt that she had to fight. She was afraid that her mother would go all the way up inside of her and she would explode. She didn't know where "down there" her mother had touched her. It felt like everywhere. As she spoke, we uncovered fantasies in which she believed that her mother had put something inside of her that had made her bad and contaminated her and was hurting her from the inside. This fantasy was linked to an unconscious but active refusal to take in and consider interpretations in the treatment. Consequently her spoken material remained superficial but under her control. She came to realize that she believed that if she took in my ideas she would be contaminated. In general Miss W felt like a no-good, dirty person. Sometimes she had conscious fantasies of smelling bad and saw this as the reason that people might not like her. She further realized that this self-experience contributed to her provoking a distance with others by becoming cool and somewhat threatening, as she had seemed with me in the consultation period. Miss W felt searing shame in telling me all this, as if she were burning; and she wanted to disappear. She felt dirty and was frightened that she could forget herself, lose control, and wipe feces all over my wall.

A dream she had shared during the early period of the treatment flashed through my mind. The dream was about a room with two beige chairs (the color of my office chairs) placed face to face. As she walked into the room, beige powder fell out of her from somewhere "down there." At that time she was contemplating intensive treatment, and her thought was that something bad was bound to happen. I reminded her of the dream and stated that we could now understand her initial fear of treatment and the possibility of our uncovering the harm done to her "down there." We could also understand her terror about the abuse and anticipation of its repetition. We spoke too about her wish to talk about the trauma and have it understood as well as to repeat it under safe circumstances so that it might be dealt with.

A pattern of relating intensely, followed by distancing either through the use of identificatory defenses or by a defensive regression into a twilight state, followed this session. With the use of the latter defense, Miss W claimed not to remember anything of the previous hour and described a strange feeling that we had not spoken in ages, even though we had had a session the day before.

When Miss W was in these defensive postures, I felt-and interpreted to her-that either the material or I had been lost to her or evacuated by her, as she had felt lost from or evacuated by her mother. I went on, with a different emphasis, that she needed to lose these memories and fantasies in order to gain control over her feelings and inner and outer reality. With work on the defenses and enactments, Miss W gradually began to allow her anger to resicte consciously within herself. She began to connect this anger to slowly emerging thoughts of being rejected and forgotten after being so intensely and inappropriately misused by her mother.

Now that Miss W felt safe in these treatment interactions, a very positive, consistent transference was established between us, with emerging fantasies of me being her mommy and she my little girl as we played putting on makeup together in front of a big mirror. This play-acting was a derivative of her childhood adoption fantasy, which created delight and pleasure. She wanted to linger in it and to make it real; she insisted that I make up dialogue as if I were really the mother with her as my child, something one might do in some forms of child treatment. As she once had used her childhood adoption fantasies to comfort herself, she now used the same defensive process, denial in fantasy, to ease the pain of her condition and to create a pathway to dissipate, or forestall experiencing, the rage and disillusionment that lay beneath the surface.

Her sense of safety in these transference experiences allowed Miss W to express wishes for closeness and attention beyond those contained in the idealized fantasy relationship. The demanding quality of these wishes increased. She had a dream of a tuna fish salad sandwich and said that it was her favorite food as a child and that she loved to take small bites out of it, let it melt and get mushy in her mouth, and savor it. In her hours with me she behaved in a like manner, taking snippets out of my interventions and mushing up what was said with a mix of affection and indifference as if I were quite irrelevant, except to fill her with ideas.

During this period of the work she also revealed that she had what she called sexual thoughts about me. We worked on her shame over the pleasure these thoughts brought to her. The content of the fantasies had the theme of her being a dominating woman while I was her captive, a plaything whom she tortured while I begged for mercy and relief. These fantasies aroused a countertransference response more in keeping with the aim of the fantasy rather than with the spoken conscious content. They seemed to convey her need to make me irrelevant as a separate sexual object. I seemed to exist in her experience at this time only as a target for her active and controlling sadistic wishes and not as a richly textured, separate oedipal object who is both desired and appreciated in its own right. Miss W confirmed my thinking by relating that what gave her shame was the pleasure in the meanness that she found within herself. This emotion gave her a feeling of aliveness, powerfulness, and definition. She explained that this sense of meanness was a feeling of powerful uniqueness within her. She was therefore not just a passive blob, a blob who only reacted to what had been done to her by her mother. Her fantasy, she said, told her about the strong wishes within herself and she liked this.

The fantasies that were more directly tied to sexual gratification also spoke to her preoedipal and pregenital needs and wishes. The nurse fantasy mentioned previously was retold by Miss W in the analysis. It remained ·unchanged in content and was her sole source of sexual gratification. This masturbation fantasy, although seemingly triangular and oedipal with anal coloration, really obscured gender differentiation. The primary emotional focus for Miss W was the nurse. In our analysis of it, we learned that the man with the explosive diarrhea symbolized for her the experience of the inside of her body when her mother abused her and when she could not achieve actual physical relief.

That this fantasy contained a disguised and defensive attempt to move to a positive oedipal position is 'not to be ruled out but has not been established thus far in the treatment. What seems more likely was that the establishment of a positive oedipal position was weakened and pulled regressively back to the fixations of the dyadic period of development. The absence of the father and brother in the treatment material could address symbolically Miss W's experience of their indifference to her as a girl child. It could further suggest the effect of their emotional absence on facilitating movement into clear gender differentiation and a positive oedipal position.

The childhood pattern of the mother-child relationship, a cumulative or strain trauma, now internalized, had negatively affected her ego's ability to regulate the conflicts around her aggressivity in an adaptive manner (Kernberg, 1990). An account of the following session illustrates her struggle.

The context for the session is Miss W's growing awareness of rage at her mother. Their telephone contact was increasing. This session occurred some time after I learned of the sexual abuse. In sessions prior to this one, Miss W had become gradually aware of some of her murderous wishes toward her mother and wanted me, at one point, literally to go through the fantasy of planning the murder of her mother. She concretely wanted my ideas on how to carry it out and in one session said in a demanding way, "So come on, give me an idea and you're going to help. So what are you doing just sitting there?" At such a moment she had the quality of a child patient who will not give the analyst the script for the drama and insists that the analyst make her independent moves. When I attempted to keep the work symbolic by stating, "This is a wish. This is a fantasy you're enacting," she became frustrated with me, which takes us to the following session.

Miss W: I feel that I've missed you. I feel that I could be hurt by someone, hit over the head, mugged, a vague feeling. I need to hear you talk, to hear your voice, to know you're here, not just your few sentences. I just imagined someone, like in a dream, coming after me, and I hide behind you. [pause] I'm wondering why I'm thinking this way. I saw this video over the weekend, a child was tied down, but I managed my feelings OK, on the surface. It was all right. I feel this undercurrent of anxiety. I need your voice for comfort, like a teddy or a "blankie" [laughs embarrassedly] Something inside isn't O.K. today. So, comfort me in a concrete way. Go ahead, I'm waiting.

Analyst: You're afraid the anger and the thoughts you have been having and talking about will hurt you and you want my reassurance and support.

Miss W: Yes, it makes me so needy. I want to try to stay with this anger. It's not easy; it's hard to believe that I could feel what I felt and think those thoughts. If I let myself get in touch with it, it's just going to be frustrating, not going to get rid of it, just have it in my mind. The feeling might be like a fire that can burn me. Once it starts, it's going to kill me, not her. [pause] It will hollow me out. I feel kind of stuck now. Last session, I remember how badly I felt. I wanted to put my head on your knee for comfort, because [pause) because I can't kill her, I can't get to her, I've never gotten to her. Your knee is like a refuge. It's fine to be there, stuck there, comforted, but not very helpful emotionally because then I'm not involved in what I'm doing. Over the weekend I thought about what we said, how I had started to feel. I got scared and made that picture of my head on your knee. What's next for me? To move away from your knee? That's not an option. To do that would bring back painful and intense feelings, so should I stay here? Short silence. It's premature, my thinking about that; it's where I am now. [silence] I feel very sad. That's where I am now. [silence] I feel very sad—that's where I am, sad and distraught.

Analyst: You ask whether you should stay near me. If it's all right to be there, I think to help yourself with that hollowed-out feeling, but you're also thinking of moving away, tell me more.

Miss W: In this feeling I couldn't walk away from you, I'm not interested in anything. I couldn't leave, overwhelmed with a feeling that I'd be all alone.

Analyst: How do you mean?

Miss W: [pause] I don't know exactly. In the image, if I walk away, the loss of physical contact, the feelings overwhelm me. I'm frightened and confused. I don't know what to do. I can't kill her. I don't know what to do with her. I can't protect myself; I can't kill her. Something bad will happen to me. I don't know what to do about it. I don't have any more ideas.

Analyst: You had an idea about being hurt, mugged, a kind of physical punishment for the feelings and fantasies you're having.

Miss W: To have these thoughts about my mother is a sin. [whispers], especially enjoying them. I think I enjoyed the fantasy when I was in it. I just muttered in my head. I wish you were dead. I have your knee now; I didn't have it· when I was little. I don't know what I used. [pause] My fantasies, I used my fantasies. I learned that here. If I left your knee now, I'm afraid of being out of it, really out of it, like I was when I was a kid. You know I remember feeling fleeting anger at her. She never understood, always accusing me. It made me frustrated. It made me angry. I couldn't make her see me. I'd tell something that happened at school, but she'd be cleaning and not say anything, or she would say it wasn't so. I'd begin to doubt myself, wonder about what she was thinking. I couldn't express my anger. I was afraid; I was confused.

I remember something now. I was young. It was before I learned not to open my mouth. It was in that kitchen. I was in that kitchen with her. I was being angry. I used words. She grabbed me by my arms and slammed me up against the wall. "Don't you ever get angry with me again," she said. I remember those angry eyes, the angry mouth. Oh, this is bad. She's going to hurt me. I never did it again in the same way. I'd get annoyed, but my feeling would disappear. I had no security about it. I was very little. I was just being myself, unself-conscious. The words just came out, bad thing to do, bad thing to do. Scary, very bad, I don't know. That's not right what she did. I couldn't defend myself. I can't defend myself. I don't ever remember wanting to kill her. Maybe, under my breath, but I was on a different floor. You don't think she heard me, do you? What I'm telling you now, what's coming up now, was below the surface. I'm putting you in the picture, preventing myself from feeling worse, I wish there had been someone there to help me. [silence]

Now your knee doesn't feel good enough, not a real person to protect me. I talked to her on the phone over the weekend. All she talked about was herself and the house, some kind of repairs needed. She went on and on. I couldn't tell her about me. I don't even know what I wanted to say. She wants to have a party. She's cleaning like crazy. She'll serve that dip. She says my father never speaks to her. She was in that kitchen of hers. I've come to hate that room. 'I want to wreck the whole house. It made her a slave. All she did was take care of it, not me. I want to get her attention. I want to make her weep. [silence] I feel frustrated, I feel depressed, I don't know how to express it, I'm supposed to relive these emotions, but I feel helpless. You get me out of this. I don't know how to do it, so do something. Help me get out of this. I feel like a blob, no words, like I'm angry at everything, but I don't know how to express it, channel it out of me. [pause] Maybe I can't stand feeling sad, depressed, like when I was a kid. I was angry for moments, I think it felt better. Now I'm rolling in it, reliving it, frustrated, I feel stuck now.

Analyst: Perhaps you're angry at me that you're feeling depressed and frustrated. Do you think it's because I didn't join you in the fantasy about killing your mother the way you wanted me to and that hurt you?

Miss W: No, I'm angry at myself. This is my fault, this mess I'm in, I'm a hopeless case. Should I blame you? It's me, it's all me. [pause] What you said so far doesn't help. I feel like I'm helpless and waiting for you to say something that's going to make a difference. I don't know what it is. [silence] You're not going to say a sentence that's going to make a difference, are you? I'm going to stay frustrated. You're not going to get me out of this frustration. I need you to say something else. That wasn't it. My feeling isn't going to be taken seriously. I have to be quiet, I'm going to be left alone with it. I don't know what to do—you won't listen to me.

Analyst: Since I cannot read your mind and don't know what this sentence is, it feels like we're stuck together here in this frustration.

Miss W: You'll abandon me. It will get buried again; I'll have to cope with it. You don't know, you'll refuse to help me. What's the use? It's hopeless.

Analyst: I think it feels hopeless to you when you feel that all communication has broken down. You feel you can't reach me, and you feel I won't reach you, similar to how it felt between you and your mother.

Miss W: Yeah, she has the same attitude you do: go figure it out yourself. Instead of trying with me, she'd ignore me, or say one thing. She'd give up, that's it. You find a way to communicate with me. I feel now this is not my fault. There's more to put into words, I can't get to it, I'm all tied up with myself. Just never mind. You don't know how to help me, you're withholding. I am angry at you, and I don't know what to do, I'm just a blob.

Analyst: You know, I just thought that, even though you feel yourself to be a blob, you are doing something with me here. I feel rather tied up with my ideas, tied up in trying to reach you. Do you think that you might be trying to bring alive with me the fantasy you had recently, of tying up your mother, imagining her being so helpless and then killing her? You're bringing it alive now with all the sad, hopeless, rageful, and guilty feelings connected with it.

Miss W: Yes, [covers her face quickly] I feel foolish with this. I feel frightened, ashamed, as though my mother caught me trying to hurt her. I feel caught now.

Analyst: Yes, as if your mother were catching you in the privacy of your thoughts. ·

Miss W: Yes, like I muttered before, like I'm practicing a secret thought, I wish she was dead. But she can't be killed. No matter how angry I am at her, I can't get to her, I can't hurt her; I can't even talk to her. I have to kill her or walk away, and I can't do either. I'm glad you have patience. I feel your patience with me, but I don't have patience right now. You're the target for my anger. Where else can I go with it? If I leave it inside, I'll explode. When I talked to my mom on the phone I tried to talk to her about my new possible deal, but she just cut me off, gave me the silent treatment and went on about her party. My possible new deal is exciting to me, I could make a nice commission and my co-workers, particularly "P," will think well of me. It's very hard work; sometimes I think I won't be able to carry it off. I tried to do some work over the weekend, but I'm preoccupied with, oh, I don't know, her, I guess, my feeling, like she's in my mind all the time, criticizing me: I'm not working fast enough; I didn't talk to the customer confidently enough; I was wrong in my numbers. It's so depressing, so frustrating. When I heard about her party, I tried to talk about her guests. She rarely has guests. She corrected my thoughts about Mrs. S; they weren't her thoughts. But it's as if I didn't speak really. She just went right on, like I can't get into her strange kingdom, except [trails off] . . .

Analyst: You seem to move away from a thought.

Miss W: Yes, except when she used me. I feel afraid to say more. It's safer to be quiet; you say it.

Analyst: What I can say is, you're afraid you'll explode with feeling and kill me. These feelings are connected with your recent fantasies and the painful memories about being physically used by your mother.

Miss W: I feel so filled with hate I can't stand it; it's such a frightening feeling. It pushes at me, I'm afraid it will spill out, leave this room, and I'll get angry at work, scream and never stop. I'm embarrassed thinking of myself like this. I feel like a little girl again, like I want to run to you, put my head on your knee, crawl onto your lap. Be safe there and get away from these horrible feelings. When I think of her on the phone, smiling about herself, her house, her party—everything is her, I want to hurt her, pulverize her. Killing isn't good enough. I want to wreck that house; it was so bleak there. She wouldn't talk to me for days, I never knew why. The weekends felt like an enormous span of time, forever with nothing to do. I'd wake up and think, oh no, it's another day. No plans, no activity, I'd try to go back to sleep and stay in bed as long as possible. I'd go downstairs. No one was there. Where was everyone? Then I'd hear her off in the background, vacuuming. No one fed me. It was so lonely, like I didn't exist. She'd only speak to me about how such and such looked in the library, or something stupid like that. I could have been dressed in rags, she'd not notice. That's how it felt. I should have yelled at her then. What a wimp I was, but she scared me. I feel right now as if I want to express my anger. I almost want to be wild with it, but it's hard for me to be that angry. It's frightening. I dread this, but I feel I've just scratched the surface.

In a subsequent session Miss W exclaimed that she wanted "to do it," that everything inside of her wanted to kill her mother. Only a split second of her own mental weakness, and her mother would be dead. Miss W thought that this would feel so good, like a volcano releasing, and this action seemed like the only way to rid herself of the boiling rage, the hatred inside of her. Her literalness was alarming, and my countertransference reaction spoke to the level of her ego regression and her anxiety.

As she went further into this regressed state of mind, an utter bleakness came over the painful, memory-laden material and evoked an emotional atmosphere of deadness. I felt, uncomfortably, that I was losing contact with her. I believed that this was an enactment of her inner experience (externalized) of losing contact with the libidinal aspects of herself as well as the representation of the object. This was an actualization of the fantasy of being killed by and killing the mother. The adaptive need for self-regulation of these frightening feelings was diminishing under the onslaught of rage. Unlike in the prior sessions, Miss W was unable to find and use the metaphor of resting her head on my knee to calm herself and reduce the emotional distance her hate was creating.

Feeling that this regressive reliving had run its beneficial course, I interpreted in such a manner as to aid her in refinding the libidinal component within herself. I tried to diminish the power of the image of the murderous self. I shared with her the thought that she was under pressure (the volcano metaphor) to get through to her mother, to make her mother notice her, that there was contained within her wish to kill tremendous frustrated need and longing. Her hateful part wanted so much for her mother to care about her, and she actively longed for care, not just from her mother but also from me. She wanted me to stay in emotional contact with her and understand her hatred. My emotional effort toward her and my interpretive slant slowly brought about a transforming experience in the treatment.

In contrast to her dread of re-creating only the explosive and overstimulating frustrations in the transference, Miss W found a feeling of safety and relief in the reality of experiencing her sadness. She felt that she had found my knee again and could rest her head and as a consequence had regained her long-lost ability to cry. This adaptive use of her oral sexual longings was akin to a transitional soothing experience. She re-created the positive introject that supported and libidinized internally the picture of her longing self. This internal structure formed the basis for the derivative longings in the adoptive-mother fantasy of her childhood but was now more rooted in the real experiences of our relationship.

The disorganizing effect of the diffuse rage had been halted as Miss W was able to regain the boundary between past and present and reality and fantasy through her ability to use both the act of and the content of interpretations.

SUMMARY

This case of childhood neglect and sexual abuse illustrates the psychological effects of trauma and how they came to be understood and worked through in the transference.

Because of the emotional deprivation she suffered through all phases of her development, Miss W had to regulate early narcissistic needs and did so through omnipotent fantasies that provided her with an illusion of control over the poorly differentiated object. She also used denial in fantasy (which did not impair her reality testing), in which she was the beloved child of idealized adoptive parents. This later defensive fantasy structure did not seem to have a family romance, oedipal meaning but, rather, followed from her splitting of the object world. She created in fantasy the good self and the idealized good object and the very early emotional nourishment that this illusion provided. Her prevalent use of projective identification, in and out of treatment, contributed to her omnipotent thinking and to a continuing experience of low-level anxiety and a weakening of reality testing. This defense posture contributed to her sense of isolation and distance from others, while at the same time she continued a private and intensely emotional overinvolvement with them. She came to learn that the people she chose to interact with (and fantasized intense but painful relationships with) unconsciously represented her mother.

The patient's ability to establish a solid foothold in the phallic oedipal position was weakened by the regressive pull of fixation points that had been established by the intense conflicts of the preoedipal period. Attempts at conflict solutions had contributed to a significant arrest in areas of her personality development and had prevented the negotiation of phallic oedipal conflicts from performing their transforming function on earlier established structures such as defense, self- and object constancy, and the content of her fantasy formations.

The shock trauma (the sexual abuse) contributed to a heightened, object-connected wish, in fantasy, to hurt and be hurt by the object for unconscious gratification and a feeling of safety. Finding or creating painful experiences gave Miss W a feeling of security in the familiarity of refinding her past and a means of coping with internal separation anxiety.

The therapeutic process of working through the emotion of hatred and its attendant fantasies contributed to the gradual shift in the internal balance of Miss W's hating and loving self-representations. The sense of herself as having been so singularly and globally dirty and bad shifted to include a more complex and nuanced inner picture. This more integrated self-representation now incorporated the once buried, thus almost atrophied, positive qualities of her self-image.

The more integrated, thus more realistic, image of herself allowed Miss W to tolerate her thoughts, wishes, and feelings and to experience them more firmly within her own boundaries. Miss W slowly became less burdened by persecutory ideas and the need for the resultant distancing maneuvers. This and other work done in the treatment led to her finding a job that provided satisfaction and allowed her, in time, to begin work toward a college degree. She also began to experience more positive interactions with other people. Her childhood longing for positive, safe connections and for companionship was finally being realized both in the real world and in her ability to use the therapeutic relationship for healing.

REFERENCES

ARLOW, J. (1969). Unconscious fantasy and disturbances of conscious experience. In: *Psychoanalysis.* Madison, CT: International Universities Press, 1991, pp. 151–175.

FREUD, A. (1936). *The Ego and the Mechanisms of Defense,* Writing 2. New York: International Universities Press.

GOOD, M. (1996). Suggestion and veridicality in the reconstruction of sexual trauma, or can a bait of suggestion catch a carp of falsehood? *Journal of the American Psychoanalytic Association* 44:1899–1224.

KLEIN, M. (1946). Notes on some schizoid mechanisms. In: *The Writings of Melanie Klein, Vol. 3, Envy and Gratitude & Other Works.* London: Hogarth Press, pp. 1–24.

KERNBERG, O. (1990). The psychopathology of hatred. In: *Rage, Power and Aggression,* ed. R. Glick & S. Roose. New Haven, CT: Yale University Press, pp. 61–79.

KRIS, E. (1956). The recovery of childhood memories. *Psychoanalytic Study of the Child* 11:54–88.

LOEWALD, H.W. (1955). Hypnoid state, repression, abreaction and recollection. In: *Papers on Psychoanalysis.* New Haven, CT: Yale University Press, 1980, pp. 33–42.

PORDER, M. (1987). Projective identification: an alternative hypothesis. *Psychoanalytic Quarterly* 26:431–451.

SANVILLE, J. (1991). *The Playground of Psychoanalytic Therapy.* Hillsdale, NJ: The Analytic Press.

VIEDERMAN, M. (1995). The reconstruction of a repressed sexual molestation. *Journal of the American Psychoanalytic Association* 43:1169–1195. a

Patsy Turrini, MSW, LCSW,
Diana Siskind, MSW, LCSW

CHAPTER 14

GERTRUDE AND RUBIN BLANCK:
THEIR CONTRIBUTIONS TO THE THEORY AND PRACTICE OF CLINICAL SOCIAL WORK AND TO THE BODY OF PSYCHOANALYTIC KNOWLEDGE

[Turrini, P. & Siskind, D. (2009). Clinical Social Work 37:32–44.]

The *Clinical Social Work Journal* and Gertrude and Rubin Blanck have had a long association going all the way back to an issue published in 1987 honoring them for their outstanding contribution to their profession. This came about in the following way. On November 17, 1984, the New York State Society of Clinical Social Work gave "A Conference and Award Presentation honoring Gertrude Blanck and Rubin Blanck for their outstanding contribution to the field of Clinical Social Work." At the end of the conference Jean Sanville, the editor of the *Clinical Social Work Journal* at that time, stood up and said that she was so impressed by the papers she had just heard that she wanted the entire content of this festschrift to the Blancks to be published in a forthcoming issue of the Journal. That issue was published in the winter of 1987, (Volume 15, #4). Rather than inviting prominent members of our profession as presenters at this important event, it gave Gertrude and Rubin pleasure to share the honor of this occasion with their students. That is just one of the many examples of their extraordinary generosity, a quality that has played an important role in the manner in which they taught and shared their considerable knowledge. They knew their material so well and in such depth that they were able to teach it with unsurpassed clarity, a rare talent and one born of their deep commitment to transmitting their knowledge to their students and to future generations of social workers practicing psychotherapy as well as other forms of social work.

We thank David Phillips for inviting us to co-author this article about the Blancks. The opportunity to do so holds particular meaning for us, like a cycle of affirmation and continuity, because the introduction to that issue of the *Clinical Social Work Journal* was written by Patsy Turrini, who had been the moderator of that memorable meeting and was a student of the Blancks at that time. One of the six papers presented was by Siskind (1987), also one of their students back then. It gives us great pleasure to write about Gertrude and Rubin Blanck, two outstanding clinicians who were our teachers, supervisors, and eventually our friends and colleagues. We are pleased to recount their contributions for our younger colleagues who did not have the benefit of studying with the Blancks and to revive for those who did study with them the memories of the pleasure and excitement we derived from the intense learning and theory building of that period, an experience that enriched our professional lives and set us on a satisfying and ever-evolving professional path that continues to this day.

While we were preparing this material, it became clear to us that their contributions are rarely studied now, and perhaps have been lost to social work training in the last two decades. Glimpses of their ideas appear in articles on attachment theory, relational theory, and mentalization propositions but rarely are they referenced to the Blancks. To remedy this neglect we will offer as much of a review of their work as time and space allow and although we will not be able to do justice to their many contributions, we hope readers will be stimulated to read their books and discover their enduring contributions.

The Blancks viewed psychoanalytic thinking as an ever-evolving branch of knowledge. The knowledge base grew in part through the effectiveness of its application. They often referred to Mendeleev, who is credited with the first version of the Periodic Table of Elements, and who left room open for new elements to be discovered. We think this view of the development of the working body of knowledge of psychoanalysis and social work theory is essential; new discoveries of the intricacies of mental structures and functions are constantly added, and the Blancks were gifted in grasping this and creating techniques that professionals could use to empower people with new psychic resources.

Gertrude and Rubin were serious clinicians and students of psychoanalytic thinking. Their scholarly approach allowed them to both teach psychoanalytic theory with exquisite clarity and expand the borders of its reach. Always crediting and honoring those psychoanalysts whose contributions they had built on, they extracted aspects of theory and made them immediately relevant to clinical work. Examples of this will appear throughout this paper.

Although known as ego psychologists, Gertrude and Rubin Blanck feared that that term could sound narrow and misleading. They preferred the term "psychoanalytic developmental object relations theory." Their mission was to enrich the therapeutic practice of clinicians of all disciplines by providing them with a solid understanding of the new infant observation studies and the therapeutic work that integrated many principles. Donnelly (2008, p. 33) says: "the power of a social work perspective to integrate contributions from many fields of knowledge and apply them to the particular purposes of our professional mission is the unique strength of social work." The Blancks would leave no stone unturned to help people.

They had a particular interest in enriching and refining the treatment approach to the more troubled patients, such as those suffering from borderline, narcissistic, and psychotic disorders. They recognized that this was an underdeveloped area of our profession and were instrumental in changing what was often a haphazard approach to psychotherapy to one based on sound understanding of the newly discovered infant mental accomplishments and internalizations—distinguishing the pre-wired elements from those requiring environmental inputs. They added an understanding of the therapeutic needs of the less structured patient. One of the ways they accomplished their goal was to give new meaning to diagnostic considerations by developing a *working diagnosis* that tracked the psychic structure of the patient and introduced the clinician to a listening mode that had broadened dimensions allowing for interventions that fitted the particularity of the patient on multiple levels. They also gave new meaning to Freud's concept of listening with "evenly suspended attention"[1] (Freud 1912). The broadened scope of this listening style was especially helpful because it expands insight into the enormous range of the emotional constellation and opened pathways into constantly evolving theory and technique.

Their approach to learning and teaching psychoanalytic theory followed the evolution of psychoanalytic knowledge beginning with Freud. They identified personality profiles (e.g., the psychosexual stages and lines of identity) in his work as well as his attention to the early origins of object relations, which they later expanded to include additional developmental lines. Among their important contributions was their organization of the developmental assessment guide mentioned earlier which outlined all the developmental lines: psychosexual development, drive taming processes, object relations, adaptive functions, anxiety level, defen-

---

[1] Sometimes referred to as "evenly hovering attention."

sive function, identity formation, and process of internalization (Blanck and Blanck 1974). This was very helpful to clinicians in that it enabled them to direct their treatment to where the patient was developmentally at a given moment.

Gertrude and Rubin's enthusiasm for psychoanalytic investigations inspired some of their students to write, to teach, and to present at scientific meetings and serve on boards of institutes. One of us (Turrini) became convinced of the importance of the mother's (parent's/caretaker's) role in promoting healthy mental functions and structures and undertook exploratory research (Turrini 1977) examining mothers' experiences and needs. The caretakers' needs and experiences constitute an environment for the child's development; thus, identifying maternal need would offer information about enabling the mother/caretaker to continue her own development while providing healthy childrearing practices for the children, practices that she may or may not have learned from her parents. From this research, the Mothers Center Model was developed and has been replicated in many parts of the country. The Model provides a community with services that include child development information, ongoing research, and advocacy for the members. This community program development is an example of how psychoanalytic information can inform social work community practices.

In another vein, Siskind applied much of her training to teaching and writing books and articles about child therapy, the importance of engaging parents in the treatment of their child, and the impact of adoption on children and parents (Siskind 1992, 1997, 1999; Hushion et al. 2006).

Hall (1998, 2004), another of their students, as well as Edward et al. (1992), Mendell and Turrini (2003) wrote books that demonstrated the influence of the Blancks in many different ways. Many others, too numerous to mention, who trained with the Blancks contributed articles and book reviews in this and other journals as well as offering teaching, supervision, and involvement in national organizations that further the place of clinical social work in the field of mental health.

While we and many of our contemporaries were exposed to Freud and to general psychoanalytic principles during our years of undergraduate and social work training, these studies tended to be rather superficial and not particularly applicable to our work with patients. It wasn't until our studies with the Blancks that aspects of psychoanalytic theory and its application began to come together in a way that was deeply meaningful to our work of providing patients with a new lease on life. Gertrude and

Rubin Blanck were masters at extracting and teaching core concepts that included study of conscious, unconscious, drives, intra- and intersystemic psychic processes, structures, and the representational inner world.

Before beginning their study of psychoanalysis, the Blancks were trained as social workers. What they drew from their study of psycho-analysis enhanced and broadened the knowledge base gained from their original studies in social work. One could say that they provided ever-increasing depth, specificity, and scientific precision to their original social work body of knowledge. We hope this paper will stimulate and encourage social workers to enrich our social work theory and practice by re-examining common human needs through the Blancks' extraordi-nary insights.

In Rubin's paper, "Practice Theory Then and Now" (Blanck 1977), he reviews the casework literature that was meaningful to him, and we get a picture of the formulations he first learned from social work. He described how social workers, out of their "hands-on" experience and observations, had frequently considered ideas that psychoanalysts were later to develop. He opens the paper in the following way: "Identifiable in the literature of earlier decades are some striking parallels to contem-porary formulations about dynamics of clinical social work practice. What is extraordinary to note is the fact that in 1940, long before Mahler's papers had been presented containing references to symbiosis and highlighting the importance of the process of separation/individuation, Gordon Hamilton had already been discussing it (pp. 95–99). No wonder Gertrude and Rubin Blanck would find Mahler's work so very valuable, for it con-tinued the knowledge base they valued and were familiar with. Rubin writes: "To cite parallels between earlier and current conceptions about practice is not to assert the equivalence of these conceptions. I do not mean to imply that there is nothing new. Indeed, during the past twenty-five years we have realized a great increase in knowledge relevant to the understanding of practice. Among other gains has been the construction *of the scientific base or rationale* for the aptness of understandings grasped intuitively by artful observers" (p. 97, italics ours).

Rubin (op. cit. 1977) charts other social work principles: the belief in self-determination, the use of the personal relationship (not alms but a friend), responsibility to promote a therapeutic relationship, the need to understand the other's reality, a comprehensive understanding of per-sonality growth, an understanding of the helping process, a diagnosis that includes an appraisal of the genetic factors influencing character development, and treatment objectives based on diagnostic appraisal of personality. Rubin concluded in that article that "the intellectual history of social work thus includes a largely intuitively based appreciation of the centrality of the relationship as a vehicle for therapeutic influence and of the helper's obligation to accept guardianship for the autonomy of the client" (p. 98).

In keeping with social work's historical commitment to the use of the relationship and its instrumentality in promoting and enabling growth and change, the Blancks' use of self in the therapeutic experience was described long before intersubjectivity and interpersonal theories were developed and in vogue. They were very thoughtful in their understanding of counter-transference reactions and would, we are sure, have believed that the 3-person psychology was not a new idea but one that was being highlighted in reaction to some of the very rigid attitudes in "classical" theory.

In another vein, Gertrude (1989) wrote that she was invited to give grand rounds at a large psychiatric hospital. While she was wandering the corridors to find the room, a social worker walked her to the auditorium but was unable to attend because she was a social worker. Gertrude writes: "It was not always that way. As a student at the Columbia University School of Social Work very many years ago, I was taught by the giants of social work: Gordon Hamilton, Fern Lowry, Dorothy Hutchinson, Lucille Austin, among others. They were openly teaching psychoanalyti-cally oriented psychotherapy. We students attended grand rounds and staff conferences at the New York State Psychiatric Institute, at Payne Whitney, and other such facilities around town. We were learning psychotherapy. It was called that. Oh Columbia, what has become of you?" (p. 1).

THEORETICAL CONCEPTS: THE ESSENTIAL CORE

In this next section, we will describe the core theoretical concepts that the Blancks drew from Hartman, Spitz, Mahler, and Jacobson, which they integrated and taught in ways that enabled their students to comprehend them well and make use of them. We recognize that much of what we are about to describe is no longer taught in graduate programs in social work or even in advanced institutes for psychoanalysis and psychotherapy. We therefore hope you will bear with us as we present this material here. Many have complained that psychoanalysis has given the world a difficult lan-guage; many ego psychologists' work is not easily read or understood. The Blancks helped undo some of the difficulty where others could not.

They were superb translators of these complex ideas. Once during a seminar we both attended, Trudy, as we called her, told us that buried in some of the lengthy and often dense books and articles that we read were "headlines." The authors did not alert us to the appearance of these headlines; rather it was our job to recognize and remember them. She was generous in helping us identify these still vital headlines and transform them into useful knowledge. We will identify some of them as we go along and also discuss how to utilize them and other important concepts to create flexible and useful developmental diagnoses. And finally, we will describe some of their contributions to technique. A friend and former student of the Blancks, Ann Bair, recently shared with us that she can pass on their books to colleagues who find their work profoundly informative. She cited as one telling point their chart on levels of anxiety by means of which her colleague recognized the concept of annihilation anxiety as explaining her confusing patient. We are heartened to hear that their work lives on.

Heinz Hartmann

We are citing four psychoanalytic contributors whom the Blancks located as offering profound information to analytic development and who can be considered as contributing to social work theory. They always credited their sources, and we are trying to demonstrate that process in reviewing the following theoreticians. In addition, the work of Hartmann, Spitz, Jacobson, and Mahler remains vivid and vital and can be used in current theory building. New discoveries need not replace earlier contributions. All can be added to the periodic analytic chart. Phillips (private communication) supports "the inter-relationship of the person in the environment and notes that Ego Psychology was a main theoretical force that brought psychoanalytic theory into social work: the idea that the ego was the force that integrated internal process and external forces." We have found their work to be very valuable in teaching, especially in its application to the treatment of seriously disturbed patients who so often make up the caseload of beginning social workers.

Heinz Hartmann, known as the father of ego psychology, began expanding psychoanalytic theory by drawing attention to normal development. He sought a general theory of the mind and drew from biology, sociology, anatomy, and supported research. He proposed that the infant ego could have conflict-free components, theorizing that each infant was born with "apparatus of primary autonomy. Each infant was born with innate ego potentialities, defined as perception, intention, object comprehension, thinking, language, recall-phenomenon, productivity, the phrases of motor development (grasping, crawling, walking" (1958, p. 8). He focused on the interaction of the infant with his "average expectable environment" and to the reciprocal adaptation that followed and shaped developing psychic structure. Current research is confirming Hartmann and the Blancks' original findings (Brazelton and Nugent 1995; Schore 2003; Weil 1978).

Hartmann's idea of "average expectable environment" is endorsed by the Blanck and Blanck (1974, pp. 28–29) who quote him: "On the side of the environment or, the average expectable environment as he called it, is foremost the mother and her maternal needs which (ideally) reciprocate the infant's needs. Behind the mother stand her husband, the "concept of family, the entire social structure, the influence of tradition and the survival of the works of man ... the works of man objectify the methods he has discovered for solving problems and thereby become factors of continuity, so that man lives so to speak, in past generations as well as in his own. Thus arises a network of identifications and ideal-formations which is of great significance for the forms and ways of adaptation" (Hartmann 1958, p. 30). Here again there is a clear link to the social work commitment to diagnose by understanding the person as existing in a certain type of environment. In discussing the important reciprocal relationship between infant and mother he introduced three very important concepts: affect adaptation, regression, and fitting together, and he writes that the mother needs the ability to temporarily regress in order to fit together with her infant, thus "serving both the maternal requirements and the infant's needs" (op. cit. p. 31).

Whereas Hartmann did not specify much more about environments, the Blancks went somewhat further in describing types of environments, especially the early caretaking environment for the infant/toddler. Seen through this lens, the therapist and the therapeutic situation become the new and growth-promoting environment for the patient, an environment that supports further development that an early environment failed to provide. Taking this one step further, the therapist, through her listening mode, needs to be able to provide empathy and understanding of the derailed structural development to "fit together" with her patient, thus employing her adaptive capacity and her ability to promote a therapeutic alliance.

Quoted by the Blanck and Blanck (1974), Hartmann presented a formula for normal development and the unfolding of the organizing process of the ego. "He presented the instrument of normal development against which to measure pathology." He distinguished between maturation—a term used for those processes that are biological—and development, for those processes that combine the biological and psychological. He directed attention to the infant's first object relations. Evolution is a "process of progressive internalizations." The individual becomes capable of increased independence over the environment. The Blancks held that specific types of caretaking were essential to the development of the innate apparatus; that appropriate caretaking fostered emergent inner tools necessary for both infant/toddler and adult health.

The Blancks and Hartmann paid attention to drives and drive neutralization. Neutralized energy was used to build ego functions when the libidinal drive held dominance over the aggressive drive. Like Mahler, they held that non-hostile aggression promoted autonomy and fueled the process of separation and individuation (Blanck and Blanck 1988). Supporting Freud's last statement on drive theory, they viewed the aggressive drive as aiding separation and the libidinal drive as maintaining connections. Drives influence the differentiation of self and object with positive affect. Good self and object experiences produce internal sensations of being loved and lovable. These are some of the points of view that guided them in creating techniques for improving the patient's self-esteem, promoting a working alliance, and aiding the development of the transference.

Although drive concepts have fallen out of favor in many places, Solms (2006) reports that current neuropsychoanalysis research is demonstrating a general theory of drives and he believes drive theory should be returned to favor and studied. He discusses the neurobiology of the libidinal drive, and says, "We humans are not exempt from the evolutionary biological forces that shaped other creatures. It is therefore difficult to form an accurate picture of how the human mental apparatus really works without using a concept at least something like Freud's definition of drive" (Solms 2002, p. 117).

Rene Spitz

Rene Spitz's observations of the innate processes and interactions with the mother demonstrated serious proof that the neonate's equipment needs to be "quickened" through the interchange with the mother (Spitz 1965). Spitz describes the process as follows:

> Although the innate equipment is available to the baby from the first minute of life, it has to be quickened; the vital spark has to be conferred on that equipment with another human being, with a partner, with the mother. Nothing less than a reciprocal relation will do. Only a reciprocal relation can provide the experiential factor in the infant's development, consisting as it does of a circular exchange in which affects play a major role. (Spitz 1965, p. 95)

He talks about the "emotional climate" created by the mother and its vital role in the development of the child. These ideas have direct bearing on the therapeutic situation and are a strong reminder that Spitz and the other early ego psychologists laid the essential foundation for attachment theory but, sadly, their contributions are generally ignored. His hospital and prison studies clearly demonstrate the dangers of absent and disconnected mothering and describe how depression, marasmus, and ever death could result from a climate lacking in even minimal human contact.

One of his outstanding contributions is his description of the three organizers of the psyche, which consist of critical nodal periods that unfold and can be observed by the appearance of specific behaviors as indicators that a new level of inner organization has occurred. These are: the smile at about 3 months (recognition of the familiar), stranger anxiety at about 8 months (true differentiation of the familiar from the stranger), and 18-month-old semantic communication and the "no" gesture. These are pre-wired expectable universal behaviors in children whose development has not been derailed. It is of great value to child therapists taking a developmental history to obtain information regarding these three manifestations of psychic development. Especially important is the appearance of the "no" gesture. The appearance of the "no" in language is called the third ego "organizer." This pre-wired capacity can be befuddling to parents who must help the child master the "no" and learn to say "yes." The inability to say "no" can be found as a developmental gap in some adults leading to a serious lack of the capacity for self-protection. Spitz's speculations, as highlighted by the Blancks, of the significance of this lack of structural acquisition shed light at times on problems of identity, individuation, and autonomy, and are clinically useful. This is one example of how the Blancks extracted from theory gems of insight that were consistently useful to many of us in understanding and helping our patients.

Altering and improving maternal self-esteem and women's self-regard for their children can take place through explanations of the expectable universal pre-wired timetables so profoundly originally explained by the Blancks (Edward et al. 1992, p. 205).

For example, it is often helpful to mention to parents who are having trouble with their "no"-saying toddlers that saying ''no'' is actually an important developmental step, and that they do have not "bad" children and they are not bad mothers. The Blancks expanded the importance of the ''no'' not only to the development of autonomy, but also to self-determination, the acquisition of self-definition and self-delineation, and *the inner capacity to say "no" to the self, a forerunner of the functions of the superego and an essential factor for self-regulation.*

The Blancks drew on Spitz's cumulative principle to track the patient's internal progress. This principle explains that each ego acquisition in an earlier developmental stage opens the pathway to allow for and join with the next developmental event. Therapists are able to use this principle to watch for evolving new structures as treatment proceeds and to understand how the derailment of one critical stage causes a derailment in the development of subsequent stages.

Margaret Mahler

The Blancks extracted from Mahler's studies of infants and toddlers the characteristics of the typical evolution of acquired structures and functions. The baby emerges from the symbiosis of the "Not Me" through the events of the separation-individuation phases, culminating in positive self- and object constancy. They warned, however, that one could not extrapolate in a simple way from Mahler's work. Their careful, deep reading of her findings enabled them to create many techniques that enabled adults in treatment to acquire inner tools and functions.

The Blanck and Blanck (1974) drew on Mahler's observation of the symbiotic experience that allowed the infant to form a sense of oneness and safe anchorage with the mother (or caretaking person). They quote Mahler as follows: "Mahler uses the term symbiosis metaphorically: 'The essential feature of symbiosis is hallucinatory or delusional, somato-psychic omnipotent fusion with the representation of the mother and, in particular, the delusion of a common boundary of the two actually and physically separate individuals'."

They believed the capacity to establish an enduring love relationship with a partner to be rooted in the symbiosis (Edward et al. 1992).

As controversial as this concept is (Silverman 2005, pp. 239–252; Stern 1985, pp. 240-242), a number of authors and researchers find it to be clinically correct (Bergman and Harpaz-Rotem 2004, p. 557; Coates 2004, pp. 589–601; Edward et al. 1992, pp. 12–32; Pine 2004, pp. 511–533; Mendell and Turrini 2003, pp. 19–41). Witnessing the pain, panic, fear, rage, or despair toddlers express when the mother is out of their sight (18 months at the height of the rapprochement crisis) is a very convincing demonstration of the trauma that infants feel when they think they are losing their mother. Mahler believed the provision of calm reassurance (I'm OK and you're OK) from the caretaker through their first 36 months enables toddlers to eventually develop a separate, individuated self capable of maintaining a positive caring image of the mother, a representation of a good object, and by 36 months to maintain that image even when the mother is physically absent. The child also develops a sense of personal substance and confidence in the self, an aspect of self-constancy. In a private discussion with Turrini, Mahler agreed that the sound of adults wailing at a funeral was similar to the wails of the toddler in the rapprochement phase whose mother is absent, attesting to the fact that before object constancy is established, the absent mother can feel as gone forever to the toddler as the fact of the mourner's sense of permanent loss.

The Blancks offer exquisitely detailed data about the sub-phases of the separation-individuation phases that lead to self- and object constancy. They carefully tracked Mahler's research findings step by step, showing the internalizations made possible by the process of moving toward and away from the mother. The symbiotic mother of safety, care, and protection is dramatically demonstrated by the Blancks' work. Their beautiful descriptions of the child's checking back and refueling dramatize the importance of the attachment object for the child. In keeping with basic social work awareness, they illuminated the facets of this biological psychological social system. Whereas the attachment researchers concentrate on one area of behavioral indicators, the Blancks employed psychoanalytic representational observation to chart the internal development of the infant learning about self and other and organizing a sense of competency. Solms (2002, pp. 123–137) cites the neurobiologist Panksepp, who describes "the seeking system" and "the panic system." "The panic system (or separation-distress system) is associated not only with panic-anxiety, but also with feelings of loss and sorrow." (His description of "distress vocalizations" or "separation calls" dovetails with the

Blanck/Mahler tracings of optimal closeness to and optimal distance from the mother. We note that diverse scientists working with different psychoanalytic foci and paradigms bear witness to various aspects of mental development (as the intersubjectivists and relational groups do). We are hopeful that those reading this material will be inspired by these observations and will incorporate them into their professional practice and research.

Recognizing that borderline personalities have not achieved these structures, the Blancks evolved techniques for helping borderline individuals to acquire positive self and object constancy. For example, Gertrude Blancks (Blanck and Blanck 1988) proposed that traits such as imitation, courage, venturesomeness, and ambition are developed in the adequately experienced practicing subphase. They defined *borderline* not as a single pathology, but a wide range of disturbances within two borders: pathology exists on the psychotic border, in between, and on the neurotic side (Edward et al. 1992).

The concept of the fulcrum (Blanck and Blanck 1979, p. 71) details the dynamics of normal development through the sub-phases, and charts the good outcome as the rapprochement subphase is successfully negotiated. The importance of the acquisition of self- and object constancy cannot be overestimated. These structures provide for steady self-esteem, a sense of substance, and an internal recognition of individuality. They also note that this acquisition allows for the capacity for transference, a full affective repertory, signal anxiety, superego formation, secondary process thought, living in the mind not just in the body, and oedipal object relations.

The Blancks understood that a pleasurable symbiosis with its protective sensations of safe anchorage becomes an affective aspect of the self continuing as an experiential memory in a preverbal form. It is in this neuro-biological bodily occurrence that Mahler's observations and that of the Blancks and Bowlby's attachment theory (Nelson 2005) come together. Clinical social work specialists in bereavement are drawing on these authors while adding their new creative observations of the types of despair and feelings of sickness that are experienced at the death of a loved one. It is likely that memory of the sense of safety and faith in the first caretaker object representation is projected into the image and representation of the new loved partner (the significant other). The model for adult grief, then, is the 3-year-old standing all day at the nursery school door waiting for the mother to return (Gwen Schwarz Borden, private communication).

Florence (2002, p. 1) says, "When someone you love dies, a part of yourself dies too." Her writing catches the delusion of the fusion of symbiotic attachment—a bodily oneness with the other. The abandonment panic, loss, and grief experience may be studied as it recapitulates the symbiosis and the separation-individuation process.

The Blancks focused a great deal of attention on the contributions of Mahler because she provided an important road map of normal development that enriched our understanding of the possible developmental derailment that could occur along the way and curtail, among other things, sound identity formation. They believed that she provided clinicians with a body of immediately useful knowledge for both the assessment of a patient and the ongoing therapeutic situation.

Edith Jacobson

Jacobson is difficult to read because her writing is so dense that it often obscures her brilliant thinking, so it was very kind of Trudy to admit to her students that she had to read *The Self and the Object World* (1964) twenty times before feeling that she really understood her. Having the benefit of Trudy's understanding of Jacobson in place, her students found that difficult as Jacobson was, she was well worth the effort because once understood her contributions become firmly available for diagnosis and treatment and enrich the understanding of the mind. Recall our idea that the Blancks spotted the headlines in the work of the giant theoreticians. Here is a quote by the Blanck and Blanck (1974) of Edith Jacobson that captures her brilliance and the complexity of her writing:

> From the ever-increasing memory traces of pleasurable and unpleasurable instinctual, emotional, ideational and functional experiences and of perceptions with which they become associated, images of the love objects as well as those of the bodily and psychic self emerge. Vague and variable at first, they gradually expand and develop into consistent and more or less realistic endopsychic representations of the object world and of the self. (Jacobson 1964, p. 19)

Jacobson offered observations on lines of identifications, from the early imitations shifting to identification, and later selective identifications. These identifications become enduring parts of the ego. By appreciating these naturally occurring developmental lines the therapist is able to trace some of the patient's identifications. The Blanck and Blanck (1994) contributed another way of understanding the process of identification, noting that a transfer of function occurs from the object representation to the self-representation. In other words, what was done for the child by the parents becomes represented as a good parent object, and then the child can include the repertoire of care into his or her self-representation and become the doer of the self-care. This dynamic process is also a potential internalization process occurring in the therapist/patient work. The patient experiences in the person of the therapist a new idea of a model and makes it her or his own. An example of this, which many of us have heard from our patients when the therapeutic alliance is strong and the transference positive, is that at times of stress they can have a conversation with us in their mind and imagine our saying to them the very thing that might soothe them and give them hope. This is an example of the Blancks' use of the therapeutic relationship, long before the current view of relationship became a separate and new therapeutic method.

In another area, The Blancks identified Jacobson's functions of the superego. *The superego maintains identity, provides a stable balance in the proportions of the drives, regulates self-esteem by maintaining harmony between the moral codes and the ego manifestations. The superego governs moods and contains attributes of a coherent, consistent defense organization. Developmental aspects enter the superego.*

As an example, the superego acquires an early maternal ego ideal composed of idealizations of neatness and nonaggression. The failure to achieve the standards of the early maternal ego ideal was found to be linked to depression in the mother (Mendell and Turrini 2003). With this brief, highly selective overview, we turn now to their contributions on Descriptive Developmental Diagnosis.

DESCRIPTIVE DEVELOPMENTAL DIAGNOSIS

The Blanck and Blanck (1974) consistently approached diagnosis and treatment based on an understanding of the level of psychic development rather than on symptoms. They note that "similar symptoms may appear in different diagnostic entities" (p. 92). A unique contribution is their diagnostic charts (1974, pp. 114–115) that provide visual lines demonstrating development from infancy through maturity. At one look the therapist can observe levels of psychosexual development, drive taming processes, object relations, adaptive function, anxiety level, defensive function, identity formation, and processes of internalization. The Blancks note that diagnosis changes as treatment proceeds by altering old structures or creating new ones. For example, by reconstructing the acquisition of a faulty body image, insight and repair can take place. Some therapists pride themselves on stating that they don't believe in diagnosing their patients because it's a way of labeling them and it feels narrow and judgmental. Anyone who has studied with the Blancks would know that what they presented as a working developmental diagnosis was anything but narrow or rigid or labeling or judgmental. On the contrary, we find that it provides the therapist with a level of attentiveness and curiosity about a patient that serves as an effective therapeutic tool. Indeed, it gives the therapist a measure of confidence that there is a way of understanding the patient's behavior no matter how puzzling and confusing it might at times be. For instance, being able to differentiate between ambivalence and ambitendency is useful in understanding some aspect of the patient's developmental position and allows the therapist to make more appropriate interventions. When a patient seems amazed that the therapist remembers what he had said at previous sessions or when a patient becomes very angry that the therapist cannot accommodate her frequent requests for schedule changes because she wants to have a haircut or wishes to see a play at the time of her appointment, both of these patients are revealing important information about themselves that they most likely are unaware of and that have diagnostic significance often dating back to preverbal times. In our opinion, to describe the first patient as having low expectations of the object and to call the second patient "entitled" is descriptive and often judgmental. But to explore the history of their communications is what treatment is all about. Thinking diagnostically allows the therapist to maintain a very open attitude and a clear perspective on all that is yet to be learned and understood about the patient, thus avoiding premature or inaccurate interventions.

Another of the Blancks' diagnostic tools, the valuable chart called "The Fulcrum of Development" (1979, p. 72) describes the ego functions acquired through the separation- individuation phases. From autism on the way to object constancy, many ego processes mature and are mastered as the toddler passes successfully through the rapprochement phase. In 1979 they indicated that ego" organization and internalization reach relatively stable points with the negotiation of the rapprochement phase. This achievement serves as a fulcrum and turns development in a favorable direction. They identified splitting as normal in early infancy, culminating in the fusion of good and bad objects in healthy development, and view splitting in older individuals as pathological and the major defense in borderline structure (Edward et al. 1992).

The Blancks stressed the importance of ego functions, providing examples of their ego-building techniques specific to each patient's particular needs through their many books and articles. When clinicians have a good grasp of the ego's functioning they can make a valuable diagnosis, a hallmark of appropriate mental health care, and perhaps this is the Blancks' most important contribution to the field. In their chapter, "Ego-Building Techniques" (1979, p. 210), they state: "Reduced to its fundamentals, ego building consists of a number of technical procedures based upon the level of the patient's organization and designed to advance the organizing process." Any therapeutic intervention that promotes ego functioning, therefore, constitutes ego building by extending the capabilities of the ego. In order to aid in recognizing these capabilities, the Blancks added to Hartmann's list of the innate pre-wired ego apparatus by defining other ego attributes (e.g., anticipation, attention, decision making, delay, identification (of various types, including selective identification), intention, intelligence, judgment, language, memory, motility, object comprehension, synthetic function, reality testing, productivity, self-preservation, soothing capacity, symbolization, thought, volition, introjection, incorporation, denial, fantasy, rationalization, repression, reaction formation, reversal, sublimation, turning against the self, undoing, object and self constancy, self-observation and self-scanning. In The Psychodynamic Diagnostic Manual (2006, p. 75), Ego Function Assessment category notes only 12 aspects of ego strength, a limited view compared to what the Blancks brought to ego descriptive studies.

The Blancks approached narcissism as a developmental line. "The term *narcissism* has come to acquire a variety of meanings. In pathology it is a form of personality disturbance; in developmental theory it is a normal developmental line and an essential prerequisite for mental well-being" (1979, pp. 50–63, 79, 176–209).

Drawing on Mahler's and Jacobson's work they observed that the child requires necessary environmental supplies in order for emerging representations to become imbued with positive libidinal cathexis (Edward et al. 1992) as the self acquires distinction from the object. They traced the development of healthy narcissism (sound secondary narcissism) through the separation-individuation phases. "Bodily libidinal supplies are especially necessary during the symbiotic phase and differentiation and practicing subphases. Narcissism takes pathological forms not only when there is affront to its phase-specific developmental formations but also if it fails to proceed as it should in equal balance with object love" (op. cit., p. 179). They defined normal narcissism as the cathexis of the self-object unit with positive affective value having its inception in the symbiotic phase. One can read the symbiotic phase as the tie of mother and baby in a feeling of safety and oneness. Here again we can observe the importance of the relationship. The Blancks say that sound, healthy secondary narcissism provides the person with self-respect, self-love and a sense of being valuable. They describe many problems that can cause pathological narcissism (e.g., parasitic symbiosis (an overly gratifying symbiosis), precocious differentiation, and under gratifying care resulting in an omnipotent object-in-fantasy (p. 181). Their understanding of narcissism is an example of their genius at theory building that is immediately relevant to diagnostic understanding and treatment approach. It goes a long way toward dispelling what is often a pejorative attitude among clinicians and provides instead a valuable insight into the early derailment of development that brought about this painful condition.

In developing their ideas on affect, the Blanck and Blanck (1979) drew upon Spitz's observations of pre-wired cumulative levels of organization in infant development. They focused on how affect is organized and channeled by the ego: "Affects in particular influence perception and the development of object relations, and anxiety is foremost among these affects" (p. 42). Such observations appeared in their writings long before the advent of the new "affect regulation" therapy. Much of the work of Schore (2003) was prefigured in 1974 by the Blancks when they hypothesized that external behavioral and affective signs were evidence of the degree and kind of internal structuralization and were therefore useful in diagnosing the patient's inner life.

The Blancks observed that many persons were not exposed to understanding their emotions and feelings. Thus, enabling patients to have words to explain what they thought and felt provided for increasingly positive inner tools, self-awareness, and an increased capacity to understand the other. Blanck (2000) said, "The coenesthetic mode of sensing is fundamental to understanding the mind-body question. This is the mode of reception that exists at the beginning of life when mind and body are one. We never abandon it, although Western civilizations play it down. Some believe that the Eastern religions and practices that, in essence, encourage reversion to the coenesthetic mode bring the individual closer to the unity of mind and body" (p. 187). The coenesthetic mode of sensing appears to be the same as current descriptions of right brain function that stores the affects and emotions.

The Blancks' recognition of the need for a good internal loving object or object representation is among their vital contributions. They taught that the good object was central to a person's development of steady self-regard and selfrespect, allowing for the capacity for independent thought and the ability to tolerate some amounts of aloneness. Sustaining libidinal ties improved an individual's feeling of well-being and sense of safety. *They believed that it is the therapist's job to maintain libidinal ties with the patient, and that all interventions need to contain that effort as an aspect of the interpretation.* Here is another forerunner of relational theory.

TECHNIQUES

The Blancks were remarkable in providing clinical studies demonstrating how some of the patterns of separation and individuation could be observed externally by the therapist, thus enabling the therapist to create interventions intended to help build the patient's psychic structure. For example, they might tell an anxious patient who had not attained object constancy where they would be on vacation, and in some instances would send postcards to reinforce their existence and connection to the patient and demonstrate that although apart they maintained this connection.

The Blancks' extensive discussion of theory and techniques for preverbal reconstruction is another of their unique contributions to technique. Their writings on preverbal reconstruction offered comprehensive explanations and guidelines for providing patients with the opportunity to understand their deepest, unconscious biological and psychological inner life. Also dictated by their developmental point of view is the idea that preverbal experience plays a vital part in the first round of development that leads to psychological birth. They demonstrate that techniques for recovering these experiences in the treatment situation exist and may pave the way to psychological birth (36 months). "These techniques involve the use of replication of object experience, dreams, persistence of maladaptive behavior, and the like" (1979, p. 14). In keeping with other psychoanalytic observers the Blancks conclude that "early experience" is not forgotten, nor is it repressed (Franck 1969). They said, "Preverbal experience has not been processed through an organized structure and therefore is not retrievable in the same way as later experience" (Blanck and Blanck

1974, p. 206). The comfort-discomfort cycle revolves mainly around the gestalt of the feeding experience in which representations of the self and object, even while still merged, lead the fortunate child toward optimistic expectations. Although never directly remembered in words, these will reflect in later attitudes toward self and others (Edward et al. 1992, p. 238). They described coenesthetic empathy (p. 238) as necessary for understanding experiences and impressions from the first years of life.

Current research and integrated reports by Schore view the emotions, bodily feelings, and esthetic experience developing in this preverbal period. Schore says, "A body of evidence shows that the right hemisphere matures before the left, a finding in line with Freud's assertion that primary process ontogenetically precedes secondary process functions. The right hemisphere is the neurobiological substrate of Freud's dynamic unconscious; this system develops in the first two years of life" (2003, p. 35). Thus current research affirms the importance of the preverbal period. It is comforting and electrifying to see new research affirming the Blancks' original contributions, especially their diagnostic recommendations and their inventive techniques.

The Blancks believed that reconstruction of the preverbal period is extremely important in understanding patients. "Many have found not only that aspects of preverbal life are recoverable but that such recovery is *essential to the complete treatment of most patients"* (1979, italics ours). They were proponents of reconstructing as completely as possible a personal biography for each patient. Because each person has a unique first 3 years of life, and no parent/environment is perfect, each reasonably normal person has assets and deficits forged in the early years. Preverbal reconstruction (Edward et al. 1992, pp. 237–238; Siskind 1987) can help structuralize and eliminate early deficits and help a person appreciate early self-assets. The reconstruction of preverbal determinants provides the opportunity for making genetic interpretations that allow patients to understand that they did the best they could under the particular conditions of their object environment. This insight often mitigates against the self-blame and sense of shame that many patients feel about what they regard as their failures.

Over the years we have had the good fortune to make a number of preverbal reconstructions. When the interpretation hits the mark, patients sit up, lean forward, and open their eyes widely, providing clues to the relevance of their early life and confirming the insight from the interpretation. The Blancks promoted and fostered observation of this uniqueness of the individual at birth and directed attention to studying how infants affected the people in their environment and how the environment affected them. This emphasis brought forth ever-expanding understanding of the ego's earliest development and led to their exquisite understanding of the technique of preverbal reconstruction. They encouraged students to create their own techniques to secure preverbal and phase-specific repair of psychic structure. At this point, patients feel deeply understood. Such an experience often engages the patient's observing ego and sets the treatment on a path that deepens the process of self-exploration.

Anticipating Jacobson, Hartmann (1958, p. 34) conceived of narcissism as "the cathexis of the self-representation." He is responsible for defining object constancy as "cathexis of the constant mental representation of the object regardless of the state of need" (op. cit. p. 35). An individual can attain an inner emotional stability which, however upset, hungry, or mad, still understands that "the other," and "others in the world" have feelings and needs that must be attended to. Gertrude Blanck taught us that the mother is the first person to help the infant/ toddler/child to understand that she, the mother, has needs and feelings that must be respected. From the child's understanding and love for the mother, the child can then identify (extrapolate) that all persons have needs and feelings. Many mothers get caught up in the idea that they must constantly give and do the major share of adapting to their children and not expect their children to feel concern and understanding in return. One comes upon parents who cannot set limits for their children or say "no" to them. Our understanding of the role of reciprocity in the development of object relations, and how ego functions develop when the capacity for dealing with frustration is allowed to grow and transform into curiosity, confidence, and eventually mastery, causes us concern about this misguided form of parenting. We also know that mothers need to be more mindful of their own needs for their own sake, as well as being good models for identification for their children. We are grateful to Gertrude Blanck for teaching these ideas that have enabled us to help many mothers understand themselves better and teach their children about common human needs. Many interventions can follow from this view of how empathy is learned and internalized.

Supporting the highest level of adaptation/functioning is another of the Blancks' core recommendations. The therapist needs to recognize that the individual is behaving and thinking in the best manner he can, given his present structural development. Knowing the components acquired through good developmental experience, the Blancks taught therapists how to diagnose the ego strengths or lack thereof, thus freeing us to appreciate the patient's behavior and thoughts. This knowledge enables the therapist to accept that human being with an unwavering non-judgmental stance. The patient is rarely wounded by the interpretation coming from this stance.

The therapist who is knowledgeable about ego development can provide interventions that help the patient acquire ego functioning, adaptive capacities, and mastery over impulses that are critical to the well-being of that individual, important for the people relating to this person, and valuable to the community.

The Blancks' criteria on the timing of termination (1988) continue to emphasize the great advantages of assessing whether the patient has acquired adequate ego functioning and internal positive representations before considering termination. They refer to the diagnosis at the termination phase as assuring completion of psychic development.

Blanck (1984, 2000) stressed Freud's observations that the 3–5-year-old child experiences both the negative and positive oedipal relationship to both parents, experiencing sexual and hostile feelings. At one moment the child will plan to marry the mother and have a baby with her, and in the next breath will decide to marry the father and have a baby with him. How the child negotiates the loss of each parent is dependent upon the capacity to feel strong and separate from the oedipal object, a challenge that patients with borderline structures cannot manage. In response to this observation Gertrude Blanck arrived at a new theoretical contribution which she described as follows: "It is suggested that, instead of a triangle, we use a straight-line diagram to depict the oedipal child moving back and forth while a parent representation remains fixed at either pole" (p. 196). Combining Arlow's (1980, p. 522) observations of the child's primal scene revenge and mortification created by the child's feeling of the parent's rejection of the child's sexual and marriage wishes helps focus on the traumatic impact of this period, and how formidable the challenge is for the less-than-structured patient. Turrini has employed the interpretation using their conceptualization, "You felt hurt and damaged when you realized your parents would not marry you. When we are born, if we have reasonable basic health, we fall in love with our parents, assume we will marry them, only to have our hopes dashed. I see that you are remembering that misery today."

PERSONAL NOTES

We are both eternally and deeply indebted to both Gertrude Blanck and Rubin Blanck. They had a long and active history as teachers, theoreticians, authors, and psychoanalysts. We both studied with them and they were our supervisors for many years. Their Institute for the Study of Psychotherapy was a beautifully run and exciting place to study and to meet colleagues in the field. Its reputation was so fine that they were overwhelmed with applicants and the institute grew every year, with classes becoming larger and larger. Most of their students were graduates of schools of social work and eager to enhance their knowledge by continuing their study beyond the MSW degrees. The Blancks had a liberal attitude about whom to accept. They felt that those who wanted to continue their studies would find an institute to accept them so they might as well attend the Institute for the Study of Psychotherapy and get the best possible training. They were equally liberal about their students' personal treatment and most willing to make referrals if so requested but left the matter of choosing a therapist up to the student, thus avoiding the revolving door referral system of many other institutes. Their respect for the autonomy of students and patients was a consistent trait they shared. Some graduates of the three-year core curriculum joined the then famous MONDAY MORNING SEMINAR, which we both attended for IS years. Trudy was the sole teacher of that seminar, teaching psychoanalysis proper and psychoanalytic psychotherapy. It was an exciting and rewarding experience.

The Blancks knew Margaret Mahler personally and professionally, and shared conversations with her with their students. Mahler once said that she became famous as a result of the Blancks' writing about her and teaching her concepts and observations. In a seminar with Mahler that we both attended, Mahler said that she often felt that the Blancks understood her work better than she did!

In 1979, Gertrude and Rubin Blanck turned over their outstanding curriculum to some of their students and several years later moved to North Carolina and joined the North Carolina psychoanalytic society. After a few years Rubin became ill and died there. After his death Gertrude returned to New York City, where she provided supervision and consultation. She lived in the building where Margaret had lived before her death. For the first few years after moving back to New York Trudy was in deep mourning. Her marriage of more than 60 years had been extraordinarily close and loving. At first her grief prevented her from resuming the type of active and productive life she had always lived. Then bravely in her mid-eighties, true believer that she was, she found an analyst for herself, and once again began her own analysis. With this wise decision in place she began to feel more hopeful, made new friends, gradually recovered her. usual energy and vitality, and eventually completed another book: *The Primer of Psychotherapy: A Developmental Perspective* (2000). In this book she reviews some of the contributions she and Rubin made in their earlier works, writes an interesting section on medication in which she supports its judicious use but stresses that "drugs cannot alter structure nor build object relations" (p. 191). "Drugs cannot provide the affective experience in self and object relations that makes us human" (p. 193). She also encourages primary prevention such as coaching to enable parents to support their children's positive development (pp. 163–166).

In her late years, Gertrude attended the New York Psychoanalytic Lectures on Neuroscience, and she ends her last book with a few words about the future:

> The future of psychoanalytic developmental psychology is intricately bound up with future discoveries in psychopharmacology and in the neurosciences. When it all comes together, we will have more precise medications that will zero in on the exact area of the brain that needs alteration. We will also know more about the effect on the brain of affective experience in life and in psychotherapy. (2000, p. 193)

In the last year of her life she battled with cancer, and when it became clear that it had reached a point beyond cure she left for Oregon to spend her final days with her daughter Susan, her son-in-law, and her two grandchildren. She died in September 2002, a short time after moving to Oregon.

When the Blancks opened the Institute for the Study of Psychotherapy, they used their living room for teaching classes. We remember the collection of their books published in various languages kept on a shelf there. *Ego Psychology* was published in Spanish, Portuguese, Gennan Book Club, and Serbo-Croat; *Marriage and Personal Development* in Italian and German Book Club, *Ego Psychology II* in German, Swedish, Italian, and Spanish, and *Beyond Ego Psychology* in Swedish and German. Of the following four books, *Ego Psychology I, Marriage and Personal Development* (1968), *Ego Psychology II,* and *Beyond Ego Psychology* (republished in 1992) between 76,000 and 77,000 books were sold. The Columbia Press staff said that this is an unusually large number of books for a text in this field. We find it strange that their work has not been referenced or assigned more often in the current American psychoanalytic journals and in social work training and we hope that this article might stimulate interest in their work.

CONCLUSION

The Blancks provided a systematic, detailed description of object relations from infancy on, and developed techniques that sought to address developmental failures and promote further ego development. We recently had contact with a BSW social worker who was faced with removing children from their mother and placing them in foster care. As she had never been exposed to the contributions of theorists such as Spitz and Mahler in her recent social work training, or to the integration of theory and technique provided by the Blancks, she was overwhelmed. Her social work training had failed to provide her with psychoanalytic concepts necessary to understand the impact of object loss or the techniques to deal with her young clients. The shortsightedness of her training stands in sharp contrast to the training provided by the Blancks. Can social work training get along without this information? We think not. Are we not throwing the new social workers to the wolves?

The Blancks' strong commitment to viewing psychoanalytic developmental object relations theory and its application to technique as an ever-evolving science of the mind was evident not only in their readiness to update their theory as their knowledge base grew and warranted revision, but to also be interested in the various schools of modem psychoanalysis that were forming around them. They believed that in many cases the roots of the new theories lay in past ideas that had been expanded and given greater prominence and validity and at times Trudy, especially, was all in favor of these developments but at other times she worried that "a part was made the whole" and she feared that this was reductionistic and a step backward.

In the last period when they were still together in New York, the Blancks organized and directed a Research Institute for the ongoing study of the development of psychic life and for the interventions and techniques that this knowledge would affect It is regrettable that their effort did not result in the establishment of a permanent research center. Perhaps their concept can be revived. However, their many books, and articles are their legacy, one that can greatly enrich the work of today's social workers, psychoanalysts, and researchers as it has enriched our lives and those of their many students and readers.

The contributions of Gertrude and Rubin Blanck to social work were outstanding. Through their tireless teachings and writings they trained thousands of students who in turn taught and wrote, and that is just what the Blancks wanted to achieve. They opened doors to us that had been closed in the past. They predicted that social workers would become the major providers of psychotherapy and psychoanalysis and they were correct. Although their contributions to psychoanalysis were unique, they will best be remembered for their contributions to psychoanalytic psychotherapy, which they elevated from a haphazard modality to one with specificity and depth. Just as Freud is the father of psychoanalysis and Hartmann the father of ego psychology, Gertrude and Rubin Blanck are the parents of psychoanalytic psychotherapy, and we are grateful for all they have done for clinical social work and for the field of mental health.

REFERENCES

American Psychoanalytic Association, International Psychoanalytical Association, Division of Psychoanalysis (39) of the American Psychological Association, American Academy of Psychoanalysis and Dynamic Psychiatry, National Membership Committee on Psychoanalysis in Clinical Social Work (2006). *Psychodynamic Diagnostic Manual (PDM).* Silver Spring, MD: Alliance of Psychoanalytic Organizations.

ARLOW, J. (1980). The revenge motive in the primal scene. *Journal of the American Psychoanalytic Association* 28:519–541.

BERGMAN, A., & HARPAZ-ROTEM, I. (2004). Revising rapprochement in light of contemporary developmental theories. *Journal of the American Psychoanalytic Association* 52(2):557.

BLANCK, G. (1984). The complete Oedipus complex. *The International Journal of Psycho-Analysis,* 65:331–339.

———— (1989). How did we let this happen? *Newsletter, Committee on Psychoanalysis, a National Membership Committee of the National Federation of Societies for Clinical Social Work,* p. 1.

———— (2000). *Primer of Psychotherapy: A Developmental Perspective.* Northvale: Jason Aronson.

———— & BLANCK, R. (1968). *Marriage and Personal Development.* New York & London: Columbia University Press.

———— ———— (1974). *Ego {sychology: Theory and Practice.* New York:

Columbia University Press.

——— ——— (1977). The transference object and the real object. *The International Journal of Psycho-Analysis* 58:33–44.

——— ——— (1979). *Ego psychology II.* New York: Columbia University Press.

——— ——— (1988). The contribution of ego psychology to understanding the process of termination in psychoanalysis and psychotherapy. *Journal of the American Psychoanalytic Association* 36:961–984.

——— ——— (1994). *Ego psychology: Theory and Practice* (2nd ed.). New York: Columbia University Press.

BLANCK, R. (1977, March). Practice theory then and now. *Smith College Studies in Social Work* 95–103.

BRAZELTON, T.B., & NUGENT, J. (1995). *Neonatal Behavioral Assessment scale.* Nyack: McKeith Press.

COATES, S. (2004). Bowlby & Mahler: A comparison. *Journal of the American Psychoanalytic Association 52*(2):579–601.

DONNELLY, J. (2008). *Social work perspectives, presented at ICCAPP conference.* Cancun, Mexico, prepublished papers.

EDWARD, J., RUSKIN, N., & TURRINI, P. (1992). *Separation/Individuation Theory and Application* (2nd ed.). New York: Brunner/Mazel.

Festshrift for G. & R. Blanck. (1987). *Clinical Social Work Journal, 15*(4). Articles by Blanck & Blanck, Dooley, M., Pieree, M., Thompson, T., Weinstein, B., Edward, J., Siskind, D., Turrini, P.

FLORENCE, S. (2002). *When you lose someone you love: A journey through the heart of grief* Watford Herts: Exley.

FRANCK, S. (1969). The unrememberable and the unforgettable: Passive primal repression. *The Psychoanalytic Study of the Child:*24:9–47. New York: International Universities Press.

FREUD, S. (1912). Recommendations to physicians on the psychoanalytic method of treatment. *Standard Edition* 12:109–120.

HALL, J. (1998). *Deepening the Treatment.* Northvale, NJ: Jason Aronson.

——— (2004). *Ego Psychology and the Problem of Adaptation.* Latham: Jason Aronson.

HARTMANN, H. (1958). *Ego Psychology and the Problem of Adaptation.* New York: International Universities Press.

HUSHION, K., SHERMAN, S., & SISKIND, D. (2006). *Understanding Adoption: Clinical Work with Adults, Parents and Children.* Latham: Jason Aronson.

JACOBSON, E. (1964). *The Self and the Object world.* New York: International Universities Press.

MENDELL, D., & TURRINI, P. (2003). *The Inner World of the Mother.* Madison: International Universities Press.

NELSON, J. (2005). *Seeing Through Tears.* Great Britain: Brunner-Routledge Taylor Francis Group.

PINE, F. (2004). Mahler's concepts of "Symbiosis" and separation-individuation: Revisited, reevaluated, refined. *Journal of the American Psychoanalytic Association* 52:511–534.

SCHORE, A. (2003). Minds in the making: Attachment, the self-organizing brain and developmentally oriented psychoanalytic psychotherapy. In *Affect Regulation and the Repair of the Self* pp. 4–57. New York: Norton.

SILVERMAN, D. (2005). Early developmental issues reconsidered: Commentary on Pine's ideas on symbiosis. *Journal of the American Psychoanalytic Association* 53:239–251.

SISKIND, D. (1987). An example of preverbal determinants in a classical analysis. *Clinical Social Work Journal* 15(4):361–367.

——— (1992). *The Child Patient and the Therapeutic Process: A Psychoanalytic Developmental Object Relations Approach.* Northvale: Jason Aronson.

——— (1997). *Working with parents: Establishing the essential alliance in child therapy and consultation.* Northvale: Jason Aronson.

——— (1999). *A primer for child psychotherapists.* Northvale: Jason Aronson.

SOLMS, M. (2002). *The brain and the inner world.* New York: Other Press.

——— (2006, May 7). *Sigmund Freud Today.* N-PSA, DVD, www.europsa.org. His lecture at the New York Psychoanalytic Society.

SPITZ, R. (1965). *The first year of life.* New York: International Universities Press.

STEM, D. (1985). *The interpersonal world of the infant.* New York: Basic Books.

TURRINI, P. (1977). Mothers center: Research, service and advocacy. *Social Work Journal* 22(6):478–483.
(for 2008, see the Internet: www.Motherscenter.org).

WEIL, A. (1978). Maturational variations and genetic dynamic issues. *Journal of the American Psychoanalytic Association 26:*461–491.

www.ingramcontent.com/pod-product-compliance
Lightning Source LLC
Chambersburg PA
CBHW072119020426
42334CB00018B/1651